Well Being
Recipes and rituals to realign the body and mind

About the Author

Danielle Copperman is a British model (IMG Models), entrepreneur (founder of Qnola), writer (Model Mange Tout blog) and cook and is also trained in Strala yoga and holistic massage. As it becomes more apparent that many aspects of 'modern living' are making us unwell, Danielle is passionate about promoting more natural and healthful rituals that can assist in handling certain stressors of the modern world (such as anxiety, digestive issues, fatigue and lack of energy, hormonal imbalances, mental illnesses and irregular breathing, to name a few). Here she shares recipes and rituals inspired by ancient traditions that she has discovered through studies, research, travel and self-experimentation. These are things that have helped her along her journey so far – from teenage model to stressed and burnt-out entrepreneur – and she hopes they will make up a part of your personal and ongoing journey to better wellbeing.

'Danielle honours that every individual is different and guides you on your journey of wellness to find your perfect state of balance.'
Bonnie Wright, actress

'Danielle Copperman inspires us to find our own way to being well through a gorgeous and seamless guide of ritual, practice and nourishment for every moment of the day. Devour her methods and enjoy sustainable wellbeing.'
Tara Stiles, Strala Yoga

Dedicated to everyone who has shaped my journey so far – my family, friends and teachers – past, present and future.

Well Being
Recipes and rituals to realign the body and mind

Danielle Copperman

Photography by Rita Platts

Kyle Books

Introduction

My journey: this book

This book is an account of my own personal journey, which I am still and will always be on. You too are on a journey, an ever-evolving one, and no single set of rules is going to support you every step of the way. This may not be what you want to hear; you may be searching for a set of guidelines that will command your life so you don't consciously have to, but the truth is, there are no guidelines that can possibly assist you at every stage of your journey. Instead, it's down to you to turn your attention inwards, to accept the responsibility for your own personal wellbeing and to educate yourself through advice and ideas combined with your own experiences to navigate your time here on Earth in a way that will allow you to live fully and to thrive. You are your greatest guide and nature and the cycles of the Universe are your greatest teachers and providers.

Deep down, *we are all well*, or are at least capable of being so, and everything we need in order to thrive is in and around us. What makes someone else well may not have the same effect on you, and what works for you one day, may not work for you another. There is no set formula designed to serve each person, each day of the year, at each moment in his or her life. In the modern world, we put so much attention and faith into fitness and diet in our mission to look and feel well, but how well you are actually depends on so much more than these physical factors: the energy within and around you, the people in your life, the spaces in which you live and work, the thoughts you think, the emotions you feel and the levels of stress in the body and mind. What we need to do to understand, manage and utilise these aspects of our lives is to rediscover lost knowledge and reconnect with our environment and our own innate intuition to find our way back to living, thinking and feeling well.

Modern editions of ancient traditions

The intention of this book is not to put you on a plan but to inspire and empower you to make one for yourself, providing you with the space and freedom to constantly grow and learn, and to enjoy it not begrudge it. The recipes and rituals are in no way prescriptive and don't promise an end result, but are offered as gentle guidance; a slight nudge in a better direction. Combining ancient ideas and wisdom from the East with modern practicality, I want to share the traditional rituals I have learnt through yoga, meditation, bodywork, energy work and Ayurveda that have been most transformational for me. You'll soon discover that you can enhance your life by simplifying it. This book aims to help you take the initial steps on a journey of clarity, self-discovery, self-improvement and eventually self-mastery that will mean you are prepared to adapt to new experiences openly and effortlessly.

My journey thus far has been inspired by many holistic and alternative teachings, systems, cultures and experiences, and this book is the culmination of the most useful and accessible tools. Some of the most ancient ideas in health and wellbeing remain relevant today, despite our modern ways and extremely different lifestyles, and there is a reason they have survived thousands of years; because they work. What I've found useful is to accept that no one ever stops being a student; we are all constantly changing and in doing so, we are constantly learning and growing. Whilst many 'gurus' in the health and wellness industry convey a sense of all-seeing, all-knowing omniscience, we are forever discovering new things (or rediscovering old ones) and research and science are constantly contradicted. No one, no matter how wise or experienced, can know everything there is to know about your personal physical, mental and emotional health, or how these factors respond to certain toxins and stresses of modern life. I have found using aspects from a variety of traditions and techniques to be most effective, most flexible and most fulfilling, long-term. A common theme amongst them being to do more things you enjoy that feel good, with less effort and minimal side effects.

Many different forms of yoga, meditation, alternative medicine, bodywork and energy work have shaped my practices, including hatha, vinyasa, ashtanga, kundalini, yin, vedic meditation and strala yoga, shiatsu and holistic massage – several of which I am qualified in. Elements of each of these appear in one or several sections of this book. What is common to all of these systems and traditions is that they treat each individual as a whole, and handle the prospect of wellbeing by considering much more than just diet and exercise. The mind, body, breath, movement and energy channels of the body (and many other aspects) influence how well you are and how well you can be, and only when you understand how to align them all will you achieve an effortless and long-lasting state of wellbeing. There are numerous tips and quick-fix methods advertised that promise noticeable results from exercising more and eating specific foods, but none of them will equip you with the sustainable knowledge of how to live well, both now and in the future. This book instead draws on systems that represent thousands of years of experienced-based techniques that can restore balance and meaning in our modern lives, which have become controlled, demanding, fast-paced and, unsurprisingly, incredibly disorientated.

No one size fits all

In the same way that no 'one size fits all', no 'one diet fits all' either. Diet and exercise merely lie on the surface of wellbeing, but in order to truly be 'well', we need to explore the connection between the body, mind, spirit and soul, and aim for alignment of all these things. We can do this by taking a holistic approach, meaning that we integrate the physical, nutritional, environmental, energetic, emotional and spiritual components that make us individuals. Each of us has unique, highly individualised needs and how we feel and what we need may vary from day to day, hour to hour, month to month and from place to place. For this reason, adopting flexible and adaptable routines is key.

The recipes

I would define my personal approach to food as 'flexitarian' and 'naturopathic' and mostly plant-based. This approach is the basis of the recipes in this book, but there is opportunity for you to modify them to suit your personal tastes. Each recipe has been constructed without meat, gluten, dairy products or refined sugar, as I find these ingredients are not cricial for our wellbeing and can cause me mental or physical unrest. However, to emphasise that no one diet fits all, I urge you to take what appeals to you and customise it. Each recipe will be a success, regardless of whether you choose to add bread or pasta, meat or dairy. The intention is purely to show you how much you can do with natural ingredients, and how little you need the highly manufactured products of modern processes and artificially refined ingredients that feature heavily in our diets today.

The rituals

Since wellbeing is influenced by more than just what you're eating, this book also offers rituals and practices, inspired by ancient traditions and slightly adapted to fit easily into busy, modern lives. They can really help to give a sense of purpose and structure to each day and I find a combination of movement, meditation, breathing exercises (pranayama), bodywork and energy work, such as Do-in, makka ho and massage, helps to reduce stress, open and centre my mind, stimulate productivity and increase positivity. I hope you can introduce some or all of these rituals and practices into your day-to-day experiences, to help handle stressful or demanding situations.

Like most things, routines change, and with constant shifts (whether global, such as seasonal, environmental, political, or in more personal circumstances like financial state, relationships, career, location) our daily routines need to remain adaptable and realistic. Most 'healthy living' programmes are often defined by rigid rules. They should be personal, flexible and fit into your life rather than adding more stress to it. You need to listen to what your body and mind are calling for and make time to provide them with whatever that may be – for example, rest, energy, nutrients or oxygen.

My intention is to offer an open-minded approach to reducing stress, regulating hormonal imbalances, clearing and lifting negative emotions, enhancing energy, eliminating energy blockages and easing digestive issues – all things I feel stand as fundamentally more important than simply changing your diet or exercise regime. When your body and mind connect on an energetic level they become powerful tools for dealing with the side effects of modern life. It is about fine-tuning and simplifying your current life and making a few better decisions. Instead of abiding by certain rules or forcing habits, it is about discovery, progression and evolution. I hope reading this book guides and inspires you to rediscover your natural flow and I hope you will gain knowledge and confidence to devise your own unique formula for feeling good through thought, food and movement. Explore my recommendations and apply the parts that make most sense to you, but above all, learn to listen to your own body and mind.

We are well

Our physical bodies have a natural self-healing ability and most of our essential biological processes operate automatically, without conscious instruction. Our bodies are designed to function in specific ways, but certain modern influences are preventing us from reaching our full potential. The essence of wellbeing is within us, we have simply lost control over it and our minds have become clouded by often contradictory information drawing us further away from our roots and what we should know. The resources we need to flourish are provided naturally by the Earth, and many of the rituals we practise require nothing more than the power of our own body and mind.

Intuition, instinct & inner wisdom

Whilst I am not professionally trained in everything I cover in this book, in some ways, that is the whole point. Professionals can help, and I have certainly benefited from their input in several ways, but in the end the only person you can fully depend on is yourself. Our bodies know what they need, and emotion, thought and instinct all work together to ensure we are on the right track. We lose our path as a result of warped and misguided thoughts, negative emotion and choosing to follow seemingly easy advice over our own natural instinct. Without the courage and trust in ourselves to follow our own intuition, we will constantly be drawn from the latest popular idea to the next.

Things like commuting to work, juggling the care of children with running a home and succeeding and achieving at school or work are stress-filled realities for many people. We eat 'on the run' (often fast or convenience foods), skip meals and depend on stimulants such as coffee, tea or alcohol to keep us going. In trying to acclimatise to the speed of modern life, we are dropping many nourishing rituals that are in fact gateways to higher living.

Diet, the food & drink industry & modern provisions

With all the 'rights and wrongs' of the food and drink and health and wellness industries, government bodies and scientific institutions, it can be hard to navigate which information or advice is reliable, which is why learning to follow your intuition is so important. The inconvenient truth is that the food and drink industry is much to blame for this disruption and our ultimate 'unwellness'. Toxins in the body are largely the result of buying and consuming products, as opposed to fresh, unaltered food, because most packaged, commercially produced 'foods' (however 'healthy', 'light' or 'skinny' they are) are made with artificial ingredients, artificial processes and without the nourishment we really need. Ingredients like bread, meat and dairy products certainly have their place in a balanced diet, but eating overly processed and refined versions of them is detrimental to our health.

Lifestyle

Beyond the way we eat, the way we live is beginning to take its toll on our health too. We are in a constant state of doing and under a considerable amount of stress, which disrupts our nervous and endocrine systems and can cause hormonal imbalances. And when our nervous system is busy coping with anxiety, our digestive system shuts down because it is not considered a priority during situations of 'fight or flight'. The energy required to digest food is considered far less important than dealing with stressful or even life-threatening situations. We experience this through symptoms of inflammation, heartburn, irritable bowel syndrome (IBS) and other common indications of digestive unrest.

Despite severe fatigue, constant stress, depression and other mental and hormonal imbalances, we try to keep going, pushing past signs that we are doing too much and need to slow down. Taking a break or even trying to get a substantial amount of sleep is seen as unproductive and a waste of valuable time that could otherwise be used to reach goals and achieve more. When people do eventually 'burn out', a restful break usually helps them journey back to health, but real rest is not something we are encouraged to do regularly enough to prevent such 'burn outs' from happening in the first place, and it's not always something people have the time or financial resources for. Luckily, there are simple tools you can use – including yoga and meditation – to start slowing down and moving with more ease, and many techniques in this book will help you reach a rested state more quickly than taking a break or sleeping more. We are rarely enouraged to stop and take a break, but I'm telling you now. By doing less you'll start achieving more, and you will find the more time out you take, the more time you have.

Factors that affect wellbeing & how to return to your 'well' state

When you start to make lifestyle changes it is important to take into account all aspects of your life and to treat yourself as a whole being, not just physically but also mentally and spiritually. You are likely to feel different every day, regardless of how 'well' your dietary habits are, and seemingly unrelated factors like your career, relationships, financial state and your environment can all influence this too. The changing seasons and the different phases of the moon can mean you feel bloated even when you haven't eaten much, and can also influence your frame of mind. With so much out of your immediate control, flexibility and adaptability are key. Broken down into sections focused on mind, breath, movement, space, and diet, this book provides everything I've found to be useful in managing and coping with the demands of modern life.

Introduction

Mind

The mind is indeed a powerful thing. Our emotions influence our thoughts and our thoughts influence our experiences. When our emotions are negative, our thoughts are negative too, and so our experiences will tend to be negative, or at least that's the way they'll seem. Furthermore, mental imbalances, including stress, anxiety and depression, can cause physical imbalances within the body. Many things affect the way we think and feel, from our own emotions to other people in our lives, our career, our financial state, our stress levels, our hormones and of course, the food that we eat. Whilst you can manage these factors in a variety of ways, adopting a more positive, open mindset can reduce stress and enhance positivity. Amongst the mental tools are meditation and mindfulness, which work to alter the energy and vibrational frequency of your thoughts, in turn calming the mind and cultivating a positive outlook. All thoughts are energetic and different thoughts have different frequencies; positive thoughts vibrating differently to negative thoughts. There are things you can do to raise the vibrational frequency of your thoughts, which, if negative, have a low frequency and so exercises to raise their frequency can help to instill a more positive mindset, and ultimately, more positive experiences. Many of the recipes and rituals in this book aim to initiate this.

Meditation & mindfulness

Meditation is a deeply nourishing mental practice that transforms the mind by slowing irrepressible thoughts. Simply focusing your mind on a single object, word or moment can help to centre the mind and promote understanding, acceptance and positivity. Once you have learnt how to train your mind in this way, regular meditation can help to manage stress and anxiety and can even lift depression. It brings balance to the nervous and endocrine systems, which are disrupted as a side effect of constant stress and activity, and by demanding your mind's full attention, meditation helps to silence scattered (and often self-limiting) thoughts, leading to increased awareness, energy, productivity and the ability to be present and open.

There are several traditional styles of meditation, but it is important to find one that resonates with you personally if you are going to practise it regularly. At first, I was certain that meditation wasn't for me. I assumed it was only for very spiritual people, and was put off by its extreme, cultish stereotypes. Since then I have experimented with many different types of meditation, from Zen meditation, visualisation and awareness, to primordial sound and

Vedic meditations. I still struggle to practise consistently, but when I do I notice the benefits instantly: my mind is refreshed and my system is calmer. There are various schools of meditation and teachers who can guide you, and nowadays you have access to apps, audios and online videos offering guided meditation, wherever you are. The Mind sections in each chapter of this book offer simple and accessible routines that will fit into each part of your day. Rather than adopting a regular practice, use these as and when you need.

As an alternative to meditation, you can explore mindfulness, which is a technique that teaches awareness of your own thoughts and feelings and encourages you to be present in every small task, from washing up to opening a door for someone. You'll also come across gratitude and journaling in this book, both in the morning and the night time chapters, which is a process used to release thoughts and empty an overloaded mind. Keeping a gratitude diary is a way of 'counting your blessings'. It is a meditative practice but as well as drawing your attention away from active or negative thoughts, it helps you to let go of them, by releasing them physically (or consciously if you prefer to do this in your head), allowing you to acknowledge and accept any thoughts and feelings you may have internalised and not dealt with.

Breath

Although we are constantly breathing, our breath is the first thing that goes when we start to become stressed. Breathing becomes short, sharp and inconsistent, instead of full, deep and regular. The power of the breath is incredible. It allows us to send vital oxygen to the brain and cells in our body, and to flush out the carbon dioxide. It adapts and changes in many situations and all of our emotional shifts are reflected in our breathing pattern. When we are scared or alarmed we hold our breath, and when we are relieved, we sigh. When we are hurt, we are often told to breathe, and this is what helps us to handle the pain. Breathing is an essential process for all living things to survive, and although we breathe automatically, and in most cases effortlessly, we rarely breathe consciously. As a result, our breathing patterns become irregular and out of sync with our bodies and our minds. Breathing meditations (known in yogic teachings as pranayama) are one of the easiest ways to rebalance and reconnect the body and mind.

Movement

Whilst exercise plays a large part in this holistic process of being 'well', I prefer to call it movement. Exercise makes me think of intense workout classes or forcing yourself to go to the gym, whilst movement is more of an open approach to using your body and keeping it active. Cardio and aerobic activity definitely have their place but not all exercise has to be overexerting, especially if that is exactly what puts you off being active at all. Sometimes a long walk or some gentle stretching can be more than enough, if that's all you feel up to. Beyond exercising for physical results and internal health, movement is also a powerful tool to redirect blocked energy within the body, and it can offer meditative benefits, connecting the body and mind on a deeper level. I try to combine the following activities with consistent cardio and strength training, for muscle definition, flexibility and mental wellbeing.

Yoga

In this book I have included my favourite yoga poses, which are influenced by many different systems and many of my past and present teachers. No specific 'style' is favoured, instead I've offered a variety of simple poses, ones that I think complement different times of the day. You'll come across standing poses, seated poses, twists, hip openers and inversions, some active and some more restorative. If you are entirely new to yoga or you're interested in receiving more constructive guidance, try attending a class or find a local teacher who can teach you the basics.

Bodywork, energy work & massage

As well as active movement, there are ways you can move and touch the body that can be both deeply energising and relaxing. Bodywork, using massage and working on specific pressure points, is a powerful way to reduce stress and tension, both mentally and physically. In 2017 I began studying shiatsu, a Japanese form of massage used to shift and redistribute energy around the body from points where it is too concentrated, to points where it is lacking. Running throughout the body are internal energy channels (known as meridians) and restriction of the flow of energy can cause all kinds of physical, emotional and pyschological ailments. Each energy channel aligns with specific organs and it is possible to remove tension, ease pain and promote mental wellbeing by simply identifying the correlating meridian and using massage, stretching and manipulation to transform its energy. One of the most important techniques I picked up was self-treatment, known as Do-in (also known as tao yin or dao yin). In this book you will find simple methods, including gentle movement and self-massage techniques, to practise on yourself to energise the body and to instil a sense of clarity and calmness. The results, for me, are more instantaneous than yoga and meditation.

Rest & sleep

As our modern lives become more hectic, sleep is an easy target as something to cut down on in order to make space for other things. Whilst some people seem able to cope just fine without sleep, beneath the surface, lack of sleep can create serious imbalances both mentally and physically.

The recipes and rituals throughout this book each have their own ways of promoting sounder sleep, be it through including certain vitamins and minerals in your diet or through mental and physical practices that work deeply into the nervous and endocrine systems to ensure our hormones (particularly melatonin, which encourages sleep, and serotonin and cortisol, which keep us alert and awake) are in balance.

A combination of meditation, movement and nutrition can aid sleep to ensure that no matter how little you manage to get, the quality of it will be optimal. And surrendering to a nurturing amount of rest can give your body and mind the break they need to rebuild and come back stronger.

Aromatherapy & smudging

Smell is one of our most powerful senses. Aromatherapy is an ancient tradition used to heal mental imbalances such as stress, fatigue, insomnia and depression. The remedial use of essential oils and plants has the power to change the way you think, feel and, ultimately, act. When you enter a spa you become enthralled with the aromas that surround you, and there is no reason why you can't bring that essence into your own home.

Proper and safe use of essential oils can help to promote a more balanced lifestyle and there are essential oils to support all kinds of situations. Some are energising and uplifting whilst others are sedative and relaxing. Some can help soothe physical imbalances whilst others work on a deeper, more psychological level. Familiarise yourself with whichever ones can serve you best and use them in candles, diffusers, atmosphere sprays, fragrance oils or simply for inhalation.

Smudging is an ancient practice that involves cleansing and refreshing energy. It involves purifying a space, or yourself, with the smoke of traditional herbs such as sage or palo santo. This is a powerful ritual to use if you want to rejuvenate your living (or working) space and remove negative energy. I find it most powerful in the morning, at the end of the day or if there's particularly negative energy in the air (i.e. after an argument).

Space & creating an optimal space to thrive In

The spaces in which you live and work can have positive and negative effects on your mental, physical and spiritual wellbeing. If you hate things about your home, you're not going to look forward to being there and you'll be in a state of frustration, finding it harder to relax and feel comfortable. If you create more positive spaces (both at home and at work), you're more likely to feel clear, content and focused, and maybe even more productive. You may find it useful to allocate specific spaces for activities, like creating a calm space to meditate, an energising space to work in and a relaxing space to sleep in.

You're likely spend most of your daytime at work, either in an office, at home, on location or on the go. If you travel a lot or attend many meetings, creating a space in which to thrive is considerably more difficult than if you sit at the same desk, day in day out. But there are still habits you can adopt to handle the stresses and toxins of such environments.

Your night-time space is perhaps the most important to get right because there are many factors that can affect your body's ability to relax and fall asleep, or stay stimulated and awake.

Here are a few simple rituals you can work into your routine to cleanse, refresh and create your optimal space.

1. *Candles and aromatherapy.* Keep candles, essential oils, natural atmosphere sprays (page 150) and crystals. If you can't light the candles, use a diffuser instead (page 153). Choose natural or homemade products and essential oils suitable for calming and reducing stress (page 298 for suggestions). I use hoodoo candles (sometimes known as magic candles or spirit candles), which are intentionally charged candles, which are believed to encourage certain experiences and opportunities. It may sound crazy, but I light my 'blockbuster' or 'power' candles during the day to encourage concentration and drive. Use smudging with sage or palo santo to cleanse and reset the energy of a room (page 16).

2. *Sound.* Sound has been used in many ancient traditions as a means of healing. Its vibrational energy touches every part of our physical being and the noises around us can impact the vibration and frequency of our cells, affecting how we feel and function mentally. Curate a soundtrack. Choose songs with a pitch, tone and frequency that raises your vibrational energy, and pay attention to the lyrics, especially if you are in need of a little motivation. If you're struggling to get out of bed, use upbeat, energetic melodies with feel-good lyrics.

If you're running late and feeling frantic, bring some peace to your day with soothing symphonies and on long, slow-paced days, set the mood for relaxing with laid-back, easygoing chill-out tunes. At a deeper level, you can explore the realms of sound healing and discover how frequency and vibrational energy can restore balance and heal from within.

3. *Light.* Make the room bright and let in as much natural light as possible throughout the day. Naturally, living beings are wired to wake in line with the sun as it rises, but artificial lighting, irregular sleeping patterns and other factors of modern life have disrupted this intended rhythm. If you have blinds, open them as soon as you wake to welcome the light in. During the day, open a window or get outside and take in a new environment to reset before returning to your space. This is a simple way to expose yourself to daylight at some point during the day, as many offices are lit artificially and this natural light can have a profound impact on your mood and mental functionality.

When you're starting to think about getting ready to sleep, begin to lower the lighting of your entire space, or at least your bedroom. Use low lighting from lamps, salt lamps, aroma diffusers with lights or even just a few candles. Light has a profound effect on your body's ability to wind down. Exposure to light is stimulating and encourages alertness, so using bright, artificial lights – including electronic devices that emit light – in the evenings can disrupt your body's ability to sleep. Even without the use of artificial lighting, if the room is too bright, naturally, this can result in frequent awakenings, lower quality sleep and insufficient rest.

4. *Declutter.* Reduce clutter and free up space to allocate to your rituals. Mess provides distraction and clutter can become toxic and suffocating, especially as it builds up or gets out of hand. If you wake to mess, you will feel distracted and frustrated. If you wake to a clear and appealing space in which you can move and dwell comfortably, you are more likely to feel more positive and appreciative. When working, make your desk a pleasant place to be, even if you don't want to be there. Organise mess as much as you can, and take a regular inventory of your belongings to decide what you need and what you don't. Once you've got rid of things that don't serve you you'll notice a sense of spaciousness and lightness, not only to the eye but within yourself as well.

When you arrive home from a long day, you can feel uninspired and unmotivated to do anything, especially tidying. But if you return home to mess or clutter, take a few moments, especially if you have excess energy (sometimes people are still buzzing and find it hard to slow down after a day of 'doing') to clear some space and reduce clutter. This will make it easier for you to relax, carry out any evening duties, and also make the space more welcoming and more comfortable if you're expecting company. Before you really wind down, take some time to remove any clutter from the space in which you will be sleeping and waking. Clear clutter off the floor or at least organise mess to make it more manageable and to create a little order.

5. *Plants.* Making room for living plants, both indoor and outdoor, can offer multiple benefits, both for the body and the senses. They brighten a space, adding colour and decoration and some also work to clear the air of toxins, drawing harmful chemicals out of the atmosphere.

6. *Colour.* Colours strongly influence the look and feel of a space, and that in turn can influence how you feel and behave in that space. Certain colours are calming whilst others are more energising and invigorating, and aggressive or garish colours can even make you feel angry or uptight. Whether you paint the walls or distribute coloured furniture and accessories around your space, be wary of disruptive colours in spaces where you want to be calm and invigorating ones in spaces where you need to be focused.

   If you're on the go and constantly out for meetings or appointments, or if you work on site/in a studio and never from an office, creating a space can be more difficult. There are, though, still ways to enhance your place of work. Use essential oil fragrance oils on your wrists or clothes, or keep them in your bag purely for inhalation. Keep music or sound-healing audios on your phone or a portable music player, to accompany you from one place to the next. This is particularly effective if you are often stressed or hurrying.

Beauty & home products

In making more natural choices and certain dietary changes, it's likely you will start to question other parts of your life that could be more natural too. By feeling more connected with the Earth and its provisions, you may feel encouraged to explore how you can utilise and work with natural options where you currently depend on manmade commercial products. Most edible natural ingredients can also have purpose in and around the home, including the bathroom and your beauty kit. Our skin is the body's largest organ and it must be nourished in the same way as the body, and this can be done with practically the exact same ingredients. Just like our dietary habits, our beauty habits have been misled by the introduction of mass-produced products made with artificial chemicals that promise quick blemish-busting or age-defying results that require very little effort on our part. Most of these products contain even more harmful components than heavily processed foods, and whilst you don't ingest them, your skin absorbs them and they still end up contaminating the body.

Unlike any other organ, our skin is constantly exposed. Daily, it faces all kinds of situations and substances, from UV rays to pollutants, and it readily absorbs products we put on it, natural or artificial. The last thing it needs is a chemical-laden moisturiser, which will prevent it from breathing properly and prohibit the absorption of things it really needs (like oxygen and light).

The beauty recipes in this book provide alternative methods that utilise natural ingredients and essential oils. These not only provide gentle options for daily rituals (such as teeth cleaning in the morning and make-up removal at night), they also offer mental healing through inhalation.

Like us, our skin can change, and how and when it does depends on so many things, from climate and environmental change to dehydration, stress and lack of sleep. Spots, dry patches or medical conditions, such as eczema, are symptoms of skin that is stressed. Since we are all unique beings, each of us will need different things from our beauty products in the same way we do from our food. Treating your skin with nourishing, natural ingredients will support its natural protective function as well as its visibly healthy appearance of long-lasting illumination and vitality. Take the remedies in this book as inspiration and apply them accordingly to your own day-to-day needs. For optimal benefits, use them in conjunction with a natural diet.

Detoxification & renewal

Exfoliation and dry brushing are simple rituals known to stimulate the lymphatic system and promote blood circulation. Exfoliation helps to remove dead skin, invigorating the new skin that lies beneath, whilst dry brushing leaves the body looking and feeling energised and vibrant (it even helps to reduce the appearance of lines and cellulite). They help to eliminate toxins and prevent build-up and blockages within the lymph system and can boost immunity.

Nature & the phases of the Universe

When it comes to health and wellbeing, many people can stick to a specific regime for a limited amount of time but almost always let things go when life gets in the way, or if they become bored. For me, what prevented this from happening was truly understanding how intrinsically we are linked to the Universe, how connected everything is and how aligned we are, or could be, with nature. I began to notice that certain cravings or symptoms coincided with the approach of a new season or the phase of the moon. I noticed the power of fresh air and the sea in calming and rejuvenating me, and really felt my body and mind respond to the warmth and light of the sun. I always knew these elements affected the growth and strength of plants and the habits of animals but was never taught about how similarly they affect us as humans. Foods that grow naturally are comprised of the natural elements of the Universe (air, aether, earth, fire, water, wind, wood and metal – depending on which systems you consider) so it is unsurprising that they help to connect us with these natural elements of the Earth. When you look at it that way, you begin to realise we ourselves are nature. We are chemically and biologically made up of and governed by the same elements as the Earth, the air, the sun, the moon, the stars, the water, the plants – we all come from the same universal source, and so it's no wonder that nature's provisions not only help us to survive, but also to thrive. It is no wonder these ingredients can heal us when we are ill, and strengthen us when we are weak. They can uplift us when we're low, they can guide us when we're lost. These natural materials are far more than fuel and sustenance, they are life forces.

Before you embark upon new dietary changes or meditative practices, you might find it interesting and useful to understand the cycles of the Earth and how they can impact your own. Whilst illness and intolerances can create inflammation and emotional unrest, it is also possible (if you are open to it) that, from time to time and in some way or another, things like seasonal change, the phase of the moon, the alignment of the stars and the weather can also be responsible for these symptoms.

Seasons

As seasons change, we do too. Our bodies adapt to each new annual cycle, acclimatising to shifts in weather, such as temperature and light. Each new cycle allows new natural provisions – roots, shoots, berries, nuts and fruits – to thrive, and this is not by coincidence. The Earth encourages materials to grow that are truly intended to support life on the planet (be it humans, animals or plants) and when we align ourselves with the rhythm of the Earth, we live in harmony with its cyclical changes, which we would do well to protect and celebrate. Aside from providing us with what we need, seasonal shifts can also affect our mental and physical health. Transitions from one season into a new one can drain our energy, affect our sleep, test our immune system and alter our mood. Eating in line with the seasons, where possible, and taking it easy (by doing less and living more gently) during these transitional times, is important in understanding why you feel the way you do, and how you can feel better.

Moon phases

It's common knowledge that the moon governs tidal energy, and since our bodies are predominantly made up of water, it should be more obvious to us that the phases of the moon can also affect how we function and feel. In researching and studying the lunar cycles and how they affect us, I found that things like whether a meal agrees with us or not can depend on the current position of the moon. When the moon is waxing, our usual eating habits tend to make us feel fuller, and it is thought that we put on or retain weight more easily at this time than when the moon is waning.

Likewise, when the moon is waning, it is likely you will feel able to eat more than usual without feeling full. At this phase in its cycle, approaching the

New Moon, our bodies are actively cleansing and detoxifying – as long as they are not disrupted by unnatural activity or infected with toxins from heavily processed foods. The moon can also affect our mood, and being conscious of the moon's phases can help you to gain understanding and be more in tune with your body. Invest in a moon calendar (I get mine from an artist on Etsy) to help manage your moods and meals and synchronise with the moon as it waxes and wanes.

Digestion & the gut

What you eat isn't half as important as how well you digest it. The gut is increasingly being referred to as 'the second brain' of the body, and apart from undertaking the activity of digestion, absorption, assimilation and delivery of nutrients from our food, the gut is also connected to our first brain, affecting our thoughts, moods and emotions. I experienced this first hand when I had intense digestive issues. Doctors would only diagnose it as IBS or mild intolerances, but over time as I began to experience other physical and mental symptoms, I self-diagnosed it as stress – not really knowing that stress could deeply disrupt the natural balance of the body. Through independent research, I found that the digestive system shuts down under stress, as our body's natural reflex is to enter 'fight or flight mode', during which digestion is simply not important. My stress levels were affecting my gut and my gut was affecting my stress levels and my mood, so I was stuck in a vicious cycle of discomfort, frustration and misery. I turned to cleansing tonics and pre- and probiotic foods to help heal my gut, and as my digestion relaxed, my mood also lifted.

We feel from the gut and the expressions 'gut instinct' and 'gut feeling' are very apt terms. Whilst serotonin is a neurotransmitter found in the brain, studies show that incredibly high levels of it are produced in the digestive tract, which is why, if the digestive system is in turmoil, we are likely to feel low and agitated, but when it is healthy, it has the potential to increase positivity and reduce physical stress. Our 'two brains' communicate intimately, and therapies that can help one, may also help the other.

For these reasons, a healthy gut is essential to living well. The recipes in this book take this into account and the rituals included are aimed at boosting digestion and replenishing the gut before loading it with food. To keep the digestive system in order, a combination of rituals to reduce stress and optimise oxygen flow are included, as well as recipes for fermented foods, which, high in good bacteria and probiotics, help the gut to thrive.

In Ayurveda, your gut is referred to as your 'fire', and depending on your doshic constitution, the way you digest food can depend on not only the ingredients you eat but also the temperature, taste and texture of food, the nature of your surroundings, and even the way you feel mentally and physically in the moment. For example, you could eat a meal in a cold city

Introduction

whilst feeling stressed, which may make you feel bloated, but you could eat the same meal whilst on holiday, when the weather is warm, whilst feeling relaxed, which may make you feel fine, or even great.

Diet & Nature's Provisions

Once your stress and energy levels are in order, you can start thinking properly about the ingredients in your diet. Whilst diet should perhaps be the most important factor in wellbeing, eating well is nowhere near as effective as it could be if you're not in the right physical state of mind to digest it.

Food is so much more than a means to satisfy hunger or to excite the taste buds; it is medicine, and if sourced well it can offer healing abilities and preventative powers through nutrition. The recipes in this book are not restricted to a specific diet or a set of rules but instead take inspiration from many different approaches with a few common themes. All the recipes use only natural ingredients. What we should eat and what our bodies need could not be any more obvious. You can find out more about the amazing ingredients used in this book on pages 292–298 and you won't find any that have been processed too far from their raw state.

All these recipes are intended to serve (alongside the rituals provided) as coping mechanisms for modern life and the common imbalances it causes. Some recipes may support specific issues, but most are designed to boost concentration, energy and positivity, ease digestion, reduce stress, and cleanse the body. You can choose the recipes that suit your diet and lifestyle, and the time and resources you have to work with.

Final thoughts

With so many factors that contribute to your wellbeing, you might be wondering how they all come together and what is most important. To summarise: a combination of a stress-free mind, a steady breath, a strong and supported digestive system, an exercised body and a set of wholesome, unprocessed ingredients are key. Together the recipes and rituals in this book are intended to help you to reach these states of being in one way or another. Using mind, breath, movement and space, I hope this book will bring you back in touch with nature and will help you to feel empowered to take control of all aspects of your life and make your own decisions to feel as well as you are designed to feel.

Morntime

Morntime

The morning, despite being widely resented, is a wonderful and sacred phase of the day – or so it should be. As we have become accustomed to modern life, we have reshaped how we wake to cope with the demands of our time. Somewhere along the way, we stopped waking naturally in line with the sun and have allowed our mornings to become possibly the most stressful time of day. Rarely fully rested, we wake to alarms (plural, of course) that stimulate our stress response and adrenaline, disturbing us from a still and peaceful state and forcing us abruptly about our morning duties before we've fully adjusted to being awake. If, instead, you wake more gently (more natural sounding alarms help), you may feel more grounded and more positive, which will set the tone for the rest of your day. Wake up earlier (if this is possible, without the constraints of early work starts or children!) to give yourself just 10–30 minutes extra. You'll feel less rushed, less stressed and will actually find you create more time for yourself, to go about your morning routines and to add some new wholesome habits to each day. Waking with the sunrise is a powerful practice to work into your routine – try to do it once a month or so as it is very inspiring and grounding.

Whilst it's easy to think adding more to your to-do list will only add more stress, creating time for yourself is important for connecting the body and mind and is a simple tactic to bring your attention inwards before dealing with the outside world. This will give you the chance to slow down and create space to acknowledge any thoughts or feelings you may be holding within, and to focus on attracting what you desire from each day. You could use the time to meditate or listen to a podcast. You might use it to journal. You could read, exercise or enjoy a drink and a proper conversation with others before going about your separate days. Explore the rituals in this section and apply some or several of the simple techniques that are designed to help you ease into each new day and stay grounded throughout. On top of practices to encourage mental clarity, you will also find a combination of exercises to help on a more physical level. Before eating, it is important that your body is in a calm enough state to deal with and digest food, which is why this section includes practices designed to determine and regulate your natural hunger upon waking, as well as mentally and physically fulfilling recipes that are easy to digest, nutritionally functional and sustainably energising. Eating whilst multitasking or stressed can in some ways cause more harm than good, or at best, seem futile and wasteful as many ingredients will go unabsorbed, so use the practices in this section to tune in and acknowledge how you feel and what you need, and then explore the recipes.

Mind

Setting Intentions

The morning is a powerful time for setting intentions. Intentions help you to bring awareness to what you want to think, feel and achieve, and can instil a sense of clarity and focus within. It is really just a matter of noticing and defining what you want, and giving it enough thought and attention to, in a way, plant a seed that will influence your higher consciousness to attract it to materialise. The way you think has the power to influence your realities and experiences, and intentions can help you to think your way to where you want to get to. It is a combination of believing in the possibility of what you want, and trusting in external forces to acknowledge your desires and encourage them to manifest into actual experiences. The concept may seem a bit 'woo woo', but even if you don't believe in the potential outcomes of manifestation, what harm is there in adopting a more positive mindset and gaining a clearer understanding of what you want, regardless of the outcome?

Your intentions are not set in stone, and can change daily – even hourly. The only thing that determines their potential is making them authentic and backing them with belief. You cannot force them or think and expect a specific kind of outcome. Intentions should be focused and direct, but also open, progressive and free, and set without expectation. Another important part of the process is being more aware of things that may begin to happen. In our fast-paced lives we rarely slow down enough to notice what's going on around us, but if you make a conscious effort to acknowledge things happening around you, you will notice that the things that you wish to attract come to you in some way. Take inspiration from the suggestions below, but before you do, understand what it is you want by asking yourself, or perhaps brainstorming or making a list, and then personalise these intentions to fit your plans.

I intend for whatever resources I need to flow into my life easily.
I intend to let go of what no longer serves me.
I intend to forgive.
I intend to take more time for myself.
I intend to stay calm in stressful situations.
I intend to spread kindness.
I intend to open my heart.
I intend to find meaning in my work.
I intend to attract abundance and wealth.
I intend to enhance my physical body and its visual and physical potential.
I intend to be grateful for my work opportunities and to accept I am exactly where I am meant to be.
I intend to perform at my best and offer everything I am capable of.
I intend to be content and not to compare myself to others.

Start the day by repeating your intention(s) for a few minutes, or however long feels right to you, each day. You can also incorporate them into yoga or meditation practices, repeating them at the beginning of a practice to instil a sense of purpose, focus and openness into your day.

Opposition Thinking, Pivoting & Positive Aspects

Something that really resonated with me at a time when I felt quite 'stuck' in my life was the Law of Attraction – a theory based on the belief that our thoughts, feelings and vibrational energy have the power to determine our experiences. It outlines how focusing on positive or negative thoughts can attract positive or negative experiences into our lives, and how our energies and actions can determine the materialisation of both our fears and desires. It's a strange concept if you aren't familiar with it, but taking inspiration from the teachings of the Law of Attraction, however lightly, will help you to think and feel more positively and, ultimately, live more fully.

The basis of the theory is 'pivoting' negative thoughts into positive ones, in order to refrain from focusing on the lack of what you want, and instead to focus on what you do want, and why you want it. Many of us internally tell a story that focuses on the things we want but do not have, and the Law of Attraction teaches that in order to attract what you desire, you should tell your story as if you already have it. Thinking negative thoughts and/or focusing on the lack of something is thought to keep you in a place of lacking, whilst thinking more positively will change the vibrational frequency of your thoughts and is more likely to attract experiences of the same frequency – the things you want.

Upon waking, maybe even before you get out of bed, think of all the things you are lucky to have and how good it is to be alive. Instead of thinking about how tired you are or that you dislike your job or other current situations, and blaming these things on other people to try and justify them, focus on how good it feels to breathe, stretch and move your body, how the bed feels beneath you. Instead of thinking negatively about the size or state of your living space, focus on how lucky you are to have a place to live at all. Try to notice the good in everything around you and look for reasons to feel good. Whenever a negative thought intrudes, replace it with a positive one; one that feels better and will encourage more confidence, inspiration and motivation within you.

Journaling & Gratitude

Journaling is another powerful way to release any negative thoughts and feelings, and frees up space to focus on things you have and are grateful for. Writing down thoughts first thing in the morning helps you to let go of anything that may be getting in the way of the desired course of your day.

Storing thoughts internally can clutter the mind and can manifest as physical tension, so try starting – not every day but on particularly challenging days – to write down anything that comes up. It could be something as simple as the dream you've awoken from, or how you feel about the day ahead. It may be something more profound, like something you are worried about or are fearful of. Whatever it is, let it out, and spend time acknowledging it in order to either appreciate it, let go of it or accept it and use it productively to move forwards.

Morntime is an influential time to practice gratitude, so take a few moments to acknowledge all that you have and all you are grateful for, which you may find comes up naturally as you start writing in a journal. When you actively express gratitude, you embody a magnetism to your desires, bringing more of what you appreciate and want into your life and speeding up the process of manifesting such things. By consciously giving thanks, you'll soon notice that you are able to change challenges and problems into possibilities, and losses and defeats into meaningful lessons that are stepping stones on your journey. By 'counting your blessings' you'll take your attention away from negative thoughts, and you'll likely find yourself feeling more positive, more fortunate, more abundant, more appreciative and considerably less affected by daily challenges or annoyances.

Morning Meditation

The morning is my favourite time to meditate, as it is a sacred, generally peaceful and untouched time, free from distractions and unaffected by unpredictable events. Whilst the morning may seem like the most unlikely part of your day in which to make time for meditation, there are many simple techniques you can adopt, and just five minutes a day can be beneficial immediately and in the long term.

Sensory Awareness Meditation

A simple meditative technique to reduce stress, align concentration and balance emotions is to use your senses to redirect your attention. This is a versatile practice, and will be different almost every time you practise it, because it is likely that scents, sights and noises will change from one day to the next. Use this technique on mornings when you find it particularly hard to focus, or feel overwhelmed with challenging thoughts, either first thing in the morning or just before starting work, to shift and reset your focus.

*   *Sensory awareness meditation may be more powerful in an unfamiliar setting, so if you can, try to change your place of practice from time to time. (It is best to practise with your eyes closed, as your senses may be influenced by things you see or you may find it hard to focus on senses other than sight if there are many visual distractions).*

1.   Find a comfortable seated position and rest your hands on your knees, in your lap or by your side.

2.   With eyes closed, bring your awareness to the rhythm of your breath. Notice how each inhalation and exhalation feels and notice where in the body you can feel the breath most. Breathe naturally with your attention on your breath until you come to a steady and comfortable breath.

3.   Begin to bring your awareness to each of your five senses. Focus on one sense at a time, noticing how it feels and how it is stimulated in the present moment. Start with whichever sense naturally grabs your attention.

Hearing will likely catch your attention first. Notice the sounds within or around you, without judgement or hostility. They may be the sounds of your own breathing or internal movements. They may be sounds made by others close by or far way, by people you know or don't know. They may be familiar or unfamiliar sounds. They may be clear or indistinguishable. Sit for a few minutes, acknowledging and accepting the sounds around you, and if any thoughts arise, simply use the sounds around you to refocus the breath.

If you find your attention drifting persistently, turn your focus to another sensation. Notice any smells around you, near or far, faint or pungent. Maybe you've lit a candle or applied some fragrance to yourself or the space around you. Maybe you smell food or plants, fresh washing or smoke. If a smell brings negative thoughts, turn your attention to more positive smells around you.

Perhaps the taste in your mouth becomes noticeable. Maybe there is a slight aftertaste from your last meal, or from smoking or brushing your teeth. If you don't smoke and/or haven't yet eaten, notice the inside of your mouth and how your tongue feels. Is it heavy or light? Is it soft or rough? How does it feel to move it slowly around the mouth? This may bring your attention to touch. How do things feel? How do your hands feel where they are resting, and what are they resting on? If rested on your body, do they feel warm or can you feel the warmth of your body beneath them? If on the floor or furniture, how does it feel? Is it cold? Is it soft or rigid? Are you comfortable? Notice the connection between your sitting bones and where you are sat. Do you feel rooted and supported by the earth beneath? Is the rest of your body comfortable in this pose? How do your clothes feel against your skin? If you want, you can even feel around you, resting your hands on any objects they fall upon and considering what they might be. Maybe this will bring your attention to your sight. Blink your eyes open gently, take in your surroundings, noticing objects, shapes, colours, materials and light. Gradually trace the room, resting on things that catch your attention, and then pause, noticing how you feel after the exercise. Close your eyes again and close the practice with a few deep breaths.

Mudras

These are a few of my favourites to use in the morning for their energising, calming and grounding intentions. Hold each mudra for 3–15 minutes, knowing that the longer you hold it the more effective it will be. You can also perform mudras at your forehead or at the point between your brows (known as the third eye).

Anjali Mudra is traditionally used as a sign of respect and greeting and is commonly used in yoga to open a practice. It alleviates stress and anxiety whilst encouraging a focused state.

1. Come to a seated position, either on the floor with your legs crossed, however is comfortable, or on a chair with your feet flat on the floor.

2. Lengthen your spine and extend the back of your neck up, so your head is facing forwards, ensuring your neck is soft, not strained. Decide whether to practise with eyes open or closed.

3. Bring your palms together at the heart's centre. Press your thumbs into the centre of your ribcage and settle here for a few minutes or for as long as feels comfortable.

Chin Mudra, also known as 'the mudra of knowledge', encourages expansion and stimulates wisdom, consciousness and knowledge, assisting you to pass challenges with ease and to feel open and empowered.

1. Follow steps 1–2 of Anjali Mudra, and rest your hands on your knees, palms facing upwards.

2. Lightly bring the tip of your thumb to meet the tip of your index finger on both hands, keeping the other fingers straight but relaxed. Settle here for a few minutes or for as long as feels comfortable.

Lotus Mudra symbolises openness and growth, and is used to cultivate faith. It calms the body and mind and encourages the mind to let go of the need to control things, allowing you to feel grounded and confident that things are as they should be.

1. Follow steps 1–3 of Anjali Mudra and get settled for a few moments.

2. Bring the tips of each thumb to touch, keeping the base of the palms and wrists together. Keep the ring, middle, and index fingers straight and spreading widely away from each other. This creates the lotus.

3. Hold your lotus in your lap, at your heart's centre or out in front of your torso or forehead. Once you are comfortable, settle here for a few minutes or for as long as feels comfortable.

Surya Mudra is a powerful mudra for getting things moving in the morning, and is valued for heating the body and boosting metabolism.

1. Follow steps 1–2 of Anjali Mudra, and rest your hands on your knees, palms facing upwards. You can also do this standing or even walking, with your hands in front of you or by your side.

2. Bend the ring finger of each hand, bringing the tip to touch the inner palm of your thumb. Fold your thumbs down over your ring fingers, keeping the other fingers straight and together. Settle here for a few minutes or for as long as feels comfortable.

Mantras

Mantras are not specifically time-sensitive and can be used at any time during the day, but I wanted to include them as a morntime practice as they fit so easily into conventional morning routines, and are a really grounding way to greet each new day.

See pages 325 to find out more about what mantras are and how they work.

Breath

The morning is an ideal time to practise pranayama (*prana* meaning life force and *ayana* meaning to extend or draw out), before your mind has the chance to start worrying too much about the day ahead. When you wake up with morning anxiety, focused breathing is a simple technique to help stop any kind of irrational thoughts and negative feelings in their tracks, preventing them from developing into a full-blown bout of stress that'll stay with you throughout the day. The following exercises are designed to ease you into each day and prepare you to cope with whatever experiences and obstacles may arise. Meditating in the morning instils not only a sense of calm but also an established sense of awareness and consciousness, which in many ways will help you experience more deeply, and feel more present in each moment.

* *Pranayama practices become more powerful when you practise over a period of time, so whilst you may only have time to practise for 5–10 minutes, try to make it a regular thing.*

* *Also, be aware not to push or strain yourself.*

* *If you are pregnant or unsure about the safety of practising pranayama, consult a teacher or healthcare professional.*

Basic Breath Observation

1. Stand, sit or lie in a comfortable position, preferably in a quiet and undisturbed environment. Rest your hands on your knees if sitting on the floor, or by your side if standing, sitting on a chair or lying down.

2. With your eyes open or closed and breathing in and out through your nose, become aware of the rhythm of your breath. Is it short and shallow? Is it deep and steady? Are you breathing into your chest or shoulders, or are you breathing fully into your abdominal area, and/or your back? There is no right or wrong way to breathe, just notice it, and begin to acknowledge and distinguish between your inhalations and your exhalations. Is one longer than the other? Are you filling and emptying the lungs fully before one breath ends and another begins? Sit and notice the rhythm of your breath, relaxing your shoulders, your neck and your head. If you feel your breath predominantly in your chest area, bring a hand to your lower abdominal, to bring the attention and the breath down into the abdomen area.

3. Stay like this for a minimum of 5 minutes, or for as long as you can or have time for. It may seem simple, but the real challenge lies in your focus and your ability to keep awareness on the breath, to calm and regulate it, and away from the thoughts of your lively mind. Inevitably – especially in the morning with an untouched to-do list and the whole day ahead of you – thoughts will enter your mind, and when they do, accept them and add them to a 'save for later' folder somewhere in your mind. You don't need them right now. Bring the attention back to the breath, and keep this rhythm of accepting and letting go of irrelevant thoughts flowing with your breath.

4. Bring the practice to a close when you physically feel more even throughout your body and more open across the chest and heart area, and when your breathing is more balanced and settled. Blink your eyes open and perhaps bring your hands into prayer, another mudra of choice or simply on your knees, and sit for a moment to readjust.

Breath Stillness

1. Stand, sit or lie in a comfortable position, preferably in a quiet and undisturbed environment. Rest your hands on your knees if sitting on the floor, or by your side if standing, sitting on a chair or lying down. Notice any internal or external sensations such as thoughts and feelings, or outside noise and distractions, and without trying to change anything, focus on nothing but settling.

2. With eyes open or closed and breathing in and out through your nose, become aware of the rhythm of your breath, relaxing your shoulders, your neck and your head.

3. Begin to deepen the breath, taking a long inhale through the nose, and exhaling fully to expel every last inch of the breath from your lungs. Observe how the breath feels entering and exiting the nose, and the way the body moves with each inhalation and exhalation. With each new breath, become aware of the point at which each inhale turns to an exhale. The brief moment at the end of an inhalation, just before an exhalation, is still and although it is not exactly a pause, it is a settling space, and bringing your awareness to it instils warmth and openness within the body. Focusing on this point will help to regulate your breath whilst also holding your attention, preventing other thoughts and feelings from drifting in or taking over. Whenever other thoughts of distraction do arise, bring your attention back to the gaps between each breath.

4. Practise for a minimum of 5–10 minutes, and bring the practice to a close when you feel more settled and peaceful.

Breath Retention (Kumbhaka Pranayama)

Antara Kumbhaka

1. Follow steps 1–2 of Breath Stillness.

2. Begin to deepen the breath, taking a long inhale through the nose, and exhaling fully to expel every last inch of the breath from your lungs. Observe how the breath feels entering and exiting the nose, and the way the body moves with each inhalation and exhalation.

3. On an inhale, notice when your lungs reach full capacity, and pause for a moment before exhaling fully. As you take your next inhalation, count the length of your breath, in seconds, pause at the top of your inhale for the same number of seconds you inhaled for, and exhale for the same number of seconds. Repeat this cycle a couple of times, and if the breath allows, gradually increase the length of each inhalation, breath retention and exhalation, keeping the ratio 1:1:1. Allow a few weeks of practising daily before extending the length of retention. Over time, increase to 8 seconds, but beginners are advised to work at 4–6 seconds. The practice should feel natural, effortless and entirely free from strain. As you retain the breath, feel as if the oxygen is sinking in and distributing itself, filling the tissues of your body.

4. You can either repeat the same counts in one practice (for example, working to a count of three for your entire practice) or you can increase the number of counts within one practice (for example, working to a count of three, inhaling, pausing and exhaling, and then increasing to a count of four, inhaling, pausing and exhaling, and then increasing again to five and maybe six, to however many seconds you can breathe comfortably).

5. Practise for up to 5 minutes, and sit in stillness for a few moments to readjust, before continuing your day. Once you are familiar with this practice and feel comfortable to develop further, work to a ratio of 1:2:3, for example, if you inhale for the count of 2, hold the breath for 4 and exhale for 6.

Morntime

Bahya Kumbhaka

1. Follow steps 1–2 of Breath Stillness (page 43).

2. Begin to deepen the breath, taking a long inhale through the nose, and exhaling fully to expel every last inch of the breath from your lungs. Observe how the breath feels entering and exiting the nose, and the way the body moves with each inhalation and exhalation.

3. Inhale gently to fill the lungs, noticing the number of seconds it takes to fill the lungs, and then exhale gradually for the same number of seconds, to fully expel the breath. Pause at the end of your exhalation for the same number of seconds you inhaled and exhaled for.

4. Practise like this for up to 5 minutes. Once you are familiar with this practice and feel comfortable to develop further, work to a ratio of 1:2:3. For example, if you inhale for the count of 2, hold the breath for 4 and exhale for 6.

Past, Present & Future Pranayama

I was introduced to this practice by a teacher and now a dear friend Pip. We frequently host events together and this practice has become routine for me since it was included in one of our first collaborations. The idea behind this practice is to follow the same tracks that your brain and ego travel along. Counting each breath in the past proves quite easy, showing how our minds are often comfortable in the past. Even if your past upsets or challenges you, it is familiar, so it is easy to get stuck there. You may notice that counting each breath in the future proves relatively difficult and frustrating. Your mind may struggle to stay consistent, or seem eager to count ahead of the breaths, showing how we wonder about and plan for the future, although there is no knowing what it holds, and so we feel off track in our actions. And the final section, counting during each breath, may seem neither easy nor difficult. You should find that counting during each breath is easier, and instils a sense of focus and clarity within. The intention of this practice is to help us cultivate the ability to stay in the present moment, with more devotion and awareness.

1. Take a comfortable seat, allowing yourself a few moments to settle. Breathe, observe the rhythm of your body, breath and mind, and find your flow.

2. Once settled, begin to count from one after each breath you take. Inhale and once you've exhaled fully, count that as one breath. For example: breathe in and out and count the number one in your head. Breathe in and out and count the number two. Do this for 4–5 minutes, with no aim to count to any specific number.

3. After 4–5 minutes, start counting each breath before you take it. For example, count the number one in your head and breathe in and breathe out. Do this for 4–5 minutes.

4. After 4–5 minutes, begin to count during each of your breaths. For example, count from the number one in your head about half way through your inhale, or anytime during your full breath. Do this for 4–5 minutes.

Movement

The morning is generally the last time of day most people want to plan any kind of extra movement. And whilst forcing yourself to run or workout when you're too tired is neither enjoyable nor wise, there are ways in which you can awaken the body through natural movement. Whether or not you intend to follow these practices with more intensive exercise, these traditional rituals have been performed for centuries to gently awaken the body, align with the breath and mind, and consquently enhance physical and mental performance. If I don't have time to fit in a proper workout, these exercises stimulate energy flow and make me feel more alive first thing in the morning.

Nauli Kriya

The Sanskrit term *kriya* translates as 'to do' and is a set of yogic exercises and techniques involving the body, mind and breath, practised daily for cleansing benefits. There are many different approaches to kriyas, but during my yogic journey I have consistently practised a few. You can think of it as separate to yoga, as it doesn't have to be performed on a mat, or during a yoga practice. Best performed on an empty stomach, it involves contracting and isolating certain muscles of the abdomen, gently massaging the organs, and is known to stimulate activity and improve digestion.

*   *If you are entirely new to yoga and pranayama, I would suggest practising first with a trained teacher. If you are pregnant, consult your doctor or a teacher before considering this practice.*

1. Stand with your feet hip-width apart and bend your knees, placing your hands firmly above them or on the thighs to support yourself. Open the chest, relax your shoulders and lengthen the spine, keeping the back of your neck long and the gaze forward.

2. Take a deep breath, and at the end of your exhale, hold the breath out of your lungs. Next, create a sort of vacuum sensation, sucking your stomach inwards and upwards, as if to tuck it into your ribcage (In Sanskrit this is termed *udiyana bhanda*). Stay here for however long feels comfortable, and release your stomach gently before your next inhalation.

3. Repeat this process, but this time as you hold your breath, release your stomach in and out, contracting and relaxing for however long feels comfortable. Then release your stomach fully before your next inhalation.

4. Repeat this sequence a few times, experimenting with the speed and force. Take deep, full breaths between each round, and rest if you feel dizzy or light-headed.

*   *Over time, you can begin to experiment with isolating each side of the abdominal muscles, and eventually both sides at the same time, to concentrate them towards the centre of your stomach and hold them there. Advanced learners may then develop a rhythmic rolling technique, almost like a wave of the abdominal muscles from one side to the other. This is extremely advanced and can take months or years to perfect, but I find simply contracting and releasing the stomach has major benefits for my digestion, as well as for my core strength.*

Do In & Self-Massage

When I started training in shiatsu I was introduced to the concept of Do-In – a self-treatment performed by practitioners before carrying out a treatment on a client. It emphasises the importance of looking after yourself in order to look after others, and I took this concept and applied it to everyday situations, not just shiatsu treatments. Whilst I understand the importance of taking care of yourself in order to function optimally, in this day and age we are influenced more to keep going and to 'power through', rather than to stop and recalibrate. To many, taking a break seems unproductive, and when I am busy and work is non-stop, self-care and time for myself is the easiest target for something to cut out of my schedule. But since learning these simple techniques (also knows as self-massage and self-shiatsu) that release tension, reduce stress and improve all kinds of misalignments in the meridians (energy channels) of the body, I feel more capable and attentive than if I were to push through, ignoring signs of fatigue and distraction.

Checking In & Grounding

This practice is for centring yourself, feeling grounded in your physical body and connecting the body and mind.

1. Sit or stand comfortably, either sitting on the floor with a straight back and relaxed shoulders, or standing with feet shoulder-width apart for support.

2. Rest your hands on your lower abdomen, just below your navel (known in shiatsu and other Eastern traditions as the hara – the physical and energetic centre of the body). As you breathe in and out, notice the expansion and contraction of your hara, and how it feels beneath your hands.

3. Close your eyes and consider how you feel right now, both mentally and physically. Is your mind busy? Do you notice any pain, tightness or discomfort? What parts of the body are you immediately aware of, and why? Then begin scanning your body from the top of your head to the tips of your toes, noticing how each part of you feels and acknowledging any sensations along the way. Become aware of your breath, breathing into each body part as you acknowledge it.

4. Now imagine, as you inhale, that fresh energy enters your body, gathering in your hara, creating warmth beneath your hands. As you exhale, imagine any tension leaving the body. Notice the areas in which you initially felt tension become lighter.

5. Spend a few minutes on this practice, and repeat if you move through it quickly. This exercise is all about bringing awareness to the physical body and for you to get to know how you feel at the beginning of each day. We constantly ask others how they are, but rarely ask ourselves how we feel. Start the day feeling more in-tune with and anchored in your body.

Tapping

Tapping is a simple routine that promotes blood circulation and energy flow, refreshing and invigorating the body. It involves tapping and massaging parts of the body, using a combination of fists and fingertips to activate them and to release any tension, emotion or energy blockages held within. This is one of my favourite rituals and can be an energising practice to include in your morning routine if you want to raise your vibrational energy and feel balanced, lighter and physically less stiff.

1. Stand with feet shoulder-width apart and bring each hand into a loose fist, keeping the wrists soft, supple and easy to rotate.

2. Starting at the head, use your fists (or fingertips if you prefer) and, with both hands, tap over the entire surface of your head. Tap the back of your head and your upper neck, then make your way around the sides and up over the top and the crown of your head. Tap for a few moments in each place, keeping the power behind your hands gentle – you are tapping, not hitting or punching.

3. Use your fingertips to massage the head and then bring the fingertips down past your forehead and across your entire face. Use a similar motion to applying moisturizer or washing your face, concentrating on the eyebrows, under eyes, cheekbones and jaw.

4. Work down the neck, squeezing and massaging however feels good. Move the head and neck to accommodate your actions, tipping the head forwards, backwards or from side to side. Massage the back of the neck and stroke down the front of the neck until you reach the chest area.

5. With one hand, hold the opposite elbow and tip your head toward the arm that is being held. Make a loose fist with the free hand, and begin tapping the opposite shoulder, focusing on the muscles around the neck and shoulder, and as far down the back as you can reach.

6. Release the supported elbow and continue working on the arms, tapping down the inside of the arms and tapping back up the back of the arms. Do this 3–5 times, ending at the shoulder rather than the wrist. Repeat steps 5 and 6 on the other arm.

7. Begin to tap across the chest area, tapping normally as you breathe out and more gently when you need to inhale.

8. Bend at the hips and fold forwards with your legs slightly bent. Release the head, neck and shoulders towards the floor and begin to tap the centre and sides of the back, moving to the lower back, the hips and then the buttocks. Use more force on the buttocks if you feel a lot of tension.

9. Tap down the outside of the legs to the ankles, and up the inside of the legs to the top of the thighs. Repeat 3–5 times, ending at the feet. Using your fingertips and focusing on one foot at a time, rub the Achilles tendon, ankles, heels and the top of the foot. (If you experience pain in the back or feel light-headed, do this sitting down, on the floor or a chair).

10. To end the practice, roll up slowly, one vertebra at a time, and stretch tall towards the sky. Release your arms, close your eyes, roll your shoulders down and away from your ears and stand, taking a few moments to notice how your body feels, and how it differs from before the practice.

* *This is a general tapping practice. There are specific points in the body that can also help heal specific issues, which should be researched and studied properly before practising.*

Shaking – arms & legs

This may seem a strange concept at first, but shaking is an amazing technque to get energy moving around the body. You can do it upon waking or even whilst waiting for the kettle to boil. It doesn't have to be done every day, but when things feel a little stiff or heavy it is such a simple technique to invigorate the body.

1. Stand with feet shoulder-width apart, arms hanging loosely by your sides.

2. Keeping it loose, start shaking your right arm, however feels good. You might shake from your shoulder and upper arm, or from the wrist and elbow. Shake for around 1 minute, and then repeat with the left arm. Then, shake both arms together, for around the same amount of time if it feels comfortable to do so.

3. Next, work on your legs, starting with the right and then the left. Move from the thigh or the feet, as if your toes are kicking water. After shaking, massage one hip and then, with your hand in a loose fist, tap down the outside of the leg, and up the inside a few times. Repeat on the other leg.

4. Finally, return to standing with feet shoulder-width apart and shake your entire body. Bending at the knees, shake from the shoulders, the core or the pelvic area, however feels good. Stop and rest, grounded and supported by your feet and take a few final moments to notice how each part of your body feels.

5. To close the practice, take a big inhale and lift your arms above your head. With your left hand, grab the right wrist and guide it gently towards the left, taking a gentle side-bend stretch. Return to the centre and repeat on the right-hand side. Lower the arms to end the practice.

Joint exercise – feet, ankles & hips

Think of this exercise as a way of 'oiling the machine', a pleasant and easy way to gently wake up the major joints and organs of the body. It will improve the flow of energy and release tension and stiffness.

1. Stand with your feet hip-width apart. Bring your weight onto one leg and stretch the other leg slightly out in front of you, pointing the toes. Flex the foot, bringing the toes to face towards you, then release, pointing the toes away from you. Repeat this for about 30 seconds, then shake the foot and repeat on the other leg.

2. Next, return to the standing position you started from and begin to turn your right foot inwards and hold, stretching the inside of the ankle for about 30 seconds. Then roll the foot onto the outer edge and hold, stretching the outside of the foot for about 30 seconds.

* *You can combine intentions or manifestations or mantras with your Do-In exercises.*

* *You can use these exercises anytime during the day, not just in the morning. They are a great way to release tension, after exercise or at the end of a long day.*

Makko Ho Stretches

There are many ways to stretch to promote blood circulation and energy flow to the organs that need it most. The lungs, large intestine, stomach and spleen are usually most active during the morning (between 3am and 11am), so these makko ho practices are focused around the energy channels (meridians) associated with these organs and the systems that require them.

Lungs & large intestines

This will activate the digestive system and encourage elimination, and exercise the lungs to ensure the breath flows optimally around the body.

1. Stand with feet shoulder-width apart and interlace your hands behind your back. Inhale, and as you exhale, bend forwards from the hips, over your legs, keeping the back straight, and lifting your arms behind you, reaching as far over your head as is comfortable towards the space in front of you. Let your head and neck hang and hold for as long as is comfortable, breathing consistently.

2. When you are ready to come up, take a deep breath in and roll up, one vertebra at a time. Settle to rest then repeat a couple more times. Close the practice by standing upright and stretching each arm across the opposite side of the body.

Stomach

This will energise the digestive system and regulate natural appetite.

1. Come to all fours with your knees and feet a little wider than hip-width apart. Gently sit back towards your heels until your seat reaches the floor between them, and sit upright with your hands in your lap (the Japanese term for this seated position is *seiza*). If this is uncomfortable, sit on a small cushion to elevate your seat and ease the stretch in your knees.

2. Settle here until comfortable, relaxing into the pose and breathing deeply. Acknowledge any sensation in the front of the thighs and down to the knees and ankles. If this is enough for you, stay here for a few breaths. If you want a more intense stretch, continue with the following steps.

3. Place your hands on the floor behind you with wrists in line with your shoulders and fingers facing towards you. Settle and breathe here for a few moments, and on an exhalation, lift your stomach and chest towards the sky, releasing your head and neck back as your gaze follows. Hold this for a few seconds, relax and come back to sitting upright. Repeat a few times and then move back through all fours to come out of the pose.

4. From all fours, bring your knees and ankles together and sit back onto your heels this time, using a cushion if extra support is required.

5. Sitting upright, lightly clasp your hands together and bring them over one knee. Gently begin to lift the knee a few inches off the ground, stretching the front of the foot and the ankle. If you are flexible, gradually lean back to deepen the stretch.

6. Do the same on the other leg, and repeat the sequence a few times on both sides. To come out of the pose, move through all fours and gently come to stand, shaking out the legs.

Morntime

Yoga Poses & Inversions

Yoga doesn't have to be a strict, dogmatic or competitive experience. Whilst some structure is crucial for safety and development, it can still be powerful to practise individual poses without working through a routine or attending a class. I like to work a few poses into my morning if I don't have time for an entire practice. Doing something, however brisk or gentle, helps to calm and centre my mind, instilling a sense of being prepared for the day ahead.

Inversions are yoga poses that involve being upside down, with the heart above the head. They are honoured for improving stamina, circulation, lymphatic drainage and confidence, as well as stimulating the nervous system in both energising and calming ways. The morning is a great time to practise inversions, to improve focus, but it is important to know how to do so safely. Below are a few simple poses for beginners. As your yoga practice develops, you might start introducing more powerful inversions, preferably with guidance from a teacher until you build strength and confidence.

Tree Pose (Vrikshasana)
This pose helps you to feel grounded, strong, powerful and present, whilst awakening the legs and releasing tension in the hips.

1. Begin by standing with your feet together, ankles and knees touching and arms loosely by your sides. Elongate through the spine, reaching the crown of your head towards the sky, and bring the palms of your hands together at the heart's centre (or use another mudra of choice (see pages 39–40 for examples).

2. On your next exhale, root down through the feet and find a feeling of steadiness and balance. Shift your weight onto your right leg, bend your left knee and hug your knee into your chest, keeping your head and neck reaching upwards.

3. With either or both hands, take your left ankle and place the sole of the foot flat on the inside of your right thigh above the knee, however high or low you can reach comfortably. Stand tall and firm on your right leg, and press the sole of your left foot into your standing leg. Push against the sole of the left foot with the thigh of the standing leg to create an even and balanced pressure. Focus on a still point directly ahead of you in line with your eyes or slightly above your eye line. Keep the chest open and high, shoulders down, hips facing forwards and pelvic floor engaged, whilst drawing the left knee out and back towards the left side.

4. Stand here for 5–20 full breaths, lengthening upwards with each inhale and rooting down through your standing leg with each exhale. Release your bent leg on an exhale, and return to standing with feet together, ankles and knees touching, and arms loosely by your sides. Repeat steps 2–4 on the other leg. Close the practice by standing with feet together, arms by your sides, and return to your natural breath.

Downward Dog

1. Come to all fours and move the spine however feels good for a few moments. When you're ready, tuck under the toes and begin to lift the knees, extending your legs and moving your hips back towards your heels. Lift the hips toward the sky, heels pushing backwards, shoulders drawing down your back away from the ears, and hands firmly on the ground.

2. Settle here and breathe deeply. If it feels good, maybe pedal your feet by bending one knee and lifting the heel, and repeating on the other leg to walk out the legs and deepen the stretch. Hold your downward dog for about five full breaths before releasing

Wall T Pose

1. Find a bare wall to work on and come to all fours with your toes tucked under, heels resting lightly on the wall where it meets the floor.

2. Come to Downward Dog, ensuring your shoulders are directly over your hands. Press your heels into the wall and then carefully begin to walk one leg up the wall, to around hip height. When you feel comfortable, slowly bring the other leg up to join it. Keeping shoulders over hands, work at straightening the legs, breathing deeply and staying focused.

3. To come out of the pose, gently walk your legs back down the wall and either walk your hands towards your feet to roll up to stand, or move through all fours to release.

* *Avoid too many or too strenuous inversions if you are menstruating, or too soon after eating, as the body is more in need of a downwards flow in these cases for blood flow and elimination. Consult your doctor or a teacher before practising inversions if you are pregnant, or injured.*

Revolved Twisted Lunge
A warming pose that energises the legs (improving strength and balance) and stimulates the internal organs (promoting detoxification and digestion).

1. Come to Downward Dog on hands and feet, heels pushing backwards, shoulders drawing down your back away from the ears, and hands firmly on the ground. As you inhale, lift your right leg off the ground and up towards the sky, and as you exhale, lower the leg, shift your shoulders over your wrists and bring the knee in towards your chest, releasing the foot onto the floor between your hands, ensuring the knee is directly over the foot.

2. From here, come to a high lunge, anchoring down through both feet, engaging the legs and lifting your hands off the ground to rest on your hips. Settle here in a high lunge, lengthening through the back and facing forwards.

3. On an inhale, straighten both legs then exhale and lift your arms overhead. As you exhale, re-bend the front leg, returning to a high lunge, and stretch the opposite arm to whichever foot is forwards straight out in front of you, as the other arm stretches back behind you. The hips remain level, whilst the chest opens up towards the direction in which you are twisting.

4. On your next inhale, come back to a high lunge and, as you exhale, twist again. Repeat a few times and then make your way back to Downward Dog and repeat with your left leg.

Cat/Cow (Marjaiasana/Bitilasana)
This is a simple, breath-regulating exercise between two poses that warms the body, loosens and activates the spine and opens the heart.

1. Come to all fours comfortably with your wrists directly under your shoulders and settle here for a moment, noticing the natural curve or arch of your back. Ensure your fingers face forwards and your knees and feet are hip-width apart. Engaging your core muscles, find a neutral spine, meaning the back is neither arched nor dipped, but flat.

2. Once settled, begin to move in any way that feels good to you. You might roll the shoulders, extend the arms whilst bending at the knees, arch or dip the back or even lift one arm at a time, twisting to one side and reaching towards the sky.

3. Then, return to a neutral spine and, on your next inhale, transition into cow pose, dropping your stomach towards the ground and creating a dip in your spine. Lift your head and chest, broaden your shoulders down and away from your ears, and extend and elongate through your lower back (sacrum), lifting it ever so slightly towards the sky. Keep your neck long and soft, and your gaze upwards and ahead.

4. As you exhale, transition into cat pose, drawing your stomach in towards your spine, rounding the back towards the sky. Release your head and neck, and engage the pelvic floor to support the lower back.

5. As you inhale, move back to cow pose, and repeat this exercise 10–20 times, or for however long feels good. Close the practice by coming to a neutral spine and returning to your natural breath.

Other Morntime Movement
On mornings when you have more time and energy, and want or need to wake up with a more vigorous, aerobic practice, natural movement exercises, home workouts and guided classes are great ways to get things moving.

1. Take a walk or go on a run locally.

2. If you find it easy to stay motivated, invest in some light weights, a skipping rope, a resistance band and any other gym equipment you tend to use and create your own bodyweight workout to practise at home. If you need more equipment and inspiration, find videos online, use an app or head to the gym, even if only for 20 minutes.

3. Attend a class, depending on your mood. Classes provide more structure and guidance, enhancing stamina and enthusiasm. Be mindful of what will assist you best each day and accept that some days maybe yoga will be demanding enough, and other days a high-intensity cardio class might be what you need. Don't force anything as it could end up being counterproductive.

Botanical Broths

Broths are usually made with animal bones and/or vegetables and used as a base for soups and stews but they have also been enjoyed as nourishing drinks in ancient traditions. Inspired by this, I've taken my daily hot water with lemon and ginger to the next level by developing lighter, more refreshing broths, made from healing fruits, roots and spices.

Rooted

Serves 6

1 litre water
2 handfuls of fresh lemon balm leaves
   (or lemongrass)
90g raw beetroot
5g liquorice root, chopped or crushed
2g rose petals
2 tbsp fennel seeds
juice and zest of 1 lime

15g fresh turmeric, sliced
small handful of dried hibiscus flowers

Elevate it: 5g chaga root powder, a handful of fresh or dried schizandra berries or dried goji berries, a small handful of fresh mint leaves or 10g fresh nettles

Heat the water in a saucepan and bring it to the boil. Add the remaining ingredients and simmer or steep off the heat for 30 minutes–1 hour. Remove from the heat, if necessary, and serve or allow to cool completely before transferring to a container to store. You can strain the liquid or transfer the liquid into a jar with all of the ingredients, to intensify the infusion over time.

Refresher

Serves 6

1.5 litres water
1 blood orange or navel orange,
   sliced into wedges
1 grapefruit or 1 lemon,
   sliced into wedges
1 green apple, chopped
15g fresh turmeric, chopped
40g fresh ginger, chopped

20g lemongrass, chopped
handful of fresh basil leaves
handful of fresh mint leaves

Elevate it: a handful of fresh or dried apricots, handful of dried goji berries, 10g fresh nettles, 2 tbsp aloe vera juice

To make this broth, follow the method for Rooted (see above).

Store in the fridge for up to 1 week.

Morntime

Making Smoothies

Full of concentrated goodness, smoothies are such powerful tools for feeling well and can completely transform your mood and energy levels in just a few sips. Easier to make and more filling than juices, they are gentler on a tired digestive system than a full meal. If you are hungry between meals, have low energy or feel unfocused, include ingredients that help improve concentration and boost energy levels (pages 297–298). And after working out, smoothies can provide a quick delivery of essential ingredients required for growth, repair and a swift recovery.

I don't think I've ever made the same smoothie twice as I rarely measure ingredients and prefer to add things as I go until I'm satisfied with the taste. Below is the core structure I generally work to. You can be flexible and creative, using whatever ingredients you have on hand or whatever the current season has to offer. As with anything, use your understanding of your own body and your intuition to choose ingredients that suit your taste preferences and dietary requirements. Add more thickening ingredients to transform these smoothies into smoothie bowls, and top them with your favourite combination of fruit, nuts, seeds and granola (pages 70 & 82).

Serves 1–2

Foundation Ingredients

Liquids (250ml)
Plant-based milk (pages 304–306)
Coconut water
Water
Homemade iced tea or infusions (page 119)

Base ingredients (100–150g)
Frozen fruits, such as avocado or berries
Elevate it: mango and acai and pitaya pulp, fresh fruits such as citrus fruit, apples, cherries and other soft fruits, fresh vegetables such as spinach, lettuce, kale, celery, carrots and beetroot

Thickeners (20–50g)
Nuts (I like cashews, almonds, Brazil nuts, walnuts and pecans)
Seeds (I like linseeds, sunflower, pumpkin and hemp seeds, and raw or soaked chia seeds)
Grains and psuedograins, such as soaked or cooked oats, soaked or cooked buckwheat and cooked quinoa, millet or rice
Nut & Seed butters
Cooked beans

Plant additions
(1–2 tbsp fresh ingredients or 1–2 tsp powdered)
Fresh herbs and spices
Ground herbs and spices
Adaptogens, tonic herbs and plant powders, such as maca, ashwagandha, chaga, reishi, lucuma, he shou wu or bee pollen

Sweeteners, to taste
Dried fruit, such as dates or apricots
More fresh fruit
Natural syrup of choice

6 ice cubes

Put all the ingredients apart from the ice in a blender and blend on a medium to high speed for 1–2 minutes, until everything is combined. Add any sweetener gradually, to suit your taste. Add the ice and then blend again on the highest speed until the ice has fully broken down and you have a silky-smooth, creamy texture. Serve instantly.

Salted Vanilla & Walnut Smoothie

Serves 2

Enjoy this gently energising drink, which is more like a milkshake than a smoothie, on an empty stomach in the morning or before or after a workout, to support muscle repair and to reduce fatigue. Elevate it with your choice of plant powders, and add 2 tablespoons of raw cacao powder for a rich, chocolatey version.

1 1/2 T
20g raw almonds (with or without skin)

2 tbsp hemp seeds or golden linseeds

2 T+
30g raw walnuts

1
100g banana, sliced and frozen

2 tbsp avocado

3/4 C
200ml filtered water or plant-based milk
(pages 304–306)

1 tsp maca powder

½ tsp ground cinnamon

0.5–1g salt

20g tahini or nut butter (page 308)   *1 1/2 T*
(I like almond butter)

2g vanilla powder   *1/2 t*

1 medjool date

6–8 ice cubes

Put all the ingredients apart from the ice in a blender and blend on a medium to high speed for 1–2 minutes, until smooth. Add the ice and then blend again on the highest speed until the ice has fully broken down and you have a silky-smooth, creamy texture. Serve instantly.

Pomegranate, Ginger, Red Grape & Rose Spirit Juice

Serves 2

This drink doesn't require a juicer and is my go-to if I'm feeling particularly low-vibe or lacklustre in the morning. Dosing up on these skin-supporting ingredients instantly floods my complexion with colour and vitality. The scent of rose water is known to reduce stress and anxiety and promote emotional wellbeing, making this not just a juice but an experience.

seeds of 1 pomegranate
400ml water
200g seedles red grapes
juice of 1 lime
3 tsp grated fresh ginger
2 tsp pure rose water
4–6 ice cubes, plus extra to serve

1½ C
7/8 <

Elevate it: ½ tsp bee pollen or ½ tsp pine pollen, ½ tsp ginseng, 1 tbsp chia seeds (soaked or raw)

Put the pomegranate seeds and water in a blender and blend for 1 minute on the highest speed, then strain into a glass or a jug and set aside.

Rinse the blender and then blend the grapes with the remaining water for 1–2 minutes on the highest speed. Strain, then return the liquid to the blender, add the pomegranate juice along with the remaining ingredients (including any elevational extras) and blend on the highest speed for 1–2 minutes, until combined. Serve over ice.

Citrus & Hibiscus Iced Green Tea

Serves 2

Iced tea always brings back memories of summer holidays and times spent abroad. Often it's loaded with sugar but this recipe can exist entirely without it. However, for those with a sweeter tooth, a little honey or natural sweetener can of course be added. You could freeze this mixture in ice-lolly moulds or use it as a base for alcoholic or non-alcoholic cocktails.

1–2 green teabags or 2–3 tbsp loose green tea
600ml boiling water
100ml grapefruit juice
8g dried hibiscus leaves
1 tsp natural sweetener (optional)

Elevate it: 1 tsp liquid probiotics, 2 tbsp kombucha or Water Kefir (page 317), 1 tsp aloe vera juice

6–8 ice cubes, plus extra to serve

Start by brewing the tea in the boiling water. Set aside whilst you muddle the grapefruit juice and hibiscus together in a glass, mug or jug, using a spatula or wooden spoon.

Once brewed, add the tea to the grapefruit mixture, along with the sweetener or any elevational extras, if using. Strain the mixture and leave to chill in the fridge for at least 2 hours before serving. Alternatively, blend with ice for 1–2 minutes to cool and serve immediately.

For a lazy option, simply put all the ingredients in a jug or jar, seal the lid and place in the fridge for 6–8 hours, or overnight, to brew and chill.

Mint or jasmine tea also work nicely as a caffeine-free option.

You can also swap the grapefruit juice for (blood) orange juice, depending on seasonal availability, and the hibiscus leaves for 10g fresh raspberries or cherries.

Making Tonics & Shots

A tonic is a medicinal plant-based drink that promises to enhance feelings of strength, vitality and general wellbeing. Tonics are not dissimilar to milks (page 304–307) or lattes (page 168–171) and can be made with the same healing herbs and adaptogenic plant powders. However, with less sweet, indulgent ingredients (like natural syrups or nut butters), more power lies in their stripped-back purity and their effects are instantaneous and long-lasting. Whether you sense the onset of illness or feel generally rundown, a tonic (even a shot-sized portion) can help soothe, enhance energy levels and prevent certain symptoms. Once you begin incorporating tonics into your daily or weekly routine, you'll notice that a glass of hot water with he shou wu or a simple shot of milk and mucuna pruriens outshines your standard cup of tea or coffee.

Plant powders, tonic herbs and adaptogens are potent ingredients and, if you are not familiar with them or unsure about how to use them, consult a herbalist or healthcare practitioner for further or specific advice. Start off by consuming a ½ tsp of your chosen ingredients per day, and gradually build up your doses once you know how your body and mind responds to them. You may not notice any changes or feel any differences at all, but the chances are things will still be shifting internally.

Tonics start with a liquid base (about 250ml) of water, coconut water, plant-based milk, fresh fruit juice or herbal tea. To this you add your chosen combination of tonic herbs and adaptogens (½–1 tsp), fresh or ground herbs and spices (½–1 tsp), fresh or puréed fruits or vegetables (1 tbsp), premade or shop-bought tinctures (2–5 drops) or medicinal pastes (½–1 tsp). If extra sweetness is desired, you can add your preferred natural sweetener, such as coconut sugar or a natural syrup, but it's best to keep them to a minimum. Fats are often included in the basic components of a tonic and they make certain vitamins and nutrients more bioavailable and easily assimilated. It is not essential but coconut oil, olive oil or ghee (¼–½ tsp) add a nice creamy texture and extra flavour.

To make a tonic, place your chosen ingredients (use those that feel particularly beneficial, depending on how you feel from one day to the next) in a mug or glass and use a fork, small whisk or electric milk frother to combine. Alternatively, put all the ingredients into a blender and blend on the highest speed for up to 1 minute, until smooth.

Serves 1

Foundation Ingredients

Liquids (250ml)
Water
Coconut water
Plant-based milk (pages 304–306)
Fresh fruit juice
Tea or herbal infusion
Coffee

Flavourings
Plant powders, such as tonic herbs and
    adaptogens (½–1 tsp)
Fresh or ground herbs and spices (½–1 tsp)
Fresh or puréed fruits or vegetables (1 tbsp)
Premade or shop-bought tinctures (2–5 drops)
Herbal pastes (pages 308–309) (½–1 tsp)

*(See page 312 for a full list of plant powders
and more details about each one)*

Sweeteners (as little as possible)
Coconut sugar or natural syrup

Fats (¼–½ tsp)
Coconut oil, olive oil, ghee (optional)

Simply combine your chosen ingredients in
a mug or glass, using a fork, small whisk or
an electric milk frother whisk, or put all the
ingredients in a blender and blend on the
highest speed for 45 seconds.

Here are some of my favourite combinations:

Water-based Tonics
Hot water or tea with he shou wu powder
Hot water with herbal paste (pages 308–309)
Hot water with cacao and coffee (or chicory)
Hot water with reishi, chaga, shilajit and
    cinnamon powders
Hot coffee with cacao and maca powder

Milk-based Tonics
Hot almond milk with cacao, maca, tocos,
    ashwagandha and mucuna pruriens
    powders and pine pollen
Hot almond milk with herbal paste
    (pages 308–309)
Hot coconut milk with astragalus, vanilla
    and cordyceps powders and ½ date
Hot hemp milk with lion's mane mushroom,
    ashitaba and maca powders and wheatgrass
Chilled almond milk with cacao, he shou wu
    and tocos and ground ginseng
Chilled coconut milk with mint leaves
    and tocos, vanilla and ashwagandha powders

Juice-based Tonics
Hot turmeric and ginger juice
Iced cucumber juice with acai, gotu kola
    and schizandra powders
Iced ginger juice with aloe vera juice
    and ginseng

Shots:
Pure aloe vera juice – *for detoxification*
Pure apple cider vinegar – *for digestion
    and acid regulation*
Ginger juice with lemon and cayenne pepper
    – *for cleansing and immunity*
Turmeric juice with black pepper – *for easing
    joint stiffness, boosting the immune system
    and enhancing concentration*
Carrot and cinnamon juice – *for skin support,
    boosting the immune system and enhancing
    oral health*

Morntime Milk

Serves 1

This morntime milk awakens the body and mind gently but powerfully. The stomach isn't always ready to digest a full meal in the morning and liquids are an ideal concentrated source of goodness that aren't too demanding on the digestive system. This milk is much lighter than a smoothie or a shake and, being high in fibre and protein, makes the perfect base for any of your favourite energising adaptogens to get you functioning fully in the morning.

1 c
1 1/2 T

240ml almond milk
15g hemp seeds
1 tsp chia or golden linseeds
1 tsp maca powder
½ tsp vanilla powder
½ tsp ground cinnamon
½ date (optional)
handful of ice

Elevate it: 2 tbsp tocotrienols, small sprinkling of bee pollen, ½ tsp mucuna pruriens powder, ½ tsp ashwagandha powder, ½ tsp he shou wu powder

Put all the ingredients apart from the ice in a blender and blend on the highest speed for 1 minute. Add the ice and then blend for a further 10–30 seconds, until the ice is combined and the liquid is smooth. Serve instantly as it is or pour over more ice.

For a hot drink, omit the ice and, once blended, transfer the milk to a small saucepan, heat through for 1–2 minutes, then serve instantly.

Ginger, Turmeric, Apple Cider Vinegar & Almond Tonic

Makes 6 shots, 1 long drink or 2 lattes

These ingredients are punchy, but their flavours are softened by almond milk. It is inspired by ancient Ayurvedic home remedies that have been used for centuries to boost the immune system and support internal unrest.

2 tbsp fresh ginger juice
    (or 2 tbsp grated fresh ginger)
4 tbsp turmeric juice
    (or 2 tbsp grated fresh turmeric)
100ml almond milk
1 tsp apple cider vinegar

pinch of black pepper or cayenne pepper
pinch of ground cinnamon

Elevate it: ½ tsp ashwagandha powder, ½ tsp ground ginseng

If you don't have a juicer, put all the ingredients in a blender and blend on the highest speed for 1–2 minutes, until everything is combined. .

Alternatively, if you do have a juicer, juice the ginger and turmeric. Transfer the juice to a blender, add the remaining ingredients and blend on the highest speed for 1 minute.

Strain into a large glass to enjoy as a long drink, or serve up a shot glass portion and store the remainder in the fridge for up to 3 days.

Orange, Ginger, Sesame & Apricot Botanical Granola

Makes about 4 servings

Preheat the oven to 140°C / gas mark 1

Line a baking tin with baking paper

I have met so many people who experienced the same shock I did when I discovered all the hidden ingredients in processed cereals, and worse, granolas, which are so innocently advertised as healthy. In reality, most granolas contain gluten (which, intolerance or not, more and more people are choosing to avoid), and are high in several kinds of sugars and hydrogenated fats. These botanical versions are gluten-, dairy- and sugar-free and are naturally flavoured and nutritionally enhanced by the power of plants and Ayurvedic spices. You can also use this granola as a topping for smoothies, smoothie bowls or desserts.

3/4 c 150g gluten-free jumbo oats
1 C ~~240g~~ sunflower seeds
1 1/2 T ~~40g~~ buckwheat (or extra sunflower seeds)
2 T ~~30g~~ almonds, chopped
1 T + 10g linseeds
1 T + 10g sesame seeds
12g ground ginger or grated fresh ginger
1 T + 10g ground or grated fresh turmeric
s t 40g apricots, dates, raisins or goji berries, chopped
pinch of salt
grind of black pepper

140ml fresh orange juice 1/2 c t
70g coconut sugar 1 4 t
1 tsp lemon juice
2 tbsp sesame oil
2 tbsp coconut oil
1 tbsp tahini or nut butter
2 tsp orange blossom water
Coconut Yogurt (page 306)

Elevate it: 1 tsp bee pollen, 1 tbsp edible dried flowers, 20g chopped walnuts, 1 tbsp maca powder, 1 tbsp acerola cherry powder

In a large bowl, mix together the oats, sunflower seeds, buckwheat, almonds, linseeds, sesame seeds, ginger, turmeric, dried fruit, salt and pepper.

Heat 100ml of the orange juice in a small saucepan over a medium heat. Add the coconut sugar and whisk until dissolved. Bring to the boil, then reduce the heat and simmer for 1–2 minutes, until the syrup thickens slightly. Remove from the heat and pour over the dry ingredients, stirring with a spatula or wooden spoon. Add the remaining orange juice, lemon juice, oils, tahini or nut butter and orange blossom water and stir until the dry ingredients are evenly coated and begin to stick together.

Tip the mixture into the prepared baking tin, spreading it out evenly, and bake for 30–35 minutes, stirring gently halfway through.

Allow to cool, stir through any of the elevational extras, if using, and serve with coconut yogurt. Store in an airtight container for up to 3 weeks.

Coconut, Miso & Buckwheat Porridge

Serves 2

Porridge is filling, high in fibre and protein, and quick and affordable to make. However, when prepared with just oats and water, it doesn't quite reach its full potential, and by making a few simple tweaks, this version will give you reason to get out of bed and will keep you thriving all through the day.

250g raw buckwheat groats
1 × 400ml can coconut milk
120ml almond milk (or water)
1 tbsp natural sweetener
2–3 tbsp coconut palm sugar
½ tsp white or brown miso paste
5–6 tbsp chia seeds
2 tbsp golden linseeds
½ tsp ground cardamom
1 tbsp coconut oil

1 tsp vanilla powder
1 tsp ground ginger
1 tbsp maca powder

For the topping
fresh fruit or veg, such as mango, peach,
    berries or grated carrot
1 tbsp cacao nibs
Qnola or granola (pages 70 & 82)
2 tbsp coconut or probiotic yogurt

To make the porridge, soak the buckwheat groats overnight or for at least 8 hours. Rinse the buckwheat and transfer to a saucepan, with the coconut milk and almond milk (or water). Bring to the boil, reduce the heat and simmer for 10 minutes, then add all the remaining ingredients. Add more miso or natural sweetener, to taste, along with any other spices or adaptogen powders you desire. Simmer for a further 20–30 minutes, stirring occasionally, until the liquid has reduced and been absorbed by the buckwheat and other seeds. Remove from the heat and serve immediately, or leave to cool and store in the fridge in an airtight container. Reheat, or stir with hot nut milk or water before serving, or enjoy chilled like bircher muesli. Serve with toppings of your choice.

Buckwheat Crepes

Serves 4–6

Pancake production was my duty in our family home from a very young age. Once I was old enough to identify eggs, milk, flour and a whisk, I became chief pancake maker, and I held the title proudly. Crepes became the centrepiece of our weekend rituals, and to this day, a weekend feels a little off without them. Serve with your favourite toppings to enhance the flavour and nutritional benefits of your morning meal even further (page 75).

200g buckwheat flour
pinch of sea salt
3 eggs
450ml almond milk
200ml water
2–3 tbsp coconut oil, melted
a selection of your favourite toppings, to serve (see page 75)

To flavour (optional)
4 tbsp beetroot powder or
    4 tbsp grated beetroot
4 tbsp blueberry powder or
    40g frozen blueberries
4 tbsp strawberry powder or
    40g frozen strawberries

Put the flour and salt in a bowl and briefly mix to combine. Make a well in the middle with your fist and fill it with the eggs. Combine the milk and water in a measuring jug and then begin whisking the flour and eggs together, adding the liquids gradually as you go. Finally, whisk in 1 tablespoon of the oil. When fully combined, strain the batter to remove any lumps and transfer to a jug. To flavour the batter, if you like, transfer to a blender along with your desired flavourings and blend for 1 minute or until smooth.

Heat about 1 tablespoon of the remaining oil in a large frying pan over a medium heat. As it begins to sizzle, carefully pour some batter into the centre of the pan, swirling to evenly coat the base, and fry for about 1 minute, until the edges come away from the pan when nudged with a spatula. Run your spatula beneath the pancake to ease it away from the pan, then flip and cook on the other side for 1 minute. Continue to flip and fry until you are satisfied with the level of brownness and crispiness.

Slide the pancake onto a large plate and keep warm in the oven on a low heat whilst you use up the remainder of the batter, piling each fresh pancake on top of the last, and keeping them all in the oven to keep warm. Serve as a stack or on individual plates with a selection of your favourite toppings

Chill any leftover pancakes in the fridge and enjoy as wraps with your favourite sweet or savoury fillings. I make a batch of filled pancakes and cut them into halves to store in the fridge as on-demand snacks or to add to packed lunches.

Caramelised Banana Surprise Pancakes

Makes 8–10 small–medium pancakes

This pancake recipe is a whole different story. With just a few extra ingredients and a slight tweak in quantities, you can transform the basic European crepe into a picture-perfect stack of the lightest, fluffiest American-style pancakes. This variation ends in a big finale of caramelised bananas, adding a warm, rich, gooey texture, whilst increasing the nutritional integrity of each bite. High in protein and valuable vitamins and minerals, these pancakes will give you a lift after a long week or just a late night.

220g buckwheat flour
1 tbsp coconut sugar, plus extra to serve
1 tsp baking powder
pinch of sea salt
1 egg
220ml plant-based milk (pages 304–306)
2 ripe bananas
3 tbsp coconut oil, melted (or butter / olive oil)

Elevate it: ½ tsp ground cinnamon or cardamom, 3 tbsp cacao powder (for a chocolatey version), handful of raw chocolate chips, 1 tbsp hemp seeds or golden linseeds

Combine the flour, sugar, baking powder and salt in a bowl.

In a separate bowl, whisk the egg and milk until pale and fluffy. In another bowl, mash one banana until almost puréed.

Gradually add the wet mixture to the dry ingredients, whisking constantly. Then add 1 tablespoon melted coconut oil (or butter) and the mashed banana and whisk a final time. If using, add any elevational extras you like, stirring through the mixture to distribute evenly.

Heat about a teaspoon of the remaining oil in a large frying pan over a medium heat. Whilst it heats, slice the second banana into rounds, about ½cm thick. Place 2–3 banana rounds onto the surface of the frying pan and cover with about 3 tablespoons of the batter. Repeat until you have 3 pancakes in the pan.

Cook for about 1–2 minutes or until air bubbles begin to appear, then flip the pancakes over with a spatula and cook the other side. Cook for about 2–3 minutes in total, flipping back and forth a couple of times to ensure they are cooked through and each side is golden.

Slide the pancake onto a large plate and keep warm in the oven on a low heat whilst you use up the rest of the batter, piling each fresh pancake on top of the last, and keeping them all in the oven to keep warm. Serve as a stack or on individual plates with a selection of your favourite toppings.

Morntime

My Favourite Pancake Toppings:
A natural syrup of your choice and a pinch of salt; chocolate sauce or chocolate
spread with raw chocolate chips, bee pollen and extra banana; chocolate
spread and coconut cream; lemon juice, passion fruit, mango and coconut
sugar; almond butter, banana and hemp seeds; avocado, spinach and pesto.

Morntime

Buckwheat, Flax & Almond Flakes

Makes about 4 servings

Preheat the oven to 140°C /gas mark 1

Whilst shop-bought breakfast cereals are quick, easy and affordable, they rarely contain ingredients that will help you to thrive, and often deliver unwanted side effects, especially if you have allergies or intolerances. For anyone looking for an alternative that is just as quick and easy to prepare, your search ends here. Enjoy these breakfast flakes with plain or flavoured plant-based milk (pages 304–306), and make a double (or triple) batch to ensure you always have some in storage.

80g ground almonds
150g buckwheat flour (or other gluten-free flour)
150g milled flaxseeds/golden linseeds
6g coconut sugar (optional)

small pinch of Himalayan pink salt
2g baking powder or arrowroot (optional)
180–200ml water
200ml plant-based milk (pages 304–306)

Put the almonds, flour, seeds, sugar, salt and baking powder or arrowroot into a mixing bowl and stir until combined. Gradually add the water and milk and mix with a spatula. Add more water if the mixture seems too thick and dry — it should be a wet paste-like consistency.

Cut some baking paper into four large rectangles and dollop about a quarter of the mixture onto each. Hold the paper at one end and spread the mixture as thinly as possible – no more than 1mm thick. It doesn't have to reach the edges of the paper, just ensure it is spread evenly and without gaps.

Carefully place each sheet of baking paper directly onto your oven racks. You want the air to circulate beneath the mixture too, to really dry them out, so using a baking tray is not advised.

Bake for 20–30 minutes (this will depend on how thinly you managed to spread your mixture). After 20 minutes, test the mixture by snapping a little bit off the edge and setting it aside to cool. If it seems crunchy enough, remove all sheets from the oven and leave to cool completely. If it still seems a little chewy, cook for a further 10 minutes, testing until you are satisfied.

Once cooled, gently peel away from the baking paper and break it into small flakes with your hands. Store in an airtight container for up to 2 weeks.

For flavoured varieties, add 1 tablespoon vanilla powder, 1 tablespoon cacao powder or ½ teaspoon ground cinnamon or cardamom in the first step.

Date, Orange, Almond & Honey Bircher

Serves 2

I was always opposed to the concept of bircher mueslis as they looked like less-appetising versions of porridge and were never something I could get excited about. Then, one morning at Dimes, my favourite restaurant in NYC, things changed. This recipe is inspired by one of their breakfast bowls, a date bircher made with almond milk and topped beautifully with fresh fruits and coconut. I only wish I could somehow bring the vibe and atmosphere of their eatery to your kitchen too, but for now, start with this and we'll figure the rest out later. You can eat this instantly or leave overnight.

200ml almond milk
120g gluten-free jumbo oats
juice and flesh of 1 large orange
40g dates, apricot or goji berries, chopped
2 tbsp chia seeds
1–2 tbsp honey

½ tsp vanilla powder
2 tbsp almond or cashew butter (optional)
your favourite toppings, to serve

Elevate it: ½ tsp orange blossom water or rose water

Mix all the ingredients apart from the nut butter together in a large bowl, stirring and gently mashing the dried fruits and squeezing out every last drop of juice from the orange. Stir through the elevational extras, if using. Refrigerate for an hour to soften, or overnight to allow the oats and seeds to absorb the liquids and become sweet, soft and creamy by the time you're ready for breakfast.

After soaking, blend a quarter of the mixture (about 4 tablespoons) in a high speed blender until smooth. Stir the blended mixture through the rest of the bircher, adding the nut butter if you think it needs thickening. Serve with a selection of your favourite toppings.

Morntime

Quick Banana, Cacao & Oat Bircher

Serves 1–2

This is my favourite thing to make if I'm in a rush, as it is highly energising, filling but not too filling, and takes just minutes to prepare. For an even creamier result, prepare this in the evening and leave it in the fridge overnight.

For the bircher
150g gluten-free jumbo oats, plus extra
    if necessary
200ml plant-based milk (pages 304–306),
    plus extra if necessary
1 ripe banana (or 1 ripe avocado)
4–5 tbsp cacao powder
1 tsp maca powder
2 tbsp milled flax or golden linseeds
1 tbsp whole chia seeds
1 tsp coconut sugar or other natural sweetener
pinch of sea salt

To serve
nut butter
fresh fruits
nuts
seeds
Qnola or Granola (pages 70 & 82)

Elevate it: 1 tbsp tocos powder, 1 tsp mucuna pruriens powder, 1 tsp ashwagandha powder

Place the oats in a large bowl and cover with the plant-based milk. Chop the banana into the bowl and use a fork to mash it into the oat mixture. Add the cacao, maca, seeds, natural sweetener and salt along with any elevational extras of your choice, and mix to combine with a fork. If the mixture seems dry, add a little more milk. If it seems too wet, add a small handful of extra oats.

Leave to soak for 5–10 minutes (or longer if you have the time). Top with any or all of the serving suggestions above.

Matcha, Avocado and Spinach Smoothie Bowl

Serves 2

The smoothie bowl is a genius concept. Descended from the traditional Brazilian 'acai bowl', which consist of frozen and puréed acai fruit, smoothie bowls can be made from pretty much any fruits or vegetables, and are a more fulfilling way to dose up on fresh ingredients than a smoothie, which is often over far too quickly. Pour into a bowl or a takeaway container, cover with your favourite toppings and enjoy the flavour and variety of a full meal with the minimal effort of a smoothie.

You can transform any smoothie into a smoothie bowl by adding thickening ingredients and reducing the amount of liquid used. Experiment with adding frozen banana, avocado, mango, soaked nuts (cashews work well), young Thai coconut flesh or even beans and pulses to your favourite smoothies and enjoy them from the bowl with a selection of toppings.

3 tbsp chia seeds
8 tbsp water
15g spinach
80ml plant-based milk (pages 304–306)
100g banana, frozen
30g avocado, fresh or frozen
10g linseeds or hemp seeds

5g vanilla powder
½ medjool date
½ tsp matcha powder
4–5 leaves of fresh herbs, such as mint or basil
pinch of salt
8–10 ice cubes
a selection of your favourite toppings to serve

First make the chia seed gel. Combine the chia seeds and water in a small bowl, stir gently and then leave to soak for about 10 minutes, stirring again after 5 minutes.

Put all the remaining ingredients apart from the ice in a blender and blend on the highest speed for about 30 seconds until everything is combined. Taste and add more vanilla, matcha or dates, as desired.

When the chia seed gel has formed, add to the blender along with the ice and blend again on the highest speed for a further 1–2 minutes, until the ice is fully broken down and the mixture thick and smooth.

Serve instantly with a selection of toppings. I like Cacao & Hemp Seed Freezer Granola (page 82), Orange, Ginger, Seasme & Apricot Botanical Granola (page 70), fresh fruits, nuts, seeds, cacao nibs, coconut and a sprinkling of adaptogens.

Cacao & Hemp Seed Freezer Granola

Serves 4–6 (makes about 700g in total)

As with most things, toppings are just as important as the base they sit upon, and this freezer granola is about to change your life. The freezer does most of the work, hardening the coconut oil around the other ingredients to make the crunchiest, most flavoursome granola you've ever tasted, with no baking necessary. Use to top smoothie bowls or enjoy with plant-based milks (pages 304–306) or yogurts (pages 306–7).

200g mixed nuts, chopped
pinch of sea salt
50g cacao powder
120g desiccated coconut
40g hemp seeds
60g ground almonds
60g sunflower seeds
5–10g bee pollen

80g coconut oil, melted
35–40g natural syrup
40g nut butter or tahini

Elevate it: 1 tsp reishi powder, 1 tsp mucuna pruriens powder, ½ tsp matcha powder, handful of cacao nibs or raw chocolate chips

Put all the dry ingredients in a large bowl and stir to combine. Add the oil, syrup and nut butter or tahini, along with any elevational extras, and stir vigorously with a spatula or wooden spoon, to ensure the dry ingredients are evenly and throroughly coated.

Transfer to a plate, freezerproof container or baking tray, scattering the mixture out evenly across the surface. (You could also form larger clusters by rolling some of the mixture together and squeezing it gently in your hands).

Place it in the freezer and allow it to harden for a minimum of 30 minutes. Store it in the freezer until ready to serve.

Morntime

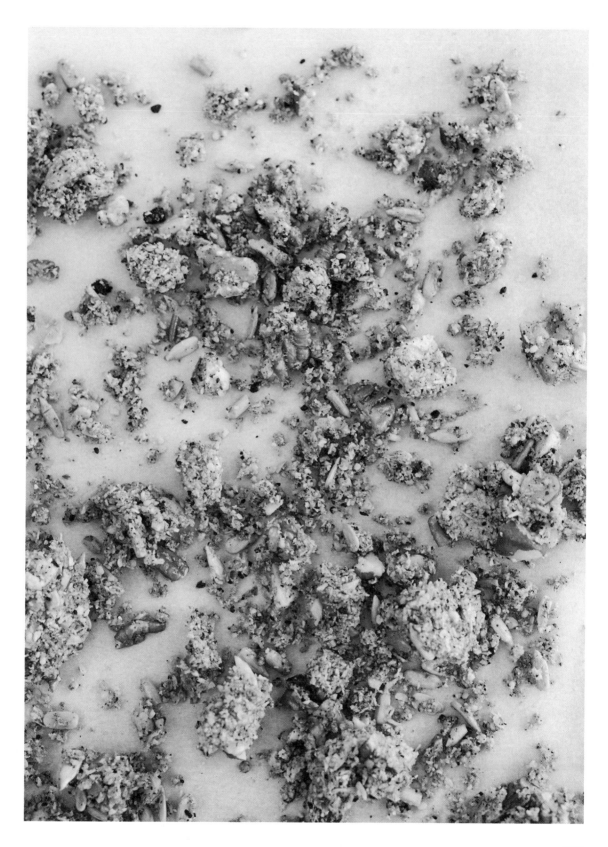

Buckwheat Waffles

Serves 4

Waffles were something I never used to make, purely because I've never owned a waffle maker. For any of you who can relate, meet the griddle pan method. Serve the waffles with a selection of your favourite toppings or slice into long strips and serve with dips, such as Coconut Cream (page 239), Chocolate Spread (page 240) and nut butter (page 308).

2 eggs
200ml plant-based milk (page 304–306)
2 tsp vanilla powder
120g buckwheat flour
100g ground almonds
1 tbsp ground cinnamon

1–2 tbsp cashew or almond butter
2 tbsp milled linseeds (optional)
pinch of salt
1 tsp baking soda
2–3 tbsp melted coconut oil

In a large bowl, whisk the eggs, milk and vanilla together until combined.

Gradually add the flour, then the almonds, cinnamon, nut butter, milled linseeds, if using, salt and baking powder, whisking constantly to combine. Lastly, add 1 tablespoon of the coconut oil and whisk a final time.

Heat about a teaspoon of the remaining oil in a large griddle pan over a medium heat. To make small, round waffles, drop large spoonfuls of the mixture onto the pan, or for larger waffles, pour the batter into the pan and spread it evenly to coat the base. Cook on one side for 1–2 minutes, until the batter firms up and you can ease the waffle away from the pan, then flip and cook the other side for the same amount of time. Lower the heat and continue to cook until each side begins to brown where the lines of the griddle pan have scorched it.

Slide the waffle onto a large plate and keep warm in the oven on a low heat whilst you use up the rest of the batter, piling each fresh waffle on top of the last, and keeping them all in the oven to keep warm.

You can replace the eggs with 4 tablespoons chia seed gel (see page 81) or ½ banana, mashed.

Double Sweet Corn Fritters with Eggs

Serves 4 (makes 6–8 fritters)

This recipe is perfect for low-energy mornings because, whilst it looks and tastes impressive, it is simple to prepare. The sweetcorn fritters stand in for conventional breakfast carbs and bring more nutrition to the table. For a very simple option, pair them with avocado or for something more extravagant, serve them with poached eggs, a selection of homemade dips, seaweed salad or greens and pickles or Sauerkraut (pages 316–317). Bacon, Coconut 'Bacon' (page 313) or smoked fish also make a nice addition.

4–8 eggs
2 avocados
1 tbsp lemon juice (optional)
pinch of salt (optional)

For the sweetcorn fritters
350g corn kernels, cooked and cooled
1 large egg (or 1 tbsp chia gel, page 81)
1 tsp ground or freshly grated turmeric
pinch of sea salt

2 tbsp extra virgin olive oil, plus extra
    for frying
60g buckwheat flour
½ tsp baking powder
small handful of fresh coriander leaves
    (or other fresh herbs)
freshly ground black pepper

Elevate it: 1 tsp shilajit powder, 1 tsp spirulina powder, 2 tbsp golden linseeds or chia seeds

First, make the fritters. Place 100g of the corn in a blender and add the egg or chia gel, turmeric, salt and oil. Add any elevate ingredients, if using, and blend on a high-speed for 30 seconds, until it forms a thick, creamy paste. Once smooth, transfer to a bowl, add the remaining corn kernels, flour, baking powder and coriander (or other fresh herbs) and stir to combine. Season to taste with salt and pepper.

Heat a little oil in a large frying pan over a medium heat and, once warm, spoon 3–4 large ladlefuls of batter – spaced apart to avoid them merging into one – into the pan. Flatten slightly with the back of a spoon and cook for 1–2 minutes, until brown and crisp, then flip and cook the other side for 1–2 minutes, until crispy. Repeat until all the batter has been used up.

Meanwhile, scramble, fry or poach your eggs. Next, prepare the avocado: cut each in half, remove the stones, and either slice thinly, lengthways, and scoop out the flesh, or into a bowl and mash with the lemon juice and salt.

Add cooled fritters to packed lunches in the place of sandwich bread.

Easy Egg Stack on Miracle Toast with Avocado Hollandaise & Herb Crisps

Serves 2

Inspired by the acclaimed eggs Benedict, this dish makes a simple but pleasing breakfast, especially if you already have a loaf of Miracle Bread in reserve. It is a high-protein, high-fibre feast, abundant in healthy fats and omegas. The herb crisps are not essential, but highly recommended.

2–4 eggs
50g watercress, spinach or other greens
handful of fresh coriander leaves
handful of fresh basil leaves
½ large courgette, grated, julienned
    or spiralised
2 tbsp extra virgin olive oil
1 tbsp lemon juice
2–4 slices of Miracle bread (page 314)
oil or Avocado 'Butter' (page 308), for spreading
1 tbsp golden linseeds, for topping
handful of chopped walnuts, for topping
sea salt and freshly ground black pepper

For the avocado hollandaise
100g avocado
80ml olive oil
1 tsp lemon juice
½ tsp apple cider vinegar
¼ – ½ tsp sea salt
5–6 tbsp boiling water

For the herb crisps
½ bunch of basil, sage or rosemary
    (or a mixture)
4 tbsp extra virgin olive oil or coconut oil
generous pinch of sea salt

First, make the hollandaise sauce. Put the avocado in a blender with the olive oil, lemon juice, salt and 2 tablespoons of the boiling water. Blend on a high speed for 30–60 seconds, until smooth, and then pause to scrape down the sides of the blender. Depending on the thickness and smoothness of the sauce, blend for a further 30–60 seconds, adding the remaining boiling water gradually to thin and bind the mixture, if needed. Once smooth, transfer to a small pot and refrigerate until ready to use.

Next, poach or fry the eggs, whichever you prefer. Whilst they cook, wash the watercress, spinach or greens and herbs, then drain and transfer the salad to a large bowl. Add the courgette to the bowl, drizzle with extra virgin olive oil and lemon juice, season with salt and pepper and stir to combine.

For the herb crisps, pick the herb leaves from their stalks. Heat the olive oil or coconut oil in a griddle or frying pan over a medium to high heat. When hot, add 10–15 leaves at a time, ensuring they don't overlap. Fry for about 4 seconds on each side, until crisp. (They burn quickly so stay attentive). Transfer to a plate lined with kitchen paper and sprinkle with a little salt.

To assemble, toast the Miracle Bread. Spread with oil or Avocado 'Butter' then lay a little salad on top. Follow with your egg and finish with 1–2 dollops of hollandaise sauce (add a little boiling hot water to thin it if it has thickened in the fridge). Garnish with the herb crisps, seeds and walnuts and serve.

To make a vibrant beetroot-stained hollandaise, add 150g cooked beetroot (chopped or grated) and 2 tablespoons beetroot powder (or beetroot juice) to the avocado hollandaise recipe, and blend until smooth.

For a turmeric hollandaise, add 2 teaspoons ground or fresh turmeric.

Turmeric Tofu Scramble

This breakfast scramble is quick and easy to prepare and offers something different to your usual scrambled eggs. It is perfect for hurried mornings but also serves as a simple, low-maintenance evening meal.

400g firm tofu
2–3 tbsp extra virgin olive or coconut oil
generous pinch of sea salt
1–2 tsp ground turmeric
½ tsp chilli flakes
½ tsp crushed garlic or garlic powder (optional)
4 tbsp plant-based milk, optional,
    (see pages 304–306)

handful of fresh coriander, basil or other
    herbs, to garnish
freshly ground black pepper

To serve
1 avocado, sliced or mashed
fresh salad greens

Start by breaking down the tofu, squeezing it gently with your hands and crumbling it until it resembles slightly overdone scrambled egg.

Heat the oil in a frying pan over a medium heat and add the tofu, salt, pepper, turmeric, chilli and garlic, if using. Keep the tofu moving around the pan to cook evenly and, if you want a softer, creamier scramble, add the milk. Cook for 6–8 minutes, stirring constantly, until the tofu begins to brown slightly.

Divide between two bowls, garnish with the fresh herbs and serve with the avocado and fresh salad greens.

Morning Millet Bowl with Herbal Hemp & Lemon Pesto

Serves 2

My breakfast habits change constantly, and whilst some days I can only just about stomach a smoothie, on others I need something heartier and brunch time, when the digestive system is reaching its energetic peak, is the ideal time of day for this. I make this wholesome millet bowl when I'm craving something more filling, particularly during the colder months. It's also a great chance to use up leftover grains or psuedograins, as well as any greens or herbs that are looking a little the worse for wear.

200g millet
4 eggs
2 tbsp extra virgin olive oil
2 handfuls of watercress
a handful of rocket

handful of kale, chopped
handful of spinach, chopped
40g sprouts (I like alfalfa, mung bean,
    sunflower or chickpea sprouts)
Herbal Hemp & Lemon Pesto (page 311)

Toast the millet in a dry saucepan or frying pan, stirring over a medium heat for 4–5 minutes, until it begins to brown. Then cook as per the packet instructions.

Meanwhile, make the pesto. Poach or fry the eggs, whichever you prefer.

Drain the millet and transfer to a bowl. Drizzle with oil, stir through the watercress, rocket, kale, spinach and sprouts and then divide between two plates or bowls. Top with the eggs and a generous spoonful of pesto.

You can replace the millet with quinoa, brown rice or other grains.

White Bean Cream Cheese with Cassava Bagels

Serves 2

Preheat the oven to 170°C /gas mark 4

Lightly grease a baking tray or line it with baking paper

In the Western world we have developed a huge array of processed breakfast convenience foods and whilst they are easy to eat and delicious, they sadly lack in nutrition. Breads and other baked goods are common breakfast choices and though we need carbs for energy, we also need vitamins, minerals, protein, healthy fats and other micronutrients. This recipe is a naturally upgraded version of the legendary cream cheese bagel. Both the cassava bagels and the white bean cream cheese are high in fibre and protein and are free from gluten and dairy. If you want more, you could add organic ham, bacon, smoked fish or sliced beetroot.

For the white bean cream cheese
200g cooked, rinsed and drained white beans
50ml extra virgin olive oil
½ tsp sea salt
2 tsp nutritional yeast
¼ tsp lemon juice
¼ tsp apple cider vinegar
20g coconut oil, melted
2–3 tbsp fresh or dried herbs, to garnish
oil, Avocado 'Butter' (page 308) or other
    butter, to serve

For the cassava bagels (makes 4)
160g cassava flour (aka tapioca flour)
160g arrowroot
50g coconut oil
1–2 tbsp natural syrup
1 tsp baking powder
1 tsp sea salt, plus extra for sprinkling
2 tbsp nutritional yeast
5 eggs
2 tbsp sesame seeds

First, make the bagels. Place all the ingredients apart from 1 egg and the sesame seeds in a large bowl and stir thoroughly to combine. Once the mixture is smooth and holds together, transfer to a lightly floured work surface and knead for 20–30 seconds, then divide into 4 pieces and work each piece into a round ball. If the mixture is too wet and sticky, add a little more cassava flour until it becomes drier and easier to handle.

Half-fill a large saucepan with water, place over a medium heat and bring to the boil. Reduce the heat slightly but ensure the water is simmering. Take a ball of dough and poke your thumb through the middle to make a hole, then drop the bagel into the water. Repeat with the remaining dough. Cook for 1–2 minutes, until they begin to float to the surface of the water.

Remove with a slotted spoon, shake off any excess water and then transfer to a baking tray. Beat the remaining egg in a small bowl or jug and then, using a pastry brush, paint the bagels with the egg mixture. Sprinkle each bagel with some sesame seeds and a little extra salt. Bake for 30–35 minutes, until golden brown (the exact time depends on the size of each bagel).

Meanwhile, prepare the white bean cream cheese. Put all the ingredients in a blender and blend on a high speed for 2–3 minutes, until smooth.

If you want to boost the flavour, experiment with adding ½ garlic clove (crushed) or herbs of your choice. Once smooth, pour into a bowl, jar or airtight container and store in the fridge until ready to serve.

Allow the bagels to cool slightly before slicing each one in half. Either crisp in the toaster or oven, or leave warm and soft as they are. Spread with coconut oil, extra virgin olive oil, Avocado 'Butter' or other butter or oil of your choice, or ignore this step and go straight in with the white bean cream cheese, spreading a thick layer on each half of the bagel. Garnish with fresh or dried herbs.

Add up to 100g more flour if the bagel mixture seems too wet – this happens to me occasionally, sometimes it's fine but sometimes it need a little extra flour to bind it together to make it manageable to form into shapes and cook.

You can serve the white bean cream cheese straight away as a smooth dip, or set it in the fridge to stiffen for 20–30 minutes if you want a harder spread.

Coconut Oil, Aloe Vera & Charcoal Toothpaste

Lasts about 10 uses

Equipment: small glass jar or pot with lid (40–50ml)

Store in the fridge or at room temperature for up to 2 months

In this alternative version to conventional toothpaste, I use activated charcoal, which is highly absorbent, meaning toxins adhere to its surface. Since charcoal is not absorbed into the bloodstream, it, and the toxins that bind to it, pass through the digestive system and are then eliminated. Charcoal is also extremely high in minerals, absorbs plaque and naturally lifts stains, helping to whiten the appearance of teeth as well as supporting overall oral health and cleanliness.

30g coconut oil, soft but not melted
2g aloe vera gel (scraped from the plant or shop-bought)
1 heaped tsp activated charcoal powder
5–6 drops spearmint essential oil

1 tsp baking soda
pinch of stevia or xylitol, to sweeten

Elevate it: 1 tsp bentonite clay, ½ tsp ground turmeric

Put all the ingredients into a small bowl and cream them together with a small spatula. Transfer to a sterilised glass jar or other pot with a lid. To use, scoop a little of the toothpaste onto your toothbrush and brush as you would normally, for about 2–5 minutes. Rinse your mouth with hot or cold water, brushing to remove every last bit of charcoal.

You don't have to use sweetener, although stevia and xylitol are thought to have antibacterial and plaque-reducing properties.

Remineralising Tooth Powder

Lasts about 20 uses

Equipment: small glass jar or pot with lid (25–50ml)

Store at room temperature for up to 4 months

This powdered formula is simple to prepare and is totally spill-safe if you travel a lot and don't want to risk oil leakages in your luggage.

6 tbsp activated charcoal powder
1 tsp baking soda

Elevate it: 2 tbsp bentonite clay powder, 1 tsp dried peppermint powder

Simply mix all the ingredients together in a bowl and transfer to a small pot.

To use, wet your toothbrush and dip it into the powder, then brush your teeth as usual, for about 2–5 minutes. Rinse your mouth well with cold water, being cautious not to swallow it.

Spearmint & Almond Mouthwash

Lasts 5–10 uses

Equipment: 1 × 150–250ml sterilised glass jar (see page 299 for sterilising instructions)

Store in the fridge for up to 2 months

Store-bought oral care products are all well and good if it's fresh breath you're after but, more often than not, the desired effects will be temporary and, in my opinion, the amount of chemicals, additives and sugars they contain is not worth a few moments of minty freshness. There are many natural ingredients (as well as dietary decisions, of course) that can help to support gum and tooth health by remineralising teeth, killing bacteria, cleaning and clearing plaque build-up, freshening breath and even halting or reversing tooth decay. This is a simple method to make your own natural mouthwash. Swig straight from the jar or store in a spray-top bottle and use as a mouth freshener.

125ml filtered water
15 drops spearmint essential oil
5 drops peppermint essential oil
1 tbsp almond or coconut oil
½ tsp stevia or xylitol

Elevate it: 1 tsp calcium carbonate powder, 1 tbsp aloe vera juice, 1 tsp baking soda, 5 drops cinnamon essential oil, 5 drops lemon or lemongrass essential oil, 1 tsp activated charcoal powder

Put all the ingredients (and any elevaional extras of your choice) into a sterilised jar, seal with a lid and shake vigorously to combine.

Transfer to a spray-top jar, if using as a breath freshener or store in the fridge in the jar.

Oil-Pulling Solution

Lasts about 8 uses

Equipment: 1 x 150–250ml sterilised glass jar (see page 299 for sterilising instructions)

Inspired by another ancient Ayurvedic practice, oil pulling is like the older, wiser sister of a mouthwash ritual. However, its ability to cleanse and reduce inflammation makes commercial mouthwash seem mediocre and a waste of time. Oils contain natural antiviral and antimicrobial properties and, as well as eliminating germs, they also remove dirt and bacteria from the mouth, thus preventing them from being absorbed into the bloodstream and entering other parts of the body. I like to use an Ayurvedic tongue scraper before this ritual.

125g coconut oil (cold-pressed and organic)
2 tbsp sesame oil (cold-pressed and organic)
2 tbsp almond oil (cold-pressed and organic)

Elevate it: ½ tsp spearmint essential oil or lemongrass esential oil, ½ tsp turmeric powder, flowers, dried petals or herbs, for infusing

Fill a small saucepan with water and bring to the boil. Place a heatproof bowl on top of the pan (creating a double boiler), then add the coconut oil. Once melted, transfer to a sterilised jar and add the sesame and almond oils, and any elevational extras, if using. (If you don't like the taste of sesame oil, you can leave it out and add another oil like olive or walnut oil, or just add extra coconut oil). Seal with a lid and shake vigorously to combine. Store in the fridge or at room temperature for up to 1 month.

Before drinking or eating anything, take about 1 tbsp of the mixture (either scooping from solid or melting briefly in a bowl of hot water) and swirl it around your mouth for 5–20 minutes. The longer you swirl the mixture, the more effective this practice will be (you can oil pull whilst you do other things). Alternatively, use the solution to brush your teeth.

You can also pour the oil pulling mixture into small, mouthful-sized moulds and set in the freezer to harden and store. You can then just pop one in your mouth and allow it to melt before swirling the oil around as instructed above.

Cocoa Butter & Shea Lip Balm

Makes approx. 100ml

Equipment: 25ml pots or 1 large pot or jar

Lasts for about 6 months

Lip balm is a life force for me. If I leave the house without it I feel lost, especially during the cold winter months. Many commercially available lip balm products contain artificial ingredients, including harmful chemicals, low-quality fillers and even plastics, which can potentially find their way inside the mouth and into the bloodstream. Although it's not a serious danger as our bodies' natural defence mechanisms will protect us, it isn't ideal and so I always prefer to make my own.

I've made my way through many different lip balms over time and this is one of my favourites. Whilst many shop-bought products leave my lips only temporarily quenched, requiring constant reapplication, I find I only need to apply this balm once or twice a day.

40g beeswax
30g shea butter
30g cacao butter
1 tbsp melted coconut oil
pinch of vanilla powder or a few drops of vanilla essential oil

4–5 drops cinnamon essential oil or other essential oil (page 303)
a few drops of honey or other natural syrup, to sweeten (optional)

Elevate it: ½ tsp maca powder, ½ tsp pink clay

Fill a small saucepan with water and bring to the boil. Place a heatproof bowl on top of the pan (creating a double boiler), then add the beeswax, shea and cacao butters, coconut oil, vanilla, essential oil and honey or other natural sweetner, if using. Mix with a spatula to combine.

When the fats have fully dissolved, transfer to a pot or sterilised jar and leave to cool in the fridge for 1–2 hours. If you have small, individual pots (you can buy affordable small pots or tubes specifically for lip balms), fill several of these, or fill one individual pot, and pour the rest of the mixture into a larger pot or sterilised jar to store for future use. When ready to use the stored lip balm, stand the jar in a double boiler and wait for the mixture to melt, then pour into your small, individual pot as before. Repeat until the mixture is used up).

Store at room temperature in your bathroom, bedroom or in your bag or make-up kit.

Use your finger to apply the balm straight from the pot. In cooler weather, you will need to allow it to melt slightly on your lips before spreading.

Morntime

Vanilla, Aloe Vera & Coconut Blossom Lip Scrub

A lip scrub is a gentle yet effective way of removing dead skin and hydrating dry or chapped lips. It is easy to make and, by using only natural ingredients, you'll ensure the new sensitive skin is refreshed and deeply nourished.

20g aloe vera gel
40g coconut sugar
1 tsp vanilla powder
20g coconut oil, softened
1–2 drops of essential oils

Elevate it: ½ tsp activated charcoal, ½ tsp pink clay

Put all the ingredients into a bowl and use a small spatula to blend them together. Once combined, transfer to a pot or a sterilised jar and leave to set in the fridge for 10–20 minutes.

When ready to use, apply to a toothbrush or your finger and scrub across each lip for about 1 minute, using circular motions. Leave to settle and soak in for 5 minutes if you can, or remove instantly by rinsing with hot water. Use a muslin cloth or a flannel to remove residual dead skin.

Morntime

Rose & Cucumber Wake-Up-Well Toning Mist

Makes about 20ml

Equipment: 50ml bottle with a spray lid (plastic or glass)

The benefits of using natural essential oils and herbal remedies in skincare is that they not only calm and support the skin in many ways, but also have the power to stimulate or settle the mind through inhalation. Facial mists are a refreshing way to prepare the skin for other products. Living in polluted cities and toxic environments means that excess oil and dirt build up on the skin's surface. Rose water helps to cleanse this off, whilst also reducing redness and inflammation and soothing many other irritations. Aromatically, rose water is known to reduce anxiety and enhance positivity, whilst cucumber water is an incredibly refreshing and hydrating ingredient that, used in the morning, ensures your skin is clean and fuelled with vital vitamins and minerals.

40ml natural cucumber water
1 ½ tsp rose water (or orange blossom water)
1 ½ tsp almond or macadamia oil

Elevate it: 4–6 small charged crystals

Put all the ingredients into a bottle, either using a funnel or a clean jug. Seal with a lid. Store at room temperature (or in the fridge for a more cooling spritz) for up to 2 months.

To use, shake vigorously before applying. Spray onto your face, after cleansing. Pat into the skin with clean, dry hands to encourage the mist to settle. Wait until fully absorbed before applying moisturiser or make-up. Alternatively, spray onto a muslin cloth and wipe your face with the cloth. Wait until fully absorbed before applying moisturiser or make-up. Use a muslin cloth or a flannel to remove residual dead skin.

Daytime

Daytime

During the day we undergo many activities and experience many thoughts, feelings, opportunities and obstacles – some of which are within our control and others that are not. The number of situations our bodies and minds are faced with each day is extremely demanding and exhausting, but in a world that is constantly 'on', particularly in fast-paced cities, it's hard to slow down, and even harder to take a break. We have evolved from human beings to human doings, and today, taking time out and occasionally doing nothing is seen as being lazy or unproductive.

For a lot of people, the bulk of the day is spent working. And for those who aren't working, the daytime still tends to be the most active and eventful time of the day. Whether working or not, we all need a break (it's a legal requirement in the workplace for a reason), yet how many of us actually stop to enjoy the opportunity of a breaktime fully? We are constantly operating, and this can put serious strains on our bodies and minds, affecting particularly our mood, brain function, energy levels and digestion. Various studies show that taking a break can actually enhance productivity, and whilst it may seem counterproductive, even just a short break can be beneficial. This chapter contains simple, accessible practices that you can do almost anywhere, which are intended to help you slow down and reset, even if only for a few minutes. I urge you to reclaim your lunch break instead of working through it, and to use it wisely. Indulging in a hobby, doing something creative or practising mindfulness, meditative exercises and pranayama will all activate different parts of your brain, so that when you do get back to work, you will feel more driven and focused for the rest of the afternoon.

The lunchtime recipes in this chapter use energising and easy-to-digest ingredients and are intended to see you through a busy day. Some can be prepared fresh and whilst others can be made in advance and taken into work as a packed lunch. Each recipe is designed to fuel the brain and energise the body, delivering essential nutrition through fresh and light ingredients that won't cause inflammation, bloating or other common side effects of processed meals and snacks. For maximum benefit when you eat these more functional options, try to combine them with some of the practices and pranayama techniques in this section. This will reduce stress and ensure your body is in an optimal state to receive, digest and absorb all that the ingredients have to offer.

Mind

Daytime Meditation

Meditation isn't only for experiencing a deep state of consciousness and stillness, it can also be used as a way to tune inwards, to check in with ourselves and to better direct the flow of our energy. The daytime is often when people are under most immediate stress, and whilst meditation is an amazing way to reduce stress, it's often difficult to fit it into busy schedules, or to switch off completely and really get into a flow. Working in a shared space makes it hard to escape distractions, or to find somewhere private to meditate without being disturbed (or judged). The practices in this section are more about being mindful. Mindfulness techniques can encourage concentration and help to keep you centred and present. These practices can be performed at your desk without attracting attention, and 5 minutes a day can produce immediate and long-term benefits. (Read more about meditation on pages 13–14 and 325.) Discover which teachings and techniques work for you and try to include them in your daily routines as often as you can.

Mantras

Mantras are not specifically time-sensitive, but I wanted to include them as a daytime practice as they fit so easily into busy routines and require little effort, no space and no equipment. They are really powerful in reducing overactive thoughts and help to instil a sense of clarity if you're feeling unfocused or overwhelmed with work and other tasks.

Mudras

These are a few of my favourites to use during the day, to encourage intuition, concentration and confidence. Hold for 3–15 minutes, knowing the longer you hold it the more effective it will be. Also see Chin Mudra on page 40.

Ahamkara mudra encourages confidence and faith, reducing self-limiting fears and reinforcing a feeling of openness and possibility.

1. Come to a comfortable seated position, either on the floor with legs crossed, however is comfortable, or on a chair with your feet flat on the floor.

2. Lengthen your spine and extend the back of your neck up, so your head is facing forwards, ensuring your neck is soft, not strained. Decide whether to practise with eyes open or closed.

3. Place the backs of your hands on your knees and bend the index finger of each hand towards the base of each thumb, and then bring your thumbs to rest on the middle of the outside of each index finger, slightly above the middle knuckle. Hold them here, keeping the other fingers outstretched loosely. Settle here for a few minutes or for as long as feels comfortable.

Hakini mudra is practised to boost thinking and concentration. It is believed to connect to the third-eye chakra, where your imagination and intuition are located, encouraging creativity and ideas.

1. Follow steps 1–2 of Ahamkara Mudra, and rest your hands on your knees, palms facing upwards.

2. Hold your hands apart in front of you, with palms facing each other.

3. Bring the fingertips of each hand to touch, and rest here gently, without applying much pressure. Settle here for a few minutes or for as long as feels comfortable.

Focused Mindful Observation

This technique is designed to connect you with the beauty of living or active things in your natural environment. We are often unaware of our surroundings as we rush from one place to the next, keeping our eyes on our phones or our minds somewhere in the past or future. Try this for around 5 minutes to enhance awareness and to cultivate concentration and refresh your mind.

1. Choose something natural that you notice in your immediate surroundings (such as insects, plants, clouds or sunlight) and study it for a couple of minutes. Become aware of its entire formation and presence, noticing its energy and considering its purpose.

*   *You can also practise this technique using non-natural objects and even daily tasks by bringing your awareness to something you can see, hear, taste, touch or smell, or to something you are doing. This helps the mind to exit the constant flow of doing and striving, even if momentarily.*

Breath

Practising pranayama is another powerful way to refresh the body and mind by renewing and repositioning energy, to reduce tension and create space for new ideas and experiences. During the daytime when stress can be at its most extreme, the breath is often affected as our natural coping mechanisms kick in.

Before practising these exercises, notice how you feel and if you are stressed or struggling with other emotions. Notice if and where you experience any tension, and work towards moving the energy focused there towards other parts of the body.

* *For anyone who sits a lot during the day, finding somewhere to sit cross-legged whilst performing the following practices will help redistribute the energy and bring it up again, towards the heart and head, which can promote brain power. Eyes can be open or closed whilst practising pranayama. I prefer to close mine.*

* *Pranayama practices become more powerful when you practise over a period of time, so whilst you may only have time to practise for 5–10 minutes, try to make it a regular thing.*

* *If you are pregnant or unsure about the safety of practising pranayama, consult a teacher or healthcare professional.*

Three-Part Breath (Deergha Swasam)

This three-part breathing technique can be performed just about anywhere and involves breathing successively into three areas of the lungs and body – the lower abdomen, the ribcage and the chest. It is a great way to oxygenate and detoxify the cells of the body through the breath.

1. Sit comfortably, either on the floor with crossed legs or on a chair. As you inhale, slowly send the breath to the bottom of the abdomen (allowing the stomach to rise as it fills with air), then the ribcage (allowing the ribcage to expand softly as it fills with air), and finally, into the chest (feeling the air fill and spread across the chest area).

2. As you exhale, let the air leave the lungs naturally, relaxing the chest first, then the ribcage, and finally, the abdomen, pulling the belly inwards to expel the air completely.

3. Next time you inhale, count your breath, and try to exhale for twice as long as you inhaled (work to a ratio of 1:2).

4. Practise for a few minutes, up to 5 minutes initially, and increase over time if you desire. Breathe comfortably and don't breathe too deeply if it causes you to strain.

*   *You can also do this practice with pauses, pausing at each stage of the inhalation and exhalation. As you inhale, feel the abdomen fill and then pause for a second, then continue inhaling, feel the ribcage fill and pause for another second. Then continue inhaling, feel the chest fill and pause for a final second. Then exhale in the same pattern.*

Skull-Shining Breath or Breath of Fire (Kapalabhati Pranayama)

This exercise is used for internal purification. It tones and cleanses the respiratory system by encouraging the release of toxins, and is intended to make you feel lighter in your body and mind. It involves short, sharp exhalations and passive inhalations, or vice versa. This is quite an advanced practice so familiarise yourself with other techniques before this one.

1. Inhale deeply and then forcefully exhale to drive all the air out of the lungs and stomach.

2. Take another full inhale, and then begin to exhale forcefully through the nose. Try to start with 6–10 short, sharp exhalations, without taking an inhale (slight inhalation will occur passively). With each short exhale, draw the belly inwards, engaging and tucking the abdomen in and up towards your ribs.

3. After you've completed a full cycle, inhale and exhale fully for a few breaths, before repeating a few more rounds (I like to do around 3–5 rounds).

4. To close the practice, settle in your seated position and return to a natural, effortless breath.

*   *Over time, increase the number of your exhales, working towards 15–30, if and when you can.*

*   *You can switch the breathing round, exhaling fully and taking short, sharp inhalations. You can also practise with longer, fuller breaths, by forcefully exhaling and emptying the lungs, and then forcefully inhaling, snapping the belly up and inwards almost as forcefully as you exhaled.*

Mindful Eating

Our modern culture runs at a high speed in order for us to fit everything in, and as a consequence, our breathing, sleeping and eating patterns have begun to suffer. Functioning at a constant fast pace is productive in many ways, but counterproductive in others. If we move through life too quickly to allow basic bodily functions to occur and focus on too many things instead of them, we stop operating at our full physical and mental potential. This is true at all times of the day, but is particularly important where eating is involved. If we don't slow down when we eat, we can end up creating more stress and imbalances within the body, and no matter how 'healthy' the food is, feeling good isn't going to come easily or occur just by eating a kale salad.

Oxygen plays an important role in the digestive process and since we restrict our intake of oxygen when we are stressed or rushed (due to shortened or restricted breathing), eating in this state is simply not the way to do it. Slowing down, taking more time to eat and ensuring you're breathing in a way that can distribute adequate oxygen around the body is an essential part of eating well.

Oxygen is just as important as any other vitamins or minerals in food, if not more, because it is essential for burning calories, breaking down food and carrying vitamins and minerals to where they are required around the body, via the bloodstream. Since the breathing pattern of stress is shallow, arrhythmic and infrequent, eating when stressed restricts oxygen from entering the system. When the blood lacks oxygen, absorption decreases, and our cells cannot obtain as much as they could from our food. Increasing oxygen, therefore, is crucial for preparing our internal systems to receive and use the food we eat.

We need to make time and oxygen major components of every meal, and start to really slow down and breathe whilst we eat, to concentrate on our food and the acts of eating, digesting, burning and absorbing. Here are two ways in which to be mindful about eating:

1. *Slow down.* Stop what you are doing, or at least try to reduce your level of activity before you start eating.

2. *Breathe.* Take a few moments before a meal to regulate your breath and check in with yourself. This can help you assess your true appetite, and also fuel the digestive process. A simple breathing practice to regulate 'stress breath' can shortcut the stress response in as little as 1 minute, which puts the body in a more optimal state to receive and use food.

Above
Coconut Creamed Mushroom Ragout
on Miracle Toast (page 142)

Pre-Meal Breathing

1. Sit comfortably and take a few deep breaths. Relax your shoulders down your back and keep your head and neck aligned with a straight spine.

2. Decide whether you want to practise with eyes open or closed, and take the option of resting one or both hands on your abdomen, which will help you feel the breath and send energy and focus to the gut.

3. Now, consciously inhale, filling your lungs just two-thirds full (this refrains you from putting further stress on the system due to full exertion of forcing the lungs to their limit). Then exhale fully, expelling all stale air from the lungs.

4. Repeat step 3 up to 10 times if you can.

* *You can also use other pranayama techniques shared throughout the book, as each will help to regulate the breath and calm the system.*

Mid-Meal breathing

1. At a few points during your meal, sit up comfortably if you have begun to slouch or hunch over your food, and take a few deep breaths. Relax your shoulders down your back and keep your head and neck aligned with a straight spine.

2. Notice how your breath is flowing as you eat. Has it become short and shallow (often a sign of eating too quickly)? However it is, consciously begin to deepen the breath with as little effort as possible (don't force the lungs full as this can be uncomfortable whilst eating).

3. Each time you pause during your meal (aim for 2–3 times depending on the size of the meal and the time available in which to eat it), take three deep breaths. As you welcome more oxygen into the body, it will be directed through the bloodstream to your cells, where it will be used to drive essential processes such as calorie burning and absorption. Consider the oxygen as a condiment or a seasoning – an actual part of the meal.

* *Try to continue these 'check-in' breaths throughout the day, to increase the oxygen in the body, which can support metabolic strength and activity, and help to keep stress levels under control.*

Check in

Once you're back on track with regulated breathing and a calmer system, take a few moments to explore your hunger and reconnect with the food in front of you – checking in with why you are eating and what you are about to eat, and how it can provide for you. Are you hungry? Is it physical hunger or emotional hunger? Are you about to eat under stress? What does the food in front of you have to offer? Is there a purpose and demand for it in your body? How will it make you feel? Where does it come from? How is it made? Is it functional?

Once you've acknowledged these questions, proceed, guided by your own intuition and instinct. Try to make more conscious decisions to eat foods that put less strain on the environment, involve less suffering (if you are eating animal products), and truly nourish and enhance you, both your body and your mind. Also, serve moderate portions, even if you might go back for more. This will help you to slow down and acknowledge your hunger, preventing mindless overeating and feelings of fullness that can be taxing on the system over time.

Continuously check in during your meal, letting your mind and body connect and really noticing your body's signals of fullness.

Be Present
Whilst you eat, remove any distractions and try to be fully involved with your meal. Try not to multitask and try to refrain from using technology. Sit down and be still, instead of eating on the move or getting up and down during a meal to do other things. And chew. Chew your food. Feel your food. Taste and appreciate your food. Use all of your senses to experience and appreciate the food, acknowledging its colours, appearance, texture, smell, flavour and any sounds (such as crunching).

The Slow Down Diet by Marc David gives more in-depth detail about the role of oxygen in digestion and was one of the books that really changed my life.

Movement

Since this time of day is probably your busiest and most restricted, I'm not going to suggest doing yoga in the middle of your workplace. If you don't have time to workout, get outside, even if only for a few minutes, even when it's grey and gloomy. Daylight, and especially exposure to sunlight, can stimulate serotonin levels, boosting your mood and positivity, which can directly affect your output and productivity. Poor air quality in buildings and artificial lighting can begin to take their toll on your respiratory system, skin and immune system, so even if it's not sunny, try to get outside for some air and natural light. Your lunch break is an opportunity to do some exercise, expel excess energy (often built up as a side effect of stress and anxiety), silence the mind, refresh thought patterns and improve your mood, circulation and metabolism. If you have an hour, walk or run locally or find a class nearby that lasts for just 30 minutes; it doesn't have to be strenuous.

* *Walking meditation involves bringing your attention to the act of walking in an effort to centre the mind, drawing its focus from doing, thinking, working and achieving. With each step you take, focus on your feet as they touch the ground, and if your mind wanders, bring it back to your actions, your surroundings, how it feels to be walking and any other sensations you notice. Keep your gaze ahead of you, and practise for just a few minutes.*

* *Earthing or grounding is a powerful method used to connect physically with the Earth. Whilst walking along city pavements doesn't have quite the intended effect, it's not hard to find somewhere natural, nurtured and alive for this practice: the grass or soil of a park or your own garden; the sand of a beach if you have access to one; even naturally formed rocky terrain.*

Daytime

Do-In

Use Do-In to improve the flow of energy and release tension and stiffness in the major joints and organs of the body. If you sit at a desk for much of the day, likely working a lot with your hands, take a moment to loosen the muscles and stimulate the flow of energy. Our hands contain major pressure points and nerve endings, and massaging these points can reduce tension and even relieve negative emotions. The neck can also suffer and hold tension if you sit hunched over a table or laptop. Below are some simple exercise you can do in the workplace to release tightness and redirect energy.

Wrists

1. Start by gently rubbing the wrist, palm and back of one hand with the other hand, and repeat on the other hand.

2. Release your arms by your sides and shake them loosely, moving from the wrists.

3. Bring your right hand up in front of you and with the palm facing downwards, take your left hand around it and gently stretch it down towards the ground. Feel the stretch in the top of your wrist and hold it for one full breath, then reposition the left hand elsewhere on the back of the right hand and stretch again, noticing if it feels any different. Do this a few times until you feel you've stretched every part of the hand.

4. Turn your right palm upwards and, with fingers together, hold them with your left hand, palm to palm. Gently stretch the fingers down to open the palm of the right hand and open up the wrist. Breathe into each stretch, then reposition the left hand elsewhere on the back of the right hand and stretch again, noticing if it feels any different. Do this a few times until you feel you've stretched every part of the hand.

5. Repeat steps 3–4 using your left hand, then bring the practice to a close by dropping the arms back to your sides and shaking the wrists out again.

Neck

1. Stand or sit comfortably, keeping your spine long. Relax your shoulders and, keeping them open and facing forward, turn your head and neck slowly to the right, looking over the right shoulder as far as is comfortable without straining. Repeat, this time turning to the left, then return to centre.

2. Allow your head to gently drop forwards, bringing the chin towards the chest and the forehead parallel to the ground. Feel the stretch along the back of the neck and top of your chest and shoulders. Breathe into the stretch and hold for 20–30 seconds. Slowly bring the head back up through centre, and gently allow it to drop backwards, releasing the throat and opening the chest. Keep the neck elongated and the shoulders relaxed so as not to restrict the chest.

3. Bring the practice to a close by returning to centre, rotating the neck however feels comfortable to give it a final stretch.

Passion Fruit, Cherry, Lime and Raspberry Smoothie

Serves 1

Passion fruit juice first came into my life when I was travelling around Central America with my cherished friend, Els. On Caye Caulker Island in Belize, we came across a colourful shack selling homemade juices and their pure passion fruit juice tasted like liquid sunshine. A similar concoction forms the base of this recipe and, combined with other lively ingredients, creates an invigorating drink to keep you feeling fresh throughout the day.

2 passion fruits
250ml water or coconut water
100g cherries, stoned and halved
35g raspberries
juice of ½ lime
3 slices of fresh ginger
4 ice cubes

Elevate it: ½ tsp schizandra powder, few fresh mint leaves, 1 tsp ground ginseng, 1 tsp baobab powder

Cut the passion fruits in half and scrape the seeds and juice into a blender. Add the water or coconut water and blend on the highest speed for 1 minute.

Strain through a sieve, rinse out the blender and then return the juice along with the remaining ingredients, apart from the ice, and blend for another minute. Add the ice and blend again, until smooth. Serve immediately.

Thicken with frozen banana, acai pulp or avocado to make a smoothie bowl, and serve with toppings of your choice as a breakfast option.

Making Teas & Herbal Infusions

Herbal infusions are probably the simplest way to work more nutrients into your diet. Not quite as potent as ingesting the ingredients whole, infusions and teas still draw nutrients from the plants you are using, which are in turn quickly and easily absorbed by the body. They help bring variety to the daily recommended amount of water we should be consuming and can be enjoyed straight or added to smoothies, juices, cocktails and even cooking.

There are several methods for infusing, and the ratio of plants to water really depends on personal taste. You can use heat or you can 'cold brew', you can use filtered water, or experiment with coconut water or even milks. Infusion time will depend on the quality and quantity of your ingredients and, again, your personal tastes. The longer the plants sit in the liquid, the more potent the infusion will become.

Foundation Ingredients

Liquids
Water
Coconut water
Plant-based milk (pages 304–306)
Liquid probiotics

Flavourings
Flowers, dried or fresh
Herbs, dried or fresh
Spices, dried or fresh
Fruit, dried or fresh
Fresh vegetables

Sweeteners
Raw or Manuka honey
Coconut palm sugar or nectar
Natural sweetener of choice

Water Infusions

Sparkling Cucumber & Mint
Add 1 cucumber, peeled and sliced thinly, and 10g fresh mint leaves to 500ml sparkling water. You could also muddle the mint in an empty jug with a wooden spoon before adding the water, to intensify the flavour.

Muddled Cherry & Rose
Put 50g stoned and chopped cherries into a jug and add 1 tsp honey and 1 tsp rose water. Muddle with a wooden spoon to infuse and then cover with 500ml water. Leave to infuse, chill in the fridge or enjoy instantly. Strain before serving.

Rose Quartz, Beetroot & Coconut Water
Put 50g cooked or raw beetroot, 1 tsp pure rose water and a rose quartz crystal into cold coconut water. You might take this opportunity to set an intention to 'programme' your crystal before adding it to the water. Leave to infuse and enjoy chilled. (You can use any kind of crystal for this if you don't have a rose quartz).

Mixed Herbal Tea
Put 2 rosemary sprigs, 8 fresh basil leaves, 20 mint leaves and any other herbs of your choice in a jug. Cover with boiling water and let steep for a minimum of 5 minutes. (Add more herbs for a stronger flavour). You can also stick to just one type of herb if you prefer. I love rosemary tea and the traditional, failsafe mint tea.

Strawberry Top Tea
Put a large handful of strawberry tops in a jug and cover with hot or cold water. Alternatively, fill a serving jug with cold water, then add the strawberry tops, stir and leave to infuse. (Add 1–2 tbsp lemon juice to make a strawberry-infused lemonade-style drink).

Iced Nettle Green Tea
Put 20g wild nettles (you can buy these from several suppliers, though handle carefully) and 1–2 green tea bags or 1 tbsp loose green tea in a jug and cover with boiling water. Set aside to steep at room temperature or in the fridge for 5–10 minutes and strain before serving.

Lavender & Sage Tea
Add 5 sprigs of fresh or dried lavender and 2 sprigs of sage to a jug of hot or cold water. Set aside to infuse for about 10 minutes, then either serve with the lavender and sage in each individual glass, or strain before serving.

Lemongrass Tea
Put 25–30g chopped lemongrass in a jug and add 1 tsp honey. Muddle with a wooden spoon, cover with 500ml boiling water. Leave to infuse, chill in the fridge or enjoy instantly.

Chaga & Astragalus Tea
Put 1 tsp chaga bark and 1 tsp astragalus root in a mug and cover with boiling water. Leave to brew for 5–10 minutes before serving.

Flowering Beetroot Tea
Add 100g raw or cooked chopped beetroot with 5g dried rose petals (or other flowers of choice), a few sprigs of mint (lemon balm or lemongrass also work nicely), 15–20g fresh ginger, lemon peel or lemon juice, to taste, to your water (hot or cold). Leave to steep for 5 minutes if hot, or 30 minutes if cold.

Cacao Nib Tea
Place 2 tbsp cacao nibs in a mug and cover with 250ml boiling water. Brew for 10–20 minutes, and then enjoy. ('Elevate it' with other roots, herbs, spices or plant powders such as vanilla beans, astragalus root, fresh ginger or cinnamon sticks.) Store in the fridge to enjoy chilled or added to smoothies, soups or stocks for an earthy flavour.

Sun Tea
Sun tea is a method of brewing tea without using any kitchen appliances. Simply fill a vessel with your chosen tea ingredients (plants or tea bags and water) and use the power of the sun to work its magic, leaving it to brew in direct sunlight for 2–5 hours, depending on how strong you like it. The ideal time to make sun tea is during the spring or summer. You might also like to charge your crystals in the sunlight and add these to the tea before drinking.

Milk Infusions

Hot Rosemary Milk

Fill a saucepan with a plant-based milk of your choice (pages 304–306) and add 3 rosemary sprigs. Bring to the boil and then simmer for 5–10 minutes. Sweeten naturally, if desired, and flavour with vanilla, maca or other plant powders.

Chamomile & Rose Milk

Fill a saucepan with a plant-based milk of your choice (pages 304–306) and add 5g dried chamomile flowers and 5g rose petals. Bring to the boil and then simmer for 5–10 minutes. Sweeten naturally, if desired, and flavour with vanilla, maca or other plant powders and bee pollen.

Peach & Astragalus Milk

Fill a saucepan with a plant-based milk of your choice (pages 304–306), then add 1–2 peaches, sliced, and 1 tbsp astragalus root. Bring to the boil and then simmer for 5–10 minutes. Sweeten naturally, if desired, and flavour with vanilla, maca or other superfood powders.

Chaga Root Milk

Fill a saucepan with a plant-based milk of your choice (pages 304–306) and add 10g chaga root. Bring to the boil and then simmer for 5–10 minutes. Sweeten naturally, if desired, and flavour with vanilla, reishi, shilajit, maca or other superfood powders.

Tips

If you don't have a teapot with a strainer or a small sieve, use a cafetière to brew your infusions.

For a more intense flavour, place your ingredients in a saucepan and bring to the boil. This brews them for longer.

Add tinctures or chia seeds to your cold infusions to elevate the flavour and nutrient-quota of your creations.

Freeze your infusions in ice-cube trays to add to soft drinks, smoothies, juices or cocktails.

Ayurvedic teas: take a look into your Ayurvedic type and use ingredients that are suited to it. Pitta types may favour cooling and cleansing ingredients (such as mint, coriander and apple). Vata types may benefit from warming, digestive-supporting ingredients (such as ginger, berries and peaches). And Kapha types should try energising ingredients (such as cinnamon, green tea, pepper and cherries).

Seasonal teas: use seasonal ingredients for infusions and teas that are suitable and supportive at specific times of the year.

Chakral teas: use ingredients associated with certain chakras if you feel energetically misaligned or 'blocked'. See more about the chakras on page 324.

Restorative Seaweed Broth

Serves 4–6

Seaweed and sea vegetables are invaluable gifts from the sea and my favourite way to use them is to enjoy the biggest nutritional hit from all their vitamins, minerals and trace elements is to brew them into a broth. This process draws out their detoxifying nutrients and all their unique vitamins and minerals, and adding a little fat to the mix also ensures fat-soluble components are easily assimilated too. I like to keep a batch in the fridge to drink, hot or cold, on an empty stomach in the morning or before lunch. However, if you can't quite come round to the idea of swapping out your morning tea, enjoy it as a hot soup or use it as a stock in other recipes.

30g dried arame
40g dried hijiki
30g dried dulse
2 tbsp coconut oil
½ tsp ground ginger or grated fresh ginger
½ tsp ground turmeric or 1 tsp grated fresh turmeric
100g mushrooms (I like chestnut, portobello, shiitake, enoki or chanterelle mushrooms)
4 tbsp tamari
2 tbsp brown miso paste
juice of ½ lime
finely chopped red chilli or chilli powder, to taste
large handful of fresh coriander leaves
sea salt

To serve
wedge of lime
chopped fresh coriander
chopped red chilli
sesame seeds

Elevate it: 100ml Chaga & Astragalus Tea (page 120), 1 tsp spirulina powder, 1 tsp reishi powder, 100g raw vegetables of choice, grated or finely sliced

Soak the seaweeds in a large bowl until they soften and triple in size (approx. 15–30 minutes).

Heat the oil in a saucepan, then add the ginger and turmeric and cook for 2–3 minutes. Add the mushrooms (along with vegetables from the 'elevate it' suggestions) and sauté for a further 5 minutes, then add the seaweed and just enough water to cover the ingredients (about 2 litres). Add the tamari, miso paste, lime juice, chilli and coriander and stir to combine. Bring to the boil, cover with a lid and simmer for 45 minutes. Taste and season further if necessary, and add any elevational extras, if using. Continue to cook for a further 15 minutes (at this point you can stir in any 'stir-throughs' of choice, see opposite) and serve immediately with a wedge of lime and some coriander leaves, chilli and sesame seeds.

Use 100g seaweed of your choice and experiment with different types, to vary the flavour and nutritional offerings. My favourites include kombu, arame, hijiki, wakame, kelp, dulse and sea spaghetti.

You could blend a quarter of the mixture in a high-speed blender and add it to the main broth to make a thicker soup.

Vegetable pastes and purées are a really delicious way to add flavour and sustenance to a broth. I like to stir through beetroot purée, sweet potato purée, sweet white miso paste, roasted garlic purée and sautéed mushroom purée. To make a stir through purée, briefly boil vegetables, add just enough water to cover them, a tablespoon of coconut or virgin olive oil and a pinch of salt and then pulse in a blender.

You can also stir coconut milk, sesame oil, an egg yolk or a little cooked fish or seafood through this broth for added flavour.

Sweetcorn Chowder

Serves 2

This recipe is inspired by a trip I took to San Francisco a couple of years ago. I was visiting for work, and on set all day, so my only time to explore was during the evenings. I was there out of season and Fisherman's Wharf was a ghost town, but I was on a mission to find the best chowder and I wasn't leaving without it. However, most places were either closed or closing, so I ended up settled on a bench, on a sidewalk that was soaked with fishy water, eating take-out chowder from a paper cup. It was everything.

This is a vegan take on that warming, soothing soup I tried and loved. The corn adds a subtle sweetness to the creamy flavour whilst the beans and quinoa bring fibre, protein and healthy fats to every mouthful. Enjoy hot in the winter or cold in the summer as a refreshing gazpacho-style soup.

150ml almond milk
350ml vegetable stock (preferably homemade)
2 tbsp nutritional yeast
300g cooked cannellini beans (or white beans)
350g cooked sweetcorn
80g cooked quinoa
60ml extra virgin olive oil
½ tsp lemon juice

1 garlic clove (optional)
herb-infused oil (page 313), to drizzle (optional)
sea salt and freshly ground black pepper

Elevate it: 1 tbsp organic Dijon mustard, 1 tbsp chaga powder, 1 tsp reishi powder

Put the milk, stock, nutritional yeast, beans, 300g of the sweetcorn, quinoa, extra virgin olive oil, lemon juice and garlic, if using, in a high-speed blender and blend for 2–3 minutes, until smooth.

Transfer to a saucepan, season with salt and pepper and add any elevational extras of your choice. Add the remaining sweetcorn and heat through before serving. Top with a drizzle of extra virgin olive oil or herb-infused oil.

If you'd prefer an entirely smooth soup, blend all the sweetcorn in the first step.

Beetroot, Carrot & Coconut Soup

Serves 4 as a main or 6 as a starter

This hearty soup uses ingredients associated with the root chakra (page 326), which works to keep us grounded with the Earth's energy and, when balanced, can increase confidence, energy and openness. Signs of a blocked or misaligned root chakra include short temper, lack of motivation, anxiety and general frustration. Eating foods associated with this chakra can help to release these emotions. Serve with Magic Vegetable 'Bread' Rolls (page 314), toasted Miracle Bread (page 314), or Crackers (page 178).

2 tbsp extra virgin olive oil or coconut oil
½ red onion, diced
2 garlic cloves, crushed
5g fresh ginger, finely chopped
1 tsp ground coriander
3 large beetroots, peeled and chopped
2 carrots, peeled and chopped

600ml vegetable or bone broth (preferably homemade, page 315)
2 × 400ml cans (800ml) coconut milk
1 tsp dried thyme or lemon thyme
sea salt and freshly ground black pepper

Elevate it: juice of ½ lime

In a large saucepan or stockpot, heat the oil over a medium heat. Once hot, add the onion, garlic, ginger and coriander and sauté for 5 minutes.

Add the beetroots, carrots and broth. Bring to the boil, then reduce the heat and simmer for 20 minutes or until the beetroot is soft.

Allow to cool slightly, transfer to a blender (work in two batches if necessary) and add the coconut milk. Blend on a medium speed for 30 seconds and then increase to the highest speed for 10 seconds. Add more broth or water to thin the soup if it is too thick.

Return to the saucepan, add the thyme, season to taste with salt and pepper and add the lime juice, if using. Heat through, then divide among bowls and serve immediately.

Top with Nut Parmesan Sprinkle (page 313), a knob of Avocado 'Butter' (page 308), herb-infused oil (page 313) or a swirl of extra coconut milk.

Blend any leftovers with a can or two of chickpeas, to make a vibrant root-vegetable dip.

Daytime

Cauliflower, Quinoa & Sweet Potato Salad with Sauerkraut, Peas & Avocado

Serves 4–6

Preheat the oven to 220°C / gas mark 7

This salad made its debut at a barbecue a few years ago, and is light, refreshing and fulfilling, without depending on heavy grains or simple carbohydrates. I wish we could eat the way we do at barbecues every day (if only the weather permitted), cooking in nature over an open fire, and sharing the occasion with those close to us. Not only does it taste better, it feels better. Serve as a main or as a side and douse with a dressing (pages 133–135) or herb-infused oil (page 313) for added flavour.

200g quinoa
150g sweet potato, cubed
2 tbsp extra virgin olive or coconut oil
pinch of sea salt
100g cauliflower
20g spinach
60g corn salad or land cress
handful of rocket

100g cooked chickpeas
100g garden peas or sweetcorn
50g sauerkraut or raw beetroot (grated)
100g hazelnuts
2 avocados, peeled, stoned and cubed
small handful of fresh coriander, basil, mint, dill or parsley leaves, chopped

Cook the quinoa as per the packet instructions. Once the quinoa is cooked, drain and rinse, then set aside.

Put the sweet potatoes in a baking tray and toss with the oil and salt. Bake for 35–45 minutes, tossing once or twice to ensure they don't overcook on one side and undercook on others.

Meanwhile, chop your cauliflower into small florets, discarding the tough middle section. Place the florets in a food-processor and blitz until it forms a rice-like consistency. Heat a frying pan over a medium heat. Add the cauliflower 'rice' and heat for 3–4 minutes, stirring constantly to avoid it burning. Once warmed through, set aside to cool.

In a large bowl, combine the spinach, corn salad or sweetcorn, cress, rocket, chickpeas, garden peas or sweetcorn and sauerkraut or beetroot.

When the sweet potatoes are cooked, remove from the oven and reduce the heat to 140°C. Put the sweet potatoes, quinoa and cauliflower into a large serving bowl, stir to combine and set aside. Once the oven has cooled, spread the nuts on a baking tray and bake for 10-15 minutes, until they begin to brown.

Add the avocado, leaves and herbs to the quinoa mixture and then top with the toasted nuts.

Late Summer Peach, Beetroot, Cherry & Ginger Salad

Serves 4

Beetroot has been used medicinally for years to heal ailments and is a trusty ingredient if you need a little boost in brainpower during the day (its nitrates increase blood flow to the brain). It is also one of the most versatile vegetables and can taste so different depending on how it's prepared. It can provide a sweet crunch to salads in summer or form the foundations of something more warming like a curry (page 226) during winter. Combined here with sweet and sour fruits and spices and creamy avocado, this salad is perfect for al fresco feasts, either as a main served with dips, or as a side salad for just about anything.

4 peaches, stoned and sliced
1 tbsp grated fresh ginger
100g corn salad or land cress
40g rocket
1 raw beetroot, thinly sliced
handful of fresh basil leaves
10 cherries, halved and stoned

2 carrots, grated, spiralised or thinly sliced with a julienne peeler
pinch of ssea alt
pinch of ground turmeric
3 tbsp extra virgin olive oil
juice of ½ orange (optional)
2 avocados, cubed

In a large serving bowl, gently stir the peaches, ginger, corn salad or land cress, rocket, beetroot, basil, cherries, carrots, salt and turmeric until combined. Add the oil (and orange juice, if using) and toss to coat, then stir through the avocado.

Serve with dips (ages 180–183) or dressings (pages 133–135) and top with toasted nuts or seeds, or Nut Parmesan Sprinkle (page 313).

Try this with grilled peaches, quarted and roasted for 10–12 minutes at 200°C or sear them in a hot griddle pan for 2–3 minutes on each side, until soft and marked slightly.

Daytime

Making Dressings

Dressings have had a lot of bad press in recent years, and whilst shop-bought dressings totally deserve it, there is definitely more to say on the matter. Not all dressings are created equal and, if you make your own – using highly nutritious ingredients – they can turn out even healthier than the food they're intended to 'dress'. Not only are they simple to make, they also add instant flavour and elevate the healing potential of any meal. Experiment with the ratios of the foundation ingredients to find a balance that suits your taste.

Foundation Ingredients

Liquids
Apple cider vinegar
Rice vinegar
Fresh lemon juice
Fresh lime juice
Fresh orange juice
Fresh grapefruit juice
Other pure fruit juices
Nut milk
Rose water
Orange blossom water

Oils
Extra virgin olive oil
Sesame oil
Coconut oil
Avocado oil
Walnut oil
Flaxseed oil
Chia Seed oil
MCT oil

Thickeners & Emulsifiers
Mustard
Tahini
Avocado
Nuts
Seeds
Tinned coconut milk
Egg yolks
Leftover cooked grains

Flavourings
Nutritional yeast
Fresh or dried fruits
Fresh vegetables
Fresh or dried herbs
Fresh or dried spices
Plant powders and adaptogens
Tamari (or soy)
Chilli
Garlic
Miso paste
Honey

My Favourite Dressings

*Each recipe serves
4–6 people*

*Store in the fridge for up
to 4 days*

Carrot & Sesame dressing
Put 2 carrots, juice of ½ orange, ½ tsp lemon or lime juice, ½ tsp tamari (or a pinch of salt), 4 tbsps extra virgin olive oil, 1 tbsp water, 2 tbsp sesame oil, ½ tsp ground ginger, ¼ tsp ground turmeric and 2 tbsp goji berries (soaked for 5 minutes in boiling water) or natural sweetener. Blend on the highest speed for 1–2 minutes until smooth and thoroughly combined.

Miso & Nori 'Umami' Dressing
Put 5 tbsp extra virgin olive oil, 4 tbsp sesame oil, 1 tsp natural sweetener of choice, 10g brown or white miso paste, 5 tbsp boiling water, 1–2 tsp tamari, 2 tsp lime or lemon juice, a pinch of ground ginger, to taste, 5g dried nori and either a pinch of garlic powder or ½ garlic clove (crushed) in a blender. Blend for 1 minute, then scrape down the sides and blend for a further 1 minute until smooth and thoroughly combined.

'Yellow Sunshine' – Turmeric & Cashew Sweet Mustard Dressing
Put 1 tsp ground turmeric, 50g cashews (ideally soaked for 1–4 hours), 80ml extra virgin olive oil, 4 tbsp boiling water, 2 tbsp hemp seeds, 2 tbsp mustard, 1–2 tsp lemon or lime juice, 1 tsp natural sweetener and a pinch of salt or a few drops of tamari in a blender. Blend on a low speed for 30 seconds and then increase to the highest speed, until smooth and thoroughly combined. (Elevate by adding fresh mint or coriander, a sprinkling of bee pollen or a handful of cooked sweetcorn).

Walnut Caesar Salad Dressing
Put 50g soaked walnuts (ideally soaked for a minimum of 2 hours) with 50ml extra virgin olive oil, 150g filtered water, 10g tahini, ½ tsp lemon juice and a pinch of salt in a blender. Blend for 1–2 minutes, until smooth and thoroughly combined. (You could also use soaked cashews, sunflower seeds or pine nuts instead of walnuts. Elevate by adding ¼ tsp spirulina, ashwgandha, chaga or wheatgrass powder or a few drops of walnut, flaxseed or chia seed oil.)

Cherry, Lime & Tahini Dressing
Cut 8 large cherries in half and remove the stones. Put them in a blender and add 1 tbsp tahini, 6 tbsp extra virgin olive oil, ½ tsp lime juice and a pinch of salt or a few drops of tamari. Blend for 1–2 minutes, until smooth and thoroughly combined. (Elevate the flavour and nutrient level by adding organic Dijon mustard, a few drops of apple cider vinegar, a pinch of wasabi paste, grated fresh ginger or a handful of fresh mint, basil, lemon balm or coriander leaves).

Simple Tamari Dipping Sauce
In a small bowl, jug or a jar, whisk together 1 tbsp tamari, 4 tbsp extra virgin olive, sesame or avocado oil, ½ tsp lemon or lime juice, 1 tbsp tahini (optional) and 1 tsp natural sweetener (optional). If using a jar, secure the lid and shake to combine.

Lime, Mint & Coconut Cream Dressing
Put 5g fresh coriander leaves, 5g fresh mint leaves, 1 x 400g can coconut milk, 2 tbsp hemp seeds, linseeds or chia seeds, juice of 1 lime, 1 tbsp honey, a pinch salt or a few drops tamari and a few chilli flakes (optional) in a blender. Blend on the highest speed for 1–2 minutes until smooth and combined. (For a thicker, more yogurt-like result, use less of the coconut milk, or add a few tbsp avocado.)

Sweet Tahini Dip
Whisk together 2 tsp tamari, 4 tbsp tahini, 4 tbsp olive oil, 1 tsp natural sweetener, 2 tsp lemon juice, ½ tsp ground ginger and either a pinch of garlic powder or ½ garlic clove (crushed) in a jug or small bowl.

Earthy Magic Mushroom Dressing
Put 2 tsp reishi powder, 1 tsp shilajit powder, 1 tsp he shou wou powder, 4 tsp miso paste, 4 tsp sesame oil, 60ml extra virgin olive oil, 4 tbsp boiling water, 2–3 tsp tamari, 2 tsp lemon or lime juice, 1 tsp apple cider vinegar, 1 tsp natural sweetener and 2 tsp tahini in a blender. Blend on a high speed for 1–2 minutes until combined.

Basic Tahini Dressing

Whisk together 100g tahini, 80ml extra virgin olive oil, 2 tsp tamari and 6 tbsp boiling water in a jug or bowl. (To elevate it, add 1 tsp sesame oil, 2–3 tbsp lemon juice, 1 tsp brown or white miso paste, 1 tsp natural sweetener, a pinch garlic powder or ½ garlic clove, crushed).

Tips

Use for salads, warm vegetables, side dishes, or main meals. Use more thickening ingredients to turn a dressing into a dip and serve with raw or cooked vegetables, crackers and other snacks. Dressings can be stored in a sealed jar or container for up to 1 week in the fridge.

Hang Loose Pokē-Style Ocean Bowl

Serves 4

Preheat the oven to 120°C / gas mark 1

Pokē, a Hawaiian-inspired delicacy, is très chic at the moment. Traditionally, it contains rice topped with tuna or salmon sashimi, a menagerie of vibrant vegetables, pickles and feisty, flavourful dressings – a bowl buzzing with fresh ingredients. This version doesn't contain fish, in case you can't get hold of sashimi-grade quality fish. The pickles, marinades and dressings bring out the flavour of the more neutral ingredients so, although it might seem like a lot of hassle, it's well worth it. Hang loose.

250g brown rice, black rice, quinoa or millet
100g edamame beans
40g kale, spinach, broccoli or other greens, raw or steamed
1 avocado
pinch of Himalayan pink salt
1 tsp lemon juice or ponzu (*optional*)
100g grated carrot, beetroot or radishes (or other raw vegetables of choice, such as spring onions, cucumber, courgette, daikon)
1 portion Quickled cucumber (page 316)
1 portion Pickled ginger (page 316)
2 tbsp sesame seeds

For the seaweed salad
15g dried hijiki or arame
1 tbsp tamari
1 tsp rice or apple cider vinegar
½–1 tsp sesame oil
¼–½ tsp honey (optional)
¼ tsp ground or grated fresh ginger
2 tbsp sesame seeds (black or white, or both)

For the marinated enoki mushrooms
200g enoki, shiitake, chestnut or portobello mushrooms or a mixture
3 tbsp rice vinegar
1 tbsp extra virgin olive, sesame or coconut oil
2 tsp apple cider vinegar
4 tbsp water
2 tbsp coconut sugar
2 tbsp tamari
½ tsp grated fresh ginger
1 tbsp fresh coriander leaves

For the baked nori crisps
6 sheets dried nori
2 tbsp sesame oil
pinch of sea salt
1 tbsp sesame seeds

Fill a saucepan with water and bring to the boil. Add the edamame beans and cook for 10–15 minutes, then drain (reserving the water), transfer to a small bowl, and set aside.

Return the reserved cooking liquid to the pan and bring to the boil again. Add the kale, spinach, broccoli or other greens and cook for 5–8 minutes until the leaves are wilted or the broccoli begins to soften but still has some bite.

Slice the avocado in half, remove the stone and then score the flesh either into cubes or thin slices, lengthways. Scoop the flesh into a small serving bowl, sprinkle with salt, drizzle with lemon juice and then place in the fridge until ready to serve.

For the baked nori crisps, cut the nori sheets into sixths, to make six small

rectangles. Place on a baking tray, brush with sesame oil and then sprinkle with the sesame seeds and a pinch of salt. Bake for 15–20 minutes, until crisp and crunchy.

For the seaweed salad, soak the seaweed in a bowl of water for 10–15 minutes, until it has tripled in size. Meanwhile, whisk together the remaining ingredients in a small bowl. Drain the seaweed and rinse it under cold water, then add it to the dressing and mix or massage the seaweed in with your hands to coat with the dressing and top with sesame seeds. Place in the fridge until ready to serve.

For the marinated mushrooms, place all the mushroom ingredients in a small saucepan, bring to the boil and then simmer for 10–20 minutes, until the mushrooms soften and the sauce thickens. Transfer to a bowl and place in the fridge until ready to serve.

When all your components are ready, divide the cooked rice or grain among four bowls. Tuck the edamame beans into one corner of each bowl. Do the same with the grated vegetables, greens, avocado, marinated mushrooms and Quickled Cucumber, and finally arrange the seaweed salad in the centre of the bowl.

Serve the Pickled Ginger on the side and either serve the nori crisps on the side or tuck 1 or 2 into each bowl.

This recipe is vegetarian but I'd encourage adding either fresh sashimi, smoked salmon, cooked fish or seafood, soft-boiled eggs for a truer pokē experience.

Serve with Lime, Mint & Coconut Cream Dressing (see page 134) or Miso, Sesame & Ginger Nori Dressing (see page 134)

Caesar Salad

Serves 1

Caesar salad may seem pretty standard, but what I really want to share with you is the walnut Caesar dressing, which brings added nutrients to the salad. Add your choice of eggs, meat or fish to make a more substantial main meal.

1 avocado
handful of kale, baby kale or spinach
small handful of rocket
½ Little Gem, sliced
½ courgette, grated
1 portion of Walnut Caesar Salad Dressing
    (page 134)

Elevate it: 10g sprouted seeds, 10g anchovies, 40g cooked garden peas, 40g cooked chickpeas, 40g cooked grains or psuedograins, 1 portion of cooked chicken, sliced or shredded, or 2 grilled portobello mushrooms, pumpkin or hemp seeds

Place the letuce in a large bowl, add the kale or spinach and rocket and toss to combine. Slice the avocado in half and remove the stone. Scoop out the flesh out, slice it and add it to the bowl. Add the courgette and any elevational extras of your choice.

Pour the dressing over the salad, tossing it to coat it evenly. Serve instantly.

Serve with Miracle Bread (page 314) or Magic 'Bread' Rolls (page 314), toasted and chopped to make croutons. Garnish with Nut Parmesan Sprinkle (page 313) or savoury Qnola.

Cauliflower, Mushroom, Chickpea & Quinoa Burgers with Portobello 'Buns'

Serves 4

Preheat the oven to 200°C / gas mark 6

A cross between falafels and burgers, these vegetable patties are a creative way to get many types of vegetables into one dish. Using grilled portobello mushrooms as 'buns' adds a delicious juiciness, but you could use Magic 'Bread' Rolls (page 314) or ordinary buns instead. I love serving these with Watercress & Nettle Pesto (page 311), Beetroot Tomato Ketchup (page 309), Cashew and Almond Mayonnaise (page 309), Tomato Goji Chilli Jam (page 309) or Hummus (page 182).

8 portobello mushrooms
3 tbsp extra virgin olive oil
80g chestnut mushrooms, diced
50g sunflower seeds or nuts, such as almonds or walnuts
30g cauliflower
70g chickpeas (or other pulses)
100g grated vegetables, such as carrot, beetroot or sweet potato
handful of fresh basil, parsley,

coriander or mint leaves
1 tsp ground cumin
1 garlic clove, crushed
50g buckwheat flour
1 egg
1 tbsp tahini
a handful of spinach, diced
150g cooked quinoa
4 lettuce leaves
sea salt and freshly ground black pepper

Wash the portobello mushrooms, pat dry and trim the stalks, then sprinkle the underside with a generous pinch of salt. Once the oven is hot, place the mushrooms, upside down, directly on the oven racks with a baking tray underneath to catch the juices. Bake for 10–15 minutes.

If you don't have any leftover quinoa, cook some from scratch (you will only need about 50g raw quinoa and double the amount of water). Simmer until all of the water has been absorbed.

Meanwhile, heat 1 tablespoon of the oil in a small saucepan, then add the chestnut mushrooms and sauté for 10 minutes.

In a food processor, blend the seeds or nuts until they form a flour-like consistency. Then, add the cauliflower, chickpeas, vegetables, fresh herbs, another tablespoon of the oil, cumin, garlic, flour, egg, cooked mushrooms, tahini and season with salt and pepper. Pulse to combine and then transfer the mixture to a bowl. Stir in the spinach and the quinoa.

Form the mixture into patties with your hands, squeezing gently to encourage it to bind. Set aside on a plate and heat the remaining oil in a frying pan over a medium heat. Place 2–4 patties at a time in the pan, and fry for 3–5 minutes until the undersides are cooked and beginning to brown. Flip the patties and cook the other sides for another 3–5 minutes. Continue to flip until the burgers are cooked through and crisp on the outside. Repeat until all of the mixture is used up.

When ready to serve, line the underside of one portobello mushroom 'bun' with a lettuce leaf and then place one pattie on top and finish with another mushroom 'bun' on top.

Coconut Creamed Mushroom Ragout
on Miracle Toast

Serves 2

The only thing that beats the smell of freshly baked bread is bread being toasted. There's something so warming and comforting about it and I used to love how the smell would linger in the air after my dad had served up one of his famous 'Copperman Fry-Up's' on weekends. Although then we would enjoy our toast with baked beans or Marmite, this creamy mushroom ragout is much more fun and filling. Try it topped with pesto (pages 310–311) or herb-infused oil (page 313).

3 tbsp extra virgin olive or coconut oil
50g kale (or other leafy greens)
500g mushrooms, such as chestnut,
    portobello and chanterelle mushrooms
300ml tinned coconut milk
2 tbsp nutritional yeast
1 tsp organic Dijon mustard
2 tbsp fresh thyme or rosemary
1 tsp salt, to taste
2–4 slices Miracle Bread (page 314)

To garnish
fresh herbs
leafy greens
hemp seeds
chopped nuts or Nut Parmesan (page 313)
    or savoury Qnola

Elevate it: few tbsp of leftover cooked grains or psuedograins, 2 tbsp soaked seaweed, 1–2 tbsp tahini, 1 garlic clove, crushed

Heat 1 tablespoon of the oil in a frying pan over a medium heat and, when hot, add your greens and sauté for 5 minutes. Add the mushrooms and sauté, stirring, for 10–20 minutes, until the mushrooms are cooked through, then gradually add the coconut milk. Bring to the boil and then simmer for 10 minutes, to reduce. Once the mixture is thick and creamy, stir in any elevational extras of your choice, then remove from the heat.

Toast the bread (I toast mine twice to make it extra crispy) and then divide between plates. Top each slice of toast with a generous serving of the mushroom ragout and garnish with fresh herbs, leafy greens, hemp seeds, nuts or Nut Parmesan Sprinkle (page 313) or savoury Qnola.

You can also serve the mushroom ragoût stirred through black or brown rice, quinoa or millet, to make a risotto-like dish.

Quinoa & Nori Sushi Rolls with Coconut Sauerkraut Slaw

Makes approx. 14 rolls

Traditional sushi uses sticky white sushi rice that can be stodgy and taxing on the digestion. Substituting it with quinoa brings many more nutrients to the table and does away with the pressures of having to get your sushi rice 'just right', which always seems something of an art. The sauerkraut slaw is a great way of getting through an endless batch of sauerkraut, and makes for a version of the traditional slaw thriving with good bacteria. If you don't have sauerkraut, just use half a red or white cabbage and some diced carrots in its place. Serve with pickles and miso, carrot or coconut-based dressings (page 134).

8–10 nori sheets
1 large sweet potato, peeled and cubed
250g cooked white quinoa (or use
    millet, buckwheat or brown rice)
1 avocado, sliced thinly, lengthways

For the sauerkraut slaw (*approx. 20 servings*)
½ red or white cabbage

½ red onion, thinly sliced
2 carrots, thinly slice
4 tbsp extra virgin olive oil
1 tsp lemon juice
1–2 tsp apple cider vinegar
200ml tinned coconut milk
salt or tamari and freshly ground black pepper
1 tsp organic Dijon mustard (optional)

For the sauerkraut slaw, place the cabbage in a large bowl. Add the onion and carrots, followed by the oil, lemon juice, vinegar, coconut milk and season to taste with salt or tamari and pepper. Use your hands to combine the vegetables and coat them evenly in the dressing. Set aside in the fridge.

Now make the sushi. Half-fill a saucepan with water and bring to the boil. Add the sweet potatoes and cook over a medium heat for 10–15 minutes, until soft. Drain and then transfer to a small bowl and mash until smooth.

Take a nori sheet and lay it flat on a dry surface. (I use a sushi mat, which helps but isn't essential.) Spread a layer of sweet potato in the middle of the nori sheet, being careful to leave about 2.5cm of space around the edge of the sheet. Layer about 2–4 tablespoons quinoa on top of the sweet potato and place a few avocado slices on top.

Starting with the end closest to you, begin to roll the nori sheet over the fillings. The first few tries may be frustrating, but you'll get the hang of it. I tend to lift and fold at the same time, using one hand to hold the nori and the other to tuck in the fillings and keep them in place. Once you have managed to roll the nori into a sausage shape, gently squeeze it with both hands (your hands must be completely dry), working from one end to the other.

Take your sharpest knife and wet it slightly. Hold the roll at one end and slice diagonally down the middle of the roll.

Repeat with the remaining ingredients. Serve instantly or store in the fridge until ready to enjoy.

For vegetable fillings, I like kohlrabi, carrot, cucumber, courgette, cabbage — chopped, leafy greens and beetroot.

If you wish to add cooked chicken, fish, tofu or tempeh, try marinating them first in a sauce of tamari, ginger, ground coriander, a natural sweetener and a little extra virgin olive oil or sesame oil.

You can also make hand rolls instead of the small, fiddly 'futomaki rolls': cut the nori sheet in half to make a smaller rectangle, spread with toppings and roll diagonally to make a cone shape that you can hold in one hand. Fill with more toppings, as desired.

Daytime

Green Pancakes with Avocado, Fennel & Chickpeas

Makes 10–12 large pancakes

Preheat the oven to 180°C /gas mark 4

As loyal as I am to sweet crepes and pancakes, this savoury option is such a game-changer for daytime meals. Fresh spinach and courgette dye the batter a wonderful earthy green and turn all the goodness of your standard trusty green juice into a delicious pancake. You could also make mini, bite-sized pancakes and top them with spreads or salad to serve as canapés.

500ml coconut drinking milk or almond milk
3 eggs
220g buckwheat flour
250ml water
1 tbsp melted coconut oil, plus extra for frying
pinch of sea salt
2 large handfuls of spinach or watercress
1 tbsp fresh basil leaves
1 large courgette, grated

For the filling
1 fennel bulb, thinly sliced
3 tbsp extra virgin olive oil
400g tinned chickpeas, drained and rinsed
2 tbsp tahini
1 tbsp nutritional yeast
1 avocado, peeled, stoned and sliced

Elevate it: ½ tsp spirulina, wheatgrass or chlorella powder

First, make the fillings. Arrange the fennel slices on a baking tray, drizzle with 1 tablespoon of the olive oil and sprinkle with a little salt. Bake for 45–50 minutes, until juicy and crisp around the edges.

Put the chickpeas in a bowl, add the tahini, 2 tablespoons of the olive oil, nutritional yeast, a generous pinch of salt and pepper, and stir to combine.

To make the pancake batter, put the milk and eggs in a high-speed blender, then add all the remaining ingredients apart from the oil and blend on a high speed for 1–2 minutes, until the mixture is smooth and develops a pale green hue. Leave in the jug of your blender for easy pouring.

Heat the coconut oil in a large frying pan over a medium heat and, once melted and hot, pour in a ladleful of batter, rotating the pan to coat the base evenly. Cook for 2–3 minutes on each side. Repeat this process until you have used up the all the batter.

Take one pancake at a time and line your fillings down the middle of it, starting with the fennel, then 1–2 tablespoons of the chickpea mixture and finally some slices of ripe avocado. Serve immediately.

Fragrance Oil

Lasts about 12 uses

Equipment: 1 × 40–50ml cosmetics bottle with a roll-on lid or spray-top lid

Store at room temperature for 4–6 months

Stress is a very common side-effect of modern life, and even if you don't consider yourself 'stressed', things like overwhelming workloads, a nightmare journey or a long queue when you're in a rush can all induce stress, contributing to your moood and mental and physical output. Using aromatherapy to keep a positive and steady mind is one simple way to ensure you cope with these situations more rationally and openly, accepting them, letting them go and continuing on your day, instead of vibrating negatively and only attracting more of the same. Choose essential oils to suit your personal preference, the season, your mood or the demands of each unique day (page 303).

2 tbsp almond oil (or other carrier oil, page 302)
6 drops bergamot essential oil
10 drops jasmine essential oil

6 drops cedarwood essential oil
10 drops ylang-ylang essential oil
10 drops frankincense essential oil

Put all of the ingredients into a bottle and secure the lid. Shake to combine.

To use, roll or spray the oil onto wrists and decolletage in the morning, before you arrive at work or throughout the day if and when new stresses arise. Shake well before each use.

If you have a spray-top lid, spray around your living or working space.

Daytime

Hand Cream

Lasts about 20 uses

Equipment: 1 x 100ml jar or pot, with a lid

Store in the fridge or at room temperature for up to 2 months

During the day our hands are constantly active and we use them to assist in more or less every daily task. A hand massage is one way to release tension and tiredness in the hands, whilst hand creams soften and moisturise the skin and prevent premature ageing and dryness (worsened during colder months). Applying these hand creams will revitalise the hands whilst releasing natural aromas that soothe and calm the mind.

Spring / Summer Aloe Hand Cream

80g aloe vera gel
20g coconut oil (or shea butter), melted

10 drops of your chosen essential oils (page 303)
1 tsp rose water

In a small bowl, whisk all the ingredients together. Once combined, transfer to your pot, secure the lid and store in the fridge.

Autumn / Winter Pink Clay & Avocado Hand Treatment

80g shea butter
25g beeswax
1 tsp pink clay
4 tsp arrowroot

25 drops amber essential oil
25 drops jasmine essential oil
2 tsp vanilla powder or extract

Fill a small saucepan with water and bring to the boil. Place a heatproof bowl on top of the pan (creating a double boiler), add the shea butter and beeswax. Stir with a spatula until melted and then remove from the heat.

Whisk in the pink clay, arrowroot, essential oils and vanilla, until combined. Pour into a pot, secure the lid and store in the fridge.

To use, apply whenever you like and allow to soak in completely. Combine application with a gentle massage to really energise the hands.

Palo Santo Atmosphere Spray

Fills a 125ml spray bottle

Equipment: 1 × 125ml bottle with a spray-top lid

If you aren't into smudging, an old Native American practice where you purify a room with the smoke of sacred herbs, but love the smell of palo santo, this atmosphere spray offers the calming aromas without the smoke or the rituals. As well as being used to clear bad energy, palo santo is thought to reduce inflammation, ease muscle pain, relieve stress and boost the immune system through inhalation, making it an ideal element to work into your daytime rituals, particularly if you're feeling stressed or strained. It is also said to repel bugs, so wear as fragrance oil where bugs are rife.

20 drops palo santo essential oil
100ml filtered water

5 drops sage essential oil
1 tbsp witch hazel

Put all the ingredients in a spray-top bottle, seal the lid and shake to combine.

To use, shake well and spray a couple of times around your desk space, your room or your entire house.

Shea Butter, Coconut & Arrowroot Deodorant Sticks

Makes about 2 individual products

Whilst deodorant is a modern necessity, a lot of commercial products contain artificial ingredients, parabens, aluminium and other toxins that, in the process of blocking pores and preventing natural perspiration, are absorbed by the skin, bringing us another set of toxins we really don't need. This natural deodorant works differently. With no artificial ingredients and scented naturally, it masks the smell of body odour, rather than blocking your sweat glands and preventing sweating, which is essential for regulating body temperature and, in some cases, removing toxins. Apply at the beginning of each day and throughout the day, if needed.

50g shea butter
40g coconut oil
40g beeswax (or you can substitute with more shea or cocoa butter)
40g arrowroot

1 tbsp baking powder
20 drops cedarwood essential oil
10 drops bergamot essential oil

Daytime

Fill a small saucepan with water and bring to the boil. Place a heatproof bowl on top of the pan (creating a double boiler), then add the shea butter, coconut oil and beeswax. Stir with a spatula until dissolved, then remove from the heat and whisk in the arrowroot, baking powder and essential oils until combined.

Divide between sections of a muffin tin, mini loaf tin, large loaf tin or a small glass, and place in the fridge to harden. Once solid, remove from the moulds. Either store in an airtight container or jar, or wrap in baking paper and store in the fridge. If using a large loaf tin, cut into smaller rectangles.

To apply, simply swipe the deodorant stick in upwards motions on each armpit until lightly coated.

Leave-In Conditioning Spray

Makes approx.150ml

Equipment: 1 × 150ml bottle with a spray-top lid

I am lucky to be blessed with pretty strong hair. On shoots, hair stylists are pleasantly surprised at the condition of it since it endures constant hassle in my line of work. I think my diet is largely to thank, but I also keep my rituals simple. I favour organic natural products and use this simple hair spray to liven up dry ends. Just spray on and leave on. Argan oil is deeply conditioning but is non-greasy, making it perfect for a spray that will refresh the smell, look and feel of your hair.

80ml filtered water
2 tbsp argan oil

10–20 drops of your chosen essential oils

Put all the ingredients into a bottle and secure the lid. Shake to combine and store at room temperature until ready to use. Spray 4–6 times all over the hair to calm frizz and nourish brittle ends. To use as a leave-in conditioner, spray 15–20 times into your hand and massage into the roots and through the lengths of your hair. You could spray into wet hair after a shower and wrap in a towel and leave for a couple of hours before rinsing too.

DIY Diffusers

Makes 1

Equipment: a small jar or glass; 6–8 reed diffuser sticks

Diffusers are an effortless way to fill your space with positive aromas and awaken the senses. If you have trouble concentrating or find yourself watching the clock after lunch, using essential oils that have the power to increase creativity and lift low moods might help you more than you think.

60ml almond or jojoba oil
25–30 drops of your chosen essential oils
    (I like citronella and bergamot)

Put the almond or jojoba oil into a jar or glass and add the essential oils. Mix vigorously with a small spoon or spatula to combine. Place the reed sticks in the jar and leave for a couple of hours, then turn the sticks upside down, to encourage the oils to travel the entire length of them. Position your diffuser where you would like to enjoy them.

Every 1–2 weeks, give the mixture a stir and turn the sticks upside down. If the scent isn't strong enough, add a few extra drops of your essential oils. Replace the sticks after a month or so.

In Between Time

In Between Time

'In between time' is that awkward stage between daytime and evening time. You've had your lunch and you've taken a break, but it's not quite time to leave work or start thinking about dinner. The late afternoon is when most people tend to hit a wall, often losing momentum and feeling unfocused, tired and maybe irritatable, depending on how their day is unfolding. This time is generally accompanied by cravings, and it is usually hard to decipher whether they are triggered by physical or emotional hunger brought on by stress, boredom or fatigue. For these reasons, it is important to check in again at this in-between phase, rather than powering through tasks you don't want to do, with energy you likely don't have. In this section you'll find practices for centring and grounding distracted and uninspired minds, plus natural movement techniques to stimulate digestion and other cellular functions that are particularly overloaded at this time of day. Use aromatherapy, home-made candles made with invigorating essential oils and soothing beauty remedies from the Beauty & Home sections of the book to increase concentration and energy even further. By taking a small break to indulge in one or several of these rituals, you may experience elevated mental performance and a fresh wave of creativity.

The recipes in this section work nicely alongside the practices and include functional drinks, sweet treats and small savoury snacks aimed to regulate appetite, soothe the mind and enhance energy levels, concentration and positivity. They are easy to graze on at work and won't make you too full for dinner, but instead will ensure you are topped up on powerful nutrients.

Mind

Chakra Meditation

The chakras are centres of spiritual energy. When we experience imbalances or feel misaligned in our body and mind, often this is a reflection of a closed chakra, one where energy is disrupted or lacking. This exercise focuses on each of the seven chakras to rebalance the flow of energy.

1. Sit comfortably, either with crossed legs on the floor or on a chair with your feet flat on the floor. Close your eyes and breathe naturally.

2. Next, bring your attention to the base of your spine, your pelvic floor. Imagine a ball glowing red and notice it expand to the size of a beach ball. This is the root chakra.

3. Bring your attention to your lower abdomen. Imagine a ball with a warm orange glow and notice it expand to the size of a beach ball. This is the sacral chakra.

4. Bring your attention to the space between your navel and your breastbone. Visualise a yellow ball and observe it as it expands to the size of a beach ball. This is the solar plexus chakra.

5. Bring your attention to the centre of your chest. Imagine a green ball and notice it grow to the size of a beach ball. This is the heart chakra.

6. Bring your attention to the neck and throat area. Visualise a turquoise ball and watch it as it expands to the size of a beach ball. This is the throat chakra.

7. Bring your attention to the space between your eyes and eyebrows. Notice an indigo ball and observe it as it expands to the size of a beach ball. This is the third-eye chakra.

8. Bring your attention to the crown of your head. See a violet ball and allow it to expand to the size of a beach ball. This is the crown chakra.

9. Bring the practice to a close by opening the eyes and settling into your seat. Take a few moments to readjust here.

Mudras

These are a few of my favourites to use in the middle of the day to enhance energy and concentration and to encourage perseverance. Hold each mudra for 3–15 minutes – the longer you hold it, the more effective the practice.

Prana mudra can be used to reduce tirednes, fatigue and nervousness.

1. Come to a comfortable seated position, either on the floor with legs crossed, or on a chair with your feet flat on the floor. Lengthen your spine and extend the back of your neck up, so your head is facing forwards, ensuring your neck is soft, not strained.

2. Rest your hands on your knees with the palms facing upwards and bend your ring finger and little finger in towards the palm of your hand. Fold your thumb over the tips of both fingers, leaving the other two fingers pointed straight.

Kali mudra is thought to break through negative thought patterns and help to overcome challenges.

1. Follow steps 1–2 of Prana Mudra, and come to rest your hands on your knees, palms facing upwards.

2. Bring your hands together and interlace your fingers. Extend both index fingers and rest them against one another.

Breath

The Cooling Breaths (Sitali & Sitkari)

These two cooling techniques are ideal for regulating body temperature. The sitali involves creating a straw-like shape with the tongue and inhaling through it; as the air passes through the tongue, it collects moisture. If you can't roll your tongue, use the sitkari method. This technique is also thought to reduce anxiety, regulate the natural appetite and hydrate the system.

Sitali

1. Sit in a comfortable position, either on the floor with crossed legs on the floor or on a chair with your feet flat, however is comfortable, ensuring the head, neck and spine are aligned.

2. Close your eyes and breathe naturally for a few moments. Relax the mouth and then drop the jaw open, as if you were about to make a low 'ah' sound.

3. Curl the sides of your tongue inwards to form a tube-like shape, and then poke it out of your mouth slightly, but with little effort.

4. Inhale deeply through the tongue, as if drinking the air in through a straw. Focus your attention on the cooling sensation of the breath and the rise of your abdomen, ribcage and chest. Retain the breath here for 5–10 counts, or release it instantly as directed in step 5.

5. Draw the tongue back inside your mouth, bring your lips together comfortably and exhale slowly through the nostrils.

6. Repeat steps 4–5 10–20 times, or however many times feels comfortable, and bring the practice to a close when you feel cooled and content.

Sitkari

1. Sit in a comfortable position, either on the floor with crossed legs on the floor or on a chair with your feet flat, however is comfortable, ensuring the head, neck and spine are aligned.

2. Close your eyes and breathe naturally for a few moments, then gently bring your lower and upper teeth together. Part your lips as much as you can to expose your teeth.

3. Inhale slowly through the teeth, letting the air flow through the gaps between each tooth, and focus on the feeling of the air against your teeth, entering the mouth, filling your abdomen, lungs and ribcage, and on the hissing sound of the breath.

4. Close your mouth, relax the jaw and the teeth and exhale slowly through the nose.

5. Repeat steps 4–5 10–20 times, or however many times feels comfortable, and bring the practice to a close when you feel cooled and content.

Nadhi Sodahana Pranayama

Nadhi sodahana is an energising, cleansing and detoxifying practice that enhances concentration. It involves alternating the breathing through the nostrils, closing off one nostril at a time to control the breath in a way that rejuvenates the nervous system and balances both sides of the brain.

1. Sit in a comfortable position, either on the floor with crossed legs or on a chair with your feet flat, however is comfortable, ensuring the head, neck and spine are aligned.

2. Decide how to use your hands to control the nostrils. You could use one thumb to close off both nostrils, clenching your fingers into a fist and keeping your thumb upright. You could use one thumb and the index finger of the same hand, tucking the remaining fingers into the palm of the hand. Or you could use one thumb and the ring finger of the same hand, keeping the middle two fingers tucked into the palm and the little finger free (Vishnu mudra).

3. If using one thumb, bring it to the right nostril and close it by pressing the thumb against it gently. Inhale deeply through the left nostril and hold your breath, then move your thumb to your left nostril and close it by pressing the thumb against it gently. Exhale through the right nostril. Keep the thumb on the left nostril and inhale deeply through your right. Hold the breath and then move your thumb to your right nostril again and close it by pressing the thumb against it gently. Exhale through the left. Repeat 10–20 times.

4. If using one thumb and your index or ring finger, bring your right thumb to the right nostril and close it by pressing the thumb against it gently. Inhale deeply through the left nostril and hold your breath, then use your finger to close the left nostril. Exhale through the right nostril. Keep the finger on the left nostril and inhale deeply through your right. Hold the breath and then replace your thumb on the right nostril to close it, exhaling through the left. Repeat 10–20 times.

5. If using Vishnu mudra, bring your right thumb to the right nostril and close it by pressing the thumb against it gently. Inhale deeply through the left nostril and hold your breath, then use your ring finger to close the left nostril. Exhale through the right nostril. Keep the finger on the left nostril and breathe in deeply through your right. Hold the breath and then replace your thumb on the right nostril to close it, exhaling through the left. Repeat 10–20 times.

Breath-Counting Meditation

This is a powerful exercise for the mind that tidies away distracting thoughts, enhancing concentration, stamina and endurance. Try this to refresh your thoughts or stay on task at work or to feel more present.

1. Sit comfortably either on the floor with crossed legs or on a chair with your feet flat on the floor. Close your eyes, bring your awareness to your breath and notice any natural patterns or rhythms.

2. On an exhale, start counting silently from one. Then inhale, pause briefly once your lungs have reached full capacity, and exhale, silently counting two.

3. Keep counting like this at the end of every exhalation until you reach ten, and then starting counting backwards, from ten to one. If thoughts intrude, you get interrupted or you become distracted and forget which number you're at, simply accept it and start again from one.

4. Once you are back to 'one', repeat the sequence, counting up to 20 or 30 or however far feels natural, and bring the practice to a close when you are ready to.

In Between Time

Movement

Dynamic Seated Spinal Twist or Washing Machine Pranayama

This invigorating and energising practice is harder than it may seem. I have practised this in yoga classes and it can get quite demanding. It is an incredibly powerful technique to release stress and tension, opening up the body and mind, and stimulating the flow of energy.

1. Sit in a comfortable position, either on the floor with crossed legs or on a chair with your feet flat, however is comfortable, ensuring the head, neck and spine are aligned.

2. Bring your hands to each shoulder, with the right hand on the right shoulder, and the left hand on the left. Rest your fingers over the front of each shoulder, with the thumbs on the backs of each shoulder.

3. As you inhale, twist your torso (keeping the chest broad and open) towards your left side, then as you exhale, rotate towards your right side. Lengthen the crown of the head towards the sky, and let it travel effortlessly with your chests and the shoulders. Pick a pace that feels comfortable for you, twisting to the left with each inhale and back to the right on each exhale. You can take long, deep breaths or shorter, more forceful, rapid breaths.

4. Continue for about 20–30 breaths, or however long feels comfortable and unstrained, and then inhale to return to the centre, facing forwards. Lower your hands to your thighs or knees and relax. Repeat if you feel inclined to, or bring the practice to a close.

Yoga Poses & Inversions

Twisting Downward Dog with Bent Knees
This is ideal for stimulating the flow of energy around the body, regulating the breath and encouraging digestion if things are slowing after lunch.

1. Come to Downward Dog (page 54) on a level, preferably soft, surface or a yoga mat if you have one.

2. Anchoring through the palms of your hands and the fingers, begin to bend your knees over to the right, allowing your hips to lower slightly and move towards the left. Hold this position for 5 breaths, and then repeat on the other side, moving your knees to the left and your hips towards the right.

3. Repeat 3–5 times, or however many times feels comfortable, and then bring the practice to a close by returning to Downward Dog and walking your feet to your hands or your hands to your feet. Roll up slowly, one vertebra at a time.

Forward Fold (Uttanasana)
This simple forward fold provides a revitalising boost of oxygen and energy, and it can help to stimulate blood flow to the brain. This posture calms the mind, relieves physical tension, improves digestion and can ease symptoms of many illnesses or discomforts.

1. Start standing tall, feet together and arms by your sides.

2. Inhale and raise your arms straight up above your head. As you exhale, fold at the hips, keeping a straight back, and bend down over your legs.

3. Relax over the legs, keeping your knees straight, and place your fingertips or palms on the floor beside your feet, or behind your ankles. To modify further, hold each elbow with the opposite hand. Hang loosely and breathe deeply for about 3–5 breaths.

4. Roll up to stand, one vertebra at a time.

*   *For a deeper stretch, as you fold forwards over the legs, swing your arms behind your back and interlace the fingers. Bring the palms together and reach the hands forwards as you bend further over your legs. To release the pose, bring the hands back towards your lower back, and roll up to stand, one vertebra at a time.*

Tapping & Shaking
Turn to pages 49–50 for instructions, and work mainly on your head, face, chest and arms for tapping and on your arms for shaking.

Makko Ho Stretches
During this in between time of day, the small intestine, bladder and kidneys are thought to be hard at work. The following meridian stretches are intended to energise these organs, stimulating digestion and elimination, and soothing digestive discomforts such as indigestion.

Index finger stretch

1. Stand loosely with your legs slightly wider than hip-width apart, and with hands just in front of you. Straighten both index fingers, pointing them upwards. Clench the rest of your fingers into a loose fist, folding your thumbs across them.

2. Now, straighten your right arm and lift it out to the right, in line with your shoulder and parallel to the ground. Your palm should be facing to the right, not to the ground, and your index finger should be pointing towards the sky. Notice the stretch and feel it along the arm and all through the finger. This may feel unusual or uncomfortable at first, but hold it here for a few breaths, breathing deeply.

3. Repeat with the left arm, and then return to the right, and repeat this pattern for a few rounds. Gradually increase the speed of transitioning between the right and left, ensuring you stretch fully through the fingers.

4. To bring the practice to a close, release your hands by your sides and give them a gentle shake.

In Between Time

Iced-Coffee Slushie

Serves 2

This is basically a sophisticated and supercharged version of a milkshake. The frozen banana, vanilla and almond milk replicate the flavour and texture of softening ice cream, whilst the maca brings mood-boosting benefits and a moreish malty essence. The coffee provides extra drive if you need a caffeine hit as the day begins to slump, but for a decaf option, replace it with chicory root – a high-fibre coffee alternative that has stress-reducing, digestion-aiding and liver-protecting capabilities.

100g frozen banana (or avocado)
125ml almond milk (or coconut drinking milk)
100ml filtered water
generous pinch of sea salt
8–10g vanilla powder
2–3 tbsp strong coffee (or 1 tbsp organic instant ground coffee or good-quality chicory powder)
2 Medjool dates

1 tbsp maca powder
200g ice cubes
crushed nuts, to serve

Elevate it: *1 tsp ground cinnamon, 1 tsp chaga powder, 1 tsp reishi powder, 2 tbsp cacao powder (for a chocolatey version)*

Put all the ingredients apart from the ice and nuts in a blender and blend on a high speed for 1–2 minutes, until smooth.

Add the ice cubes and blend again for 30 seconds or until all the ice has broken down and the mixture is thick but completely smooth. Divide between two glasses, top with crushed nuts and serve instantly.

Make ice cubes out of plant-based milk or coffee and use them instead of standard ice cubes to intensify the flavour.

Making Lattes

Warm milk-based drinks flavoured with powerful plants have been used as soothing and preventative home remedies in Eastern traditions for centuries. You'll likely be familiar with the Ayurvedic turmeric milk or chai latte, known to boost the immune system and reduce inflammation, but it doesn't stop there. Silky smooth nut milks are a delicious way to distribute the goodness of powdered plants around the body efficiently, and you can easily experiment to develop a latte suited to your ever-changing tastes and needs. Lattes are quick to make and easy to digest, attuning your internal systems with minimal effort. For iced versions, use refrigerated milks and add ice accordingly.

Serves 1

Foundation Ingredients

Base Liquids (250ml)
Plant-based milks (pages 304–306)
Water
Coconut water

Thickeners (1–2 tbsp)
Nuts and nut butters (such as pecans, almonds, cashews, walnuts, Brazil nuts, hazelnuts, almond butter, cashew butter, hazelnut butter)
Seeds and seed butters (such as tahini, sesame seeds, hemp seeds, linseeds)

Fats (½–1 tsp)
Cacao butter
Creamed coconut and coconut butter
Coconut oil
Ghee
Organic butter
Avocado
MCT oil

Flavourings (to taste, ½–1 tsp)
Adaptogens and tonic herb powders (such as reishi, cordyceps, he shou wu, maca, cacao, mucuna pruriens, ashwagandha)
Freeze-dried plant powders (such as blueberry, beetroot, raspberry, wheatgrass, baobab, spirulina, coconut milk powder)
Ground kitchen herbs and spices (such as turmeric, cinnamon, nutmeg, vanilla)
Fresh plant juices (such as ginger, turmeric, carrot, beetroot
Rose water or orange blossom water

Sweeteners (to taste)
Coconut palm sugar
Coconut nectar
Raw honey or manuka honey
Date paste
Agave syrup
Palm jaggery
Rice syrup
Dates
Stevia

In Between Time

In Between Time

A Few of My Favourites

Reishi & Rhodiola cappuccino

Heat 280ml coconut, oat or almond milk in a small saucepan over a medium heat for 45 seconds–1 minute, stirring occasionally. Put 1 tsp reishi powder, ½ tsp rhodiola, 1–2 shots coffee or 1–2 tsp instant coffee granules (or 2 tbsp chicory powder), ½ tsp vanilla powder, pinch of salt, ½ tsp maca powder and ½ tsp melted cacao butter or coconut oil in a high-speed blender. Add the hot milk and blend on a high speed for 1–2 minutes, until smooth and frothy. Pour into a glass or mug and enjoy.

Charcoal Iced Latte

Put 350ml water in a blender and add 50g hemp seeds (or soaked almonds or cashews), 2g activated charcoal powder, 1 tsp vanilla powder and 4–6 ice cubes. (Elevate by adding 5–6 fresh mint leaves, ½ tsp ashwagandha powder, ½ tsp tocotrienols or ½ tsp maca powder). Blend for 1–2 minutes, until smooth and frothy. Pour into a glass or mug and enjoy.

Wheatgrass Coconut Latte

Heat 250ml coconut milk in a small saucepan over a medium heat for 45 seconds–1 minute, stirring occasionally. Put ½–1 tsp wheatgrass, 2 tbsp coconut milk powder (or creamed coconut), ½ tsp vanilla powder and ½ Medjool date in a high-speed blender and blend for 1–2 minutes, until smooth and frothy. Pour into a glass or mug and enjoy.

Hazelnut Butter, Coconut & Cacao Mocha

Heat 250ml coconut milk in a small saucepan over a medium heat for 45 seconds–1 minute, stirring occasionally. Put 1 tbsp cacao powder, ½ tsp maca powder, 1 tbsp hazelnut butter, 1 shot coffee (or 1 tsp instant coffee powder or 1 tbsp chicory powder), 1 tsp natural sweetener and a pinch of salt in a high-speed blender and add the hot milk. Blend for 1–2 minutes, until smooth and frothy. Pour into a glass or mug and enjoy.

Apple Cider Vinegar Latte

Heat 250ml plant-based milk (pages 304–306) in a small saucepan over a medium heat for 45 seconds–1 minute, stirring occasionally. Put 1 tsp apple cider vinegar, a dash of fresh turmeric juice (or ground turmeric), a dash of fresh ginger juice (or ground ginger) and a few drops of natural syrup and add the hot milk. Blend for 1–2 minutes in a high-speed blender, until smooth. Pour into a glass or mug and enjoy.

Avocado Latte

Heat 220ml plant-based milk (pages 304–306) in a small saucepan over a medium heat for 45 seconds–1 minute, stirring occasionally. Put 1–2 shots coffee (or 1–2 tsp instant ground coffee or 1–2 tbsp chicory powder), 20g avocado, ½ tsp vanilla powder and ½ tsp natural syrup in a high-speed blender and add the hot milk. Blend 1–2 minutes until smooth. If the mixture is too thick for you, add a little more milk before pouring into a glass or mug to enjoy.

Blueberry & Acai Latte

Heat 250ml plant-based milk (pages 304–306) in a small saucepan over a medium heat for 45 seconds–1 minute, stirring occasionally. Put 20g frozen blueberries, 10g acai pulp (or 1 tbsp acai powder), ½ tsp vanilla powder, 15g creamed coconut (or coconut butter) and a pinch of salt in a high-speed blender. Blend until smooth and frothy. Pour into a glass or mug and enjoy.

Magic Mushroom & Chicory Power Latte

Heat 250ml plant-based milk (pages 304–306) and 50ml water in a small saucepan over a medium heat for 45 seconds–1 minute. Put 1 tsp reishi powder, ½ tsp he shou wu powder, 1 tsp chaga powder, 1–2 tbsp chicory powder, ½ tsp vanilla powder, 1 tsp cacao powder, 1 tsp maca powder, ½ tsp ground cinnamon, ½ tsp ashwagandha or mucuna pruriens powder, ½ date (or ½ tsp natural syrup) and ½ tsp coconut oil in a high-speed blender and add the hot milk. Blend for 1–2 minutes. Pour into a glass or mug and enjoy.

Charcoal Tahini Maca Latte

Put 350ml boiling water or plant-based milk, 1 tbsp tahini, 50g hemp seeds (or soaked almonds or cashews), 2g activated charcoal powder, 1 tsp vanilla powder and 1 tsp maca powder in a high-speed blender. Blend for 1–2 minutes, until smooth and frothy. Pour into a glass or mug and enjoy.

Let's Go! Reishi & Tahini Hot Chocoloate

This is liquid nourishment at its finest. Unlike many wellness elixirs, it feels far too delicious to have any real health benefits, but, of course, it does. If you tend to crave chocolate or coffee during this 'in between' stage of the day, replace your usual pick-me-up with this hot chocolate. It has just as much, if not more, potential to alter your physical and mental performance. High in tryptophan, which boosts serotonin levels, this drink delivers just the emotional and energetic lift that you likely need as the pace of the day begins to lag.

250ml coconut or almond milk
80ml water
2 tbsp cacao powder
1 tbsp tahini
1 tbsp maca powder
1 tsp natural syrup
1 tsp coconut oil
 pinch of sea salt

1 tsp vanilla powder
1 tsp reishi powder

Elevate it: pinch of matcha powder, 40g cooked quinoa, generous pinch of ground turmeric, 2 cinnamon sticks, ¼ tsp finely chopped fresh chilli or a pinch of chilli flakes

Pour the milk and water into a saucepan and bring to the boil over a medium heat. Reduce the heat and allow to simmer for 1–2 minutes.

Whisk in the cacao powder, tahini, maca, natural syrup, coconut oil, salt and any elevational extras. Once the cacao and tahini have dissolved, remove from the heat. If you used any solid ingredients, such as cinnamon sticks or chilli, strain the mixture. If you used quinoa, transfer the mixture to a high-speed blender, add an extra splash of nut milk or hot water, if needed, to thin, and blend for 1–2 minutes until smooth. Serve immediately.

In Between Time

Creamy Greens Afternoon Smoothie

Serves 2

The mention of another green smoothie may be yawn-inducing, but this is a delicious variation of the vegetable-based drinks you might be used to. It takes many powerful greens and combines them with creamy nuts and seeds to become more of a shake than a smoothie. High in protein, fibre, minerals and phytonutrients, I often turn to this drink after a workout to assist the repair and rebuilding of muscles, and to replace any sodium and potassium lost during a workout.

250ml almond or coconut milk or coconut water
30g spinach
100g frozen banana
5g avocado (10g for a thicker option)
1 tsp vanilla powder
1 heaped tsp maca powder
25g hemp seeds
1 tbsp almond butter

1 tsp chia seeds
6 ice cubes
pinch of Himalayan pink salt

Elevate it: *1 tsp chaga powder, 1 portion of Plant-Powered Protein Powder (page 312), 1 tsp mixed greens powder, ½ tsp matcha powder*

Put all the ingredients apart from the ice in a blender and blend for 2–3 minutes, until smooth. Taste and add more vanilla, maca, almond butter, salt or any of the elevational extras until you are satisfied with the flavour.

Add the ice and blend for a further 1–2 minutes, until all the ice is broken down and the mixture is completely smooth. Serve immediately.

Apple Cider Vinegar Mushroom Crisps

Serves 1–2

Preheat the oven to 150°C /gas mark 2

Line two baking trays with baking paper

Unique in flavour and addictive in texture, these mushroom crisps make a natural and nutritious alternative to regular crisps and are easy to snack on whilst on the go. You can also add them crushed to salads, stir them through a batch of carbonara (page 223) or use them to top main meals.

1 tsp apple cider vinegar
2 tbsp extra virgin olive or coconut oil, melted
1 tbsp tamari
½ tsp lemon juice

200g button or chestnut mushrooms, thinly sliced
2 tbsp white sesame seeds, to garnish

Combine the apple cider vinegar, oil, tamari and lemon juice in a bowl. Add the mushrooms and stir to combine, or use your hands to coat the mushrooms in the marinade.

Arrange the mushrooms on the prepared baking trays. Place in the oven and bake for 45–60 minutes. The timing will depend on the size and thickness of your mushrooms. Test the mushrooms after 45 minutes by taking one or two out of the oven and allowing them to cool for 5 minutes. If they are crispy enough, remove the trays from the oven. If they need longer, continue to bake for a further 10–12 minutes, until you are happy with the result.

Sesame & Charcoal Crackers

Around this time of the day, I either fancy something sweet or something crunchy. These crackers are easy snacking and delicious au naturel, but also take well to dips and spreads (pages 180–183) or a variety of toppings. You could also crumble them into salads in the place of croûtons.

Makes 18–20

Preheat the oven to 180°C /gas mark 4

150g buckwheat flour
2 tbsp nutritional yeast
2 tbsp sunflower seeds
4 tbsp olive or coconut oil, melted
1 tsp activated charcoal powder, plus extra
    if necessary

5 tbsp water
2 tbsp white or black sesame seeds
2 tbsp chopped dried nori (optional)
sea salt

Put the flour, yeast, seeds, oil and charcoal into a food processor and blend for 1–2 minutes, until the seeds have broken down and the mixture is smooth. With the machine still running, gradually add the water until the mixture begins to form a doughy ball (you may not need to use all of the water, or you may need to add a little more).

Transfer the mixture onto a large piece of baking paper and lay another sheet of baking paper on top. Use a rolling pin to roll the dough out until it is no more than 3mm thick. Remove the top layer of baking paper and sprinkle the dough with the sesame seeds, nori, if using, a little salt and a little extra charcoal powder, if desired.

Return the top layer of baking paper and roll across the dough toppings to ensure the seeds and nori are pressed into the mixture. Use a sharp knife to score the dough into 5cm squares, rectangles or other shapes (use a cookie cutter if you want to make round crackers). Scoring the dough makes it easier for you to make individual crackers once it is baked. Transfer the dough on the baking paper directly onto the racks of the oven and bake for 20–25 minutes, until the dough is dry and crispy to touch. Allow to cool on a cooling rack for 10–20 minutes before breaking into crackers along the scored lines. Store in an airtight container at room temperature.

Variations

For a beetroot variation, substitute the charcoal with 20g raw grated beetroot and top with extra sunflower seeds.

For a herbal variation, substitute the charcoal with 5g fresh herbs of your choice (I like basil, thyme or rosemary) and top with 2 tbsp dried herbs.

In Between Time

Making Dips & Spreads

Dips and spreads can be concentrated forms of powerful ingredients and are easy, quick and tasty ways to artfully enhance the flavour and functional abilities of a meal. You can use them for dipping your favourite raw or cooked vegetables, crackers (page 178), toast, bread rolls and other snacks. You can even thin dips and spreads with a little water to make dressings for salads.

Foundation Ingredients

Liquids
Oils (such as extra virgin olive oil, coconut oil, avocado oil, walnut oil, flaxseed oil, sunflower oil or chia seed oil)
Filtered water
Apple cider vinegar

Thickeners
Nuts (such as almonds, cashews, walnuts, pine nuts, hazelnuts)
Seeds (such as sesame seeds, pumpkin seeds, sunflower seeds)
Pulses (such as chickpeas, white beans, cannellini beans, black beans, puy lentils, mung beans)
Avocados

Flavourings
Vegetables and fruits (such as leafy greens, avocados, tomatoes, red peppers, broccoli, cauliflower, peas, sweetcorn, carrots, beetroot)
Herbs and spices (such as basil, parsley, coriander, mint, sage, thyme, lemon balm, chilli, ginger, cinnamon, sumac, turmeric)
Fresh citrus juices (such as lemon, lime, orange, grapefruit)
Organic Dijon mustard
Sea salt
Nutritional yeast
Tamari
Tahini
Plant powders (such as tonic herbs and adaptogens, pages 297–298)

A Few of My Favourites

Serves 6–10, depending on serving rituals

Turmeric & Sweetcorn Hummus

Put 60ml olive oil, 1 tin chickpeas, 250g sweetcorn, 4 tbsp water, 20g tahini, generous pinch of salt and ½ tsp turmeric in a blender and blend on a high speed for 2–3 minutes. If the blender's having difficulty blending smoothly, add a dash more oil or a little water. Transfer to a small bowl and chill in the fridge until ready to serve.

Red Pepper Hummus

Preheat the oven to 180°C/gas mark 4. Slice 2 large red peppers and chop 4 large tomatoes and arrange them in a baking tray together. Roast for 30–40 minutes and then place them in a blender along with 4 tbsp tahini, ½ ripe avocado, 1 x 400g can chickpeas (drained and rinsed), 60ml extra virgin olive oil, 2 garlic cloves, 1 tsp tamari and ½ tsp lemon juice. Blend on a high speed for 2–3 minutes, until smooth. If the blender's having difficulty blending smoothly, add a dash more oil or a little water. Transfer to a small bowl and chill in the fridge until ready to serve.

Puy Lentil & Black Olive Hummus

Put 100g cooked puy lentils, 1 x 400g can chickpeas (drained and rinsed), 80ml olive oil, 50g black olives, pitted, juice from ½ fresh lemon, 3 tbsp tahini, ¼ cup water and fresh thyme, oregano or basil leaves into your blender and blend on a high speed for 2–3 minutes. If it's not blending smoothly, add a dash more oil or water. (For a more filling option, add 50g whole chickpeas and 50ml water. To elevate, add fresh herbs of your choice. Transfer to a small bowl and chill in the fridge until ready to serve).

Pea & Mint Hummus

Put 150g cooked garden peas, ½ x 400g can chickpeas (drained and rinsed), 60ml extra virgin olive oil, pinch of salt, ½ tsp lemon juice, 1 large handful of fresh mint leaves, ½ avocado and a small handful of spinach into a blender and blend on a high speed for 2–3 minutes. If the blender's having difficulty blending smoothly, add a dash more oil or a little water. Transfer to a small bowl and chill in the fridge until ready to serve.

Red Pepper & Goji Muhammara

Preheat the oven to 180°C/gas mark 4. Chop 1 red pepper, 1 tomato and ½ onion (red or white) into chunks. Arrange them in a baking tray and add 1 whole clove of garlic, drizzle with a little oil and roast for 30–40 minutes. Transfer them to a blender and add 4 tbsp extra virgin olive oil, 110g walnuts (or macadamia nuts), 35g goji berries, 1 tbsp nutritional yeast, ½ fresh red chilli, 1 tsp lemon juice, ½ tsp salt, 1 tsp paprika and black or cayenne pepper, to taste. (Elevate it by adding ½ tsp reishi or shilajit powder.) Blend on a high speed for 2–3 minutes, until thick and smooth. Transfer to a small bowl and chill in the fridge until ready to serve.

Walnut Pâté

Put 200g walnuts, 80ml olive oil, 120ml chickpea water (either the water from a can of chickpeas or can also use normal water), 10g tahini, ½ tsp lemon juice and a generous amount of salt in a blender and blend on a high speed for 2–3 minutes. If the blender's having difficulty blending smoothly, add a dash more oil or a little water. (For a more filling option, similar to houmous, add 50g tinned chickpeas (rinsed) and 50ml boiling water. To elevate the flavour, add fresh herbs of your choice.) Transfer to a small bowl and chill in the fridge until ready to serve.

Beetroot & Walnut Dip

Preheat the oven to 200°C/gas mark 7. Cut 150g raw beetroots into small wedges and arrange in a baking tray. Sprinkle with a little salt and then roast for 40–45 minutes. Transfer to a blender along with 60g walnuts, 20g tahini, 100g tinned chickpeas (drained and rinsed), 60ml extra virgin olive oil, 100ml boiling water, ½ tsp lemon juice, 1 tbsp nutritional yeast, ½ tsp apple cider vinegar and a generous pinch of salt. Blend on a high speed for 2–3 minutes, until smooth. Transfer to a small bowl and chill in the fridge until ready to serve.

Roasted Carrot & Macadamia Dip

Preheat the oven to 190°C/gas mark 5. Place 200g carrots (about 4) into a baking tray and roast for 30 minutes. Reduce the heat to 150°C/gas mark 2 and then add 60g macadamia nuts to the same tray. Bake for a further 15 minutes, until the carrots are soft and the macadamia nuts are turning golden. Remove from the oven and transfer to a blender. Add 200g tinned cannellini beans (rinsed), 80ml extra virgin olive oil, a small handful of basil leaves, 1 tsp ground turmeric, ½ tsp sumac, 2 tbsp tahini, 4 tbsp hot water, 1 tsp lemon juice, a generous pinch of salt and blend on a high speed for 2–3 minutes, until smooth. Add a little more oil or hot water if the mixture is too thick. Transfer to a small bowl, jar or airtight container and chill in the fridge until ready to serve.

Chanterelle Mushroom Pâté
Heat 2 tbsp coconut oil in a frying pan and add 150g sliced chestnut mushrooms, 150g sliced chanterelle mushrooms, 1 crushed garlic clove and salt and pepper, to taste. Sauté over a medium heat for about 10 minutes, until the mushrooms become soft and buttery. Remove from the heat and transfer to a blender and add 3 tbsp coconut oil, 2 tbsp olive oil, 6 tbsp coconut milk (solid part only), ¼ tsp lemon juice, ½ tsp ground turmeric, 1–2 tsp nutritional yeast and ¼ ripe avocado (or 1 tbsp tahini). Blend on a high speed for 2–3 minutes, adding a splash of boiling water to thin and combine, if needed. Season to taste, adding more salt, pepper, lemon juice, nutritional yeast or turmeric, as desired. Transfer to a bowl and chill in the fridge for 30–45 minutes, until set.

Serve on toast, in sandwiches, with savoury pancakes or as a side to salad.

Stir into soups or dissolve 2 tbsp in a mug or bowl of hot water for an instant soothing soup.

Add more coconut milk and some water to make a creamy chanterelle mushroom sauce to go on pasta or to use in risotto dishes.

Coconut Blondies

Serves 2

Preheat the oven to 180°C /gas mark 4

The blondie is a unique invention. Not quite a brownie but so much more than a cake, it combines the gooeyness and chewiness of a brownie with the lighter, less intense flavours of vanilla sponge. Although this recipe uses banana, the flavour is hidden by the rich cacao butter and vanilla. If you really aren't a banana fan, you can replace it with the same amount of roasted butternut squash or sweet potato mashed into a purée.

120g coconut oil, soft, plus extra for greasing
60g cacao butter
2 tsp vanilla powder
generous pinch of sea salt
200g coconut sugar
2 eggs, plus 1 egg yolk
4 tbsp cashew or almond butter (or tahini)
200g bananas, mashed
200g buckwheat flour

½ tsp bicarbonate of soda
large handful of Dark Chocolate chunks
    (page 194)
Nuts, to decorate

Elevate it: 1 tsp ashwagandha powder, 1 tbsp maca powder, 2 handfuls fresh berries or cherries

Grease a standard 33 × 22cm baking tin with coconut oil.

Bring a small saucepan of water to the boil. Place a heatproof bowl on top of the saucepan (creating a double boiler), and add the cacao butter and coconut oil. Once melted, remove from the heat and whisk in the vanilla and salt.

Place the coconut sugar, eggs, cashew or almond butter and 150g banana into your blender and blend until thick, creamy and smooth.

In a large bowl, combine the banana mixture with the cacao and vanilla mixture and whisk or stir to combine. Gradually add the buckwheat flour and then the bicarbonate of soda. Finally, stir in the remaining mashed banana and any elevational extras, along with the dark chocolate chunks.

Tip the cake mix into your prepared baking dish and bake for 30–35 minutes, until the surface forms a crust and is beginning to crack. Remove from the oven and, once the baking dish is cool enough to handle, slice around the edges and gently ease the cake out onto a cooling rack. Allow to cool before slicing. Once sliced, store in an airtight container, either at room temperature (for a cakier blondie) or in the fridge (for a fudgier blondie) for up to 1 week. Decorate with nuts of your choice.

In Between Time

Carrot Cake with Cashew Cream Frosting

Makes 1 loaf

*Preheat the oven to 150°C
/gas mark 2*

I made this carrot cake loaf for British *Vogue* a few years ago, when they did a shoot with one of my flatmates at our house. It's always such a crowd-pleaser as it takes a recipe that everyone knows and loves and makes it naturally better for you. You could swap carrots for beetroots, parsnips or other root vegetables in this recipe, or use a combination of them all to add flavour and nutritional variety.

2 eggs
150g coconut oil, melted, plus extra
    for greasing
150g coconut sugar
2 large carrots, grated (approx. 300g)
1 tsp vanilla powder
100g Medjool dates, chopped
75g walnuts or pecans, chopped
170g buckwheat flour
80g ground almonds
50g desiccated coconut

generous pinch of sea salt or tamari
2 tsp ground cinnamon
1 tsp allspice
½ tsp ground nutmeg
½ tsp baking powder
½ tsp bicarbonate of soda
1 quantity Cashew Buttercream (page 239)

To decorate
edible flowers
crushed nuts

Grease a 900g loaf tin with a light coating of oil (or a muffin tin, to make smaller, individual cakes).

Beat the eggs with an electric whisk until smooth, then add the oil, sugar, carrots, vanilla, dates and nuts and continue to whisk until well combined. Add the flour, almonds, coconut, salt, spices, baking powder and bicarbonate of soda and stir with a wooden spoon until combined. Pour the mixture into the prepared loaf tin (or muffin tin) and smooth out and level off the surface. Bake for 1 hour and 15 minutes (1 hour for the muffins) or until a skewer inserted into the centre of the cake comes out clean.

Allow to cool slightly, then slide a small knife around the edges of the cake to free it from the tin. Ease it out gently and stand it upright on a cooling rack, then leave to cool completely.

When the cake is completely cool, use a small spatula or the back of a spoon to spread the buttercream over the top. Garnish with edible flowers and crushed nuts.

Chicory, Chaga, Pecan & Tamari Salted Brownies

Makes 12

Preheat the oven to 180°C /gas mark 4

Brownies are great – we know that – but these ones are even greater than the standard sugar/butter/flour varieties as they contain ingredients that nourish the body, mind and soul. The pecans bring a lovely flavour to the mixture whilst also adding healthy fats and protein and the chicory adds a mocha-like undertone to the intensity of the cacao. Together, these plant-powered ingredients form a perfectly rich and gooey brownie – with not a bar of chocolate in sight!

20g pecans
30g buckwheat flour
2 tsp arrowroot
3 tbsp chicory powder (or instant coffee)
2 eggs
180g coconut sugar
80g cacao butter

100g coconut oil, plus extra for greasing
60g raw cacao powder, plus extra for dusting
1–2 tsp tamari

Elevate it: 1 tsp shilajit powder, 1 tsp reishi powder, 5g fresh basil or rosemary leaves, 2 handfuls of Dark Chocolate chunks (page 194)

Grease a standard 34.5 × 24 × 4cm baking tray with a little oil, and dust with a sprinkling of cacao powder.

Make the pecans into a flour by blending them in a food processor or blender for 1 minute, until they form fine crumbs. Transfer to a small bowl and stir in the flour, arrowroot and chicory, until combined.

In a large bowl, beat the eggs with the coconut sugar until smooth and frothy.

Fill a small saucepan with water and bring to the boil. Place a heatproof bowl on top of the pan (creating a double boiler), then add the cacao butter and oil and whisk until melted. Remove from the heat and whisk in the cacao powder and tamari. Allow to cool for 10 minutes.

Add the chocolate mixture to the eggs and whisk to combine. Gradually add the flour mixture, whisking constantly until all of the flour is added and the mixture is smooth and thick. Stir in any elevational extras of your choice. Pour the brownie mixture into the prepared baking tray and bake in the oven for 18–20 minutes, until the surface crusts and begins to crack.

Remove from the oven and, once the baking tray is cool enough to handle, slice around the edges of the tray and lift the brownie onto a cooling rack. Leave to cool and then cut into rectangles to serve. Store in an airtight container, either at room temperature (for a cakier brownie) or in the fridge (for a fudgier brownie).

Walnut Chocolate Biscuits
& Millionaire's Shortbread

*Makes 12–16 chocolate fingers
or 10–12 chocolate digestives*

*Preheat the oven to 160–170°C
/ gas mark 3–4*

The biscuits many of us have come to adore are sadly a product of industrialised food production, made exclusively from highly refined ingredients. They're delicious, but not tools for longevity or to enhance overall health in the way that the ingredients in the following recipes are. Living in Britain, where a cup of tea is nothing without a biscuit to dunk in it, it would be wrong to go completely without, so instead, go with alternatives.

30g walnuts
30g sunflower seeds
4 tbsp coconut sugar
2 tbsp water
100g buckwheat flour
pinch of sea salt
½ tsp vanilla powder
2 tbsp natural syrup

25g coconut oil
1 quantity melted chocolate (page 194)

For the Millionaire's Shortbread
1 ½ quantity Almond & Date Salted Caramel
    (page 240)
1 ½ quantity Dark Chocolate (prepared up
    to the end of step 2, page 194)

Put the walnuts, seeds, sugar and water in a food processor and blend until they form a paste. Transfer to a bowl and, using a wooden spoon, stir in the flour, salt, vanilla, natural syrup and oil. Use your hands to form a dough, which you can now be used to make whichever biscuit suits your mood.

To make Chocolate Rounds
Break the dough into 10–12 pieces and roll each one into a ball. Gently flatten each ball with the palm of your hand, then arrange the biscuits on a baking tray, spaced evenly apart. Alternatively, roll the pastry out flat and use a cookie cutter to cut out the biscuits. Bake for 12–15 minutes, until the edges begin to brown, then allow to cool whilst you prepare the chocolate.

Take one biscuit at a time, hold it between your fingertips and use a pastry brush to brush a layer of chocolate onto the surface. Place the uncoated side down on a cooling rack and repeat until all the biscuits have been painted. Place in the freezer for 5–10 minutes to set. Paint the biscuits a second, or even a third, time (setting them in the freezer between each coating) until all the chocolate is used up. Store in an airtight container at room temperature or in the fridge for up to 2 weeks.

To make Chocolate Fingers
Break the dough into 12–16 pieces and roll each one between your palms into a finger shape, about 6cm in length and 1cm wide. Arrange them on a baking tray and then bake for 15 minutes.

In Between Time

Once the fingers have cooled, using tongs or a fork, dip one finger at a time into the chocolate, then lift them out, place on a cooling rack and repeat until all the fingers are coated.

Place in the freezer for 5–10 minutes to set, and then dip a second, or even a third time (ensuring the chocolate is still liquid and setting them in the freezer between each coat), until all the chocolate is used up. Store in an airtight container at room temperature or in the fridge for up to 2 weeks.

To make Millionaire's Shortbread

Roll the dough out to fit the base of a 20 x 20cm square tin. Press down with your fingertips so the dough meets the edges and is compact and bake for 15–18 minutes, until the edges start to brown. Set aside to cool.

Spread a layer of the caramel evenly over every inch of biscuit, reaching to the edges of the baking tin. Follow this with a top layer of chocolate. The amount of caramel and chocolate you want to use is entirely up to you. Store in the fridge for up to 1 week.

In Between Time

Pecan Cookie Dough Balls

Makes 10–15

When I was in school, my friends and I would walk home together and, more often than not, we would take a detour to buy a packet of raw cookie dough, with no intention of making cookies. My fondest memories are of those afternoons spent at my friend Georgia's house, where we'd pass the slab of cookie dough between us, taking bites straight from the packet. These pecan cookie dough bites are inspired by that memorable ritual, but are made with more natural ingredients than that of our former addiction.

100g pecans
2 tbsp desiccated coconut
200g buckwheat flakes or jumbo oats
140g Medjool dates, halved and stoned
60g coconut oil, at room temperature
½ tsp sea salt
1 tbsp ground golden linseeds
½ tsp lemon juice or zest
2 tbsp chia seeds
1 tbsp boiling water

2 tbsp tinned coconut milk (solid part only)
2 tbsp natural syrup
1 tsp maca powder
100g Dark Chocolate (page 194) or shop-bought raw or dark chocolate, broken into chunks

Elevate it: 1 tsp mesquite powder, 1 tsp mucuna pruriens powder, 1 tbsp lucuma powder,

Put the pecans, coconut and buckwheat or oats in a food processor and blend for 1 minute or until they form a floury consistency. Add the dates and blend for 30 seconds, then pause the machine and add the remainder of the ingredients (except the chocolate) and any elevational extras of your choice. Blend again for a further 1–2 minutes until fully combined. The mixture should form a large dough-like ball that holds together when pressed.

Transfer to a large bowl and stir in the chocolate, kneading with your hands to combine. Divide the mixture into 10–15 pieces and either roll each one into a ball or roll them out with a rolling pin to flatten them into round cookies. Arrange on a cooling rack or baking tray and place in the freezer. Leave for 30 minutes–1 hour.

When ready to eat, allow to thaw for 5 minutes before enjoying.

Variations
To coat in chocolate, follow steps 1–2 for making Dark Chocolate (page 194) and roll each 'frozen' cookie dough ball in the chocolate before placing on a cooling rack. Return to the freezer and, once set, dip a second time for a thicker coating. If using cookie shapes, follow the same instructions, or dip just half of the cookie in the chocolate.

Bee Pollen, Chaga & Sunflower Seed Bars with a Coconut 'Yogurt' Base

Makes approx. 12 bars

Preheat the oven to 160°C /gas mark 3

Line a 33 × 23cm baking tray with baking paper and grease the paper lightly with a little coconut oil

The only things worse than snack foods are 'healthy' snack foods. With no refined sugars and lots of fibre and protein, these sunflower bars are inspired by the falsely advertised granola bars that, although high in sugar and additives, are commonly advertised as healthy. These alternatives are simple to make, and fit just as easily into busy lives.

1 tbsp coconut oil, for greasing
80g sunflower seeds, plus extra to decorate
80g natural syrup of your choice (about 8 tbsp)
sprinkling of bee pollen, plus extra
    to decorate
pinch of sea salt
2 tbsp golden linseeds
10g raw or activated buckwheat groats
10g quinoa pops

1 bar of creamed coconut
1 tsp vanilla powder
Handful of nuts of your choice
100g oats
200g bar of creamed coconut

Elevate it: 1 tsp chaga powder, 1 tsp maca powder

Put half the sunflower seeds in a blender or food processor with the natural syrup and blend until a pale paste begins to form. Once smooth, transfer to a bowl and stir in the remaining sunflower seeds along with the other ingredients apart from the creamed coconut.

Tip the mixture onto the prepared baking tray and spread it out to 4–5mm thick. Press down lightly with your fingertips to ensure it is compact and there are no gaps. If you have leftover mixture, spread it onto a second baking tray. Use a sharp knife to gently score the mixture into small rectangles, squares or other shapes of your choice. (I make mine into approximately 8cm × 4cm rectangles.) Top with extra sunflower seeds and bee pollen and then bake for 25–30 minutes, until golden brown and crisping at the edges. Once cooked, set aside to cool for 30 minutes – 1 hour.

Meanwhile, prepare the coconut yogurt coating. Fill a small bowl with boiling water. Place the creamed coconut in the water (do not cut the plastic wrapper) and let it melt for 10 minutes, massaging it a little to help. Once it's melted, cut the end of the wrapper and pour the mixture into a small bowl.

Break the cooled biscuits into pieces along the lines you scored and then use a pastry brush to paint the creamed coconut onto the bottom of each biscuit. Set them upside down on a baking tray and place in the freezer for 5 minutes. Paint a second layer, or even a third, if you would like to. Once set, store in an airtight container at room temperature or in the fridge for up to 2 weeks.

You could also dip the bars in dark chocolate instead of the coconut 'yogurt'.

Chocolates

Cacao is a truly magical ingredient. Whether in bean, butter, paste, liquor or powder form, it opens up so many culinary doors. I use one basic recipe to make chocolate, which can be used to coat fruits or other snacks, or to make individual chocolates or bars. I spike the mixture with my favourite adaptogen powders, or fill each one with a caramel, ganache or truffle-like mousse.

Basic Chocolate Recipe

Makes approx. 300g chocolate and will cover approx. 25–30 individual chocolates

Dark Chocolate
100g cacao butter
pinch of sea salt
40g cacao powder
1 tbsp coconut sugar or natural syrup

Elevate it: adaptogens, tonic herbs and other plant powders of your choice, chia seeds, 1–2 drops of food-grade essential oils, 1–2 drops of natural plant tincture or extract

White Chocolate
100g cacao butter
pinch of sea salt
1 tbsp melted creamed coconut
    or cashew butter
1 tsp vanilla powder
1 tbsp natural syrup

To make either the dark or white chocolate, fill a small saucepan with water and bring to the boil. Place a heatproof bowl on top of the pan (creating a double boiler), then add the cacao butter and salt.

Once the cacao butter has melted, remove from the heat and whisk in the cacao powder (for dark chocolate) or the creamed coconut/cashew butter and vanilla powder (for white chocolate). Either add your natural sweetener and any elevational extras, and whisk until combined, or transfer the mixture to a blender and blend on a high speed for 1–2 minutes, until smooth.

Pour into a chocolate bar mould, small container or small confectionery moulds and sprinkle with your favourite toppings. Freeze until set.

Add to hot plant-based milk to make a rich hot chocolate. For a creamier option, add 10g avocado or 50g cashews before blending.

For chocolate chunks, pour into a loaf tin and place in the freezer for 30 minutes–1 hour. Once set, use the end of a wooden spoon to break the chocolate into pieces. Alternatively, remove the slab of chocolate and cut into chunks with a knife.

In Between Time

In Between Time

Chocolate Cookie Crunch Bars

Makes 6-8

Preheat the oven to 150°C /gas mark 2

Chocolate doesn't need much improvement, but if you can add some cookie crumbs to the mix, why wouldn't you? Rather than adding actual cookies, I've fashioned just as good a crunch out of crushed, toasted nuts here, bringing increased flavour and enhanced benefits to your natural chocolate creations, without any unnecessary additives.

1 quantity Dark Chocolate (page 194)

For the cookie crunch
50g hazelnuts
50g almonds
20g coconut oil, melted

10g cacao powder
10g natural syrup
1 tbsp almond butter
½ tsp bee pollen
½ tsp maca powder
pinch of sea salt

Start by making the cookie crunch. Spread the nuts out on a baking tray and roast for 10–15 minutes, until golden. Remove from the oven and allow to cool for a few minutes, then crush, either in a food processor or using a sharp knife.

Transfer the nuts to a bowl and add the coconut oil, cacao powder, natural syrup, nut butter, bee pollen, maca and salt. Stir to combine and then transfer to a freezer-proof container. Press the mixture down firmly to ensure it is compact and then place in the freezer to set for 20–30 minutes.

Meanwhile, make the chocolate according to the instructions on page 194 and fill a container or chocolate bar molds with chocolate.

Roughly break or chop the cookie mixture into small chunks in its container and then scatter the cookie crunch over the chocolate (some of it will sink, which is what you want). Place in the freezer and allow to set for 20–30 minutes. Enjoy straightaway or store in the fridge or freezer.

Chocolate Salted 'Nolo' Caramels

Makes approx. 20 nolos

With a nutritional nudge from nature, these chewy, chocolatey treats are high in fibre and completely free from refined sugars, whilst retaining an irresistible chocolate-coated chewiness.

1 quantity Almond & Date Caramel (page 240)
1 quantity Dark Chocolate (page 194)
pinch of sea salt
edible dried flowers, to decorate

Elevate it: 1 tsp rhodiola or other plant powders of your choice

Start by making the caramel.

Once the caramel is set, use a small spatula to scrape it onto a clean surface. Wet your hands and form the caramel into about 20 small balls, approximately 2cm thick. Arrange on a cooling rack and then place in the freezer to set. Allow 1–2 hours for the balls to harden.

When the balls are more or less solid, prepare the chocolate to liquid stage (page 194). Using a fork, dip one caramel ball at a time in the liquid chocolate, turning it to coat thoroughly, then lift it out and place on the cooling rack and repeat with the other balls, working quickly. Place the chocolate-dipped balls in the freezer and leave to set for 5–10 minutes, then dip a second time. Sprinkle with a pinch of salt or other plant powders or dried flowers, to decorate, and then return them to the freezer for a final time (or dip them a third time if you have leftover chocolate mixture). Once set, store in the fridge or freezer.

See photograph on page 195.

Almond Florentines

Makes approx. 10

Preheat the oven to 140°C /gas mark 1

There are many good memories attached to these Florentines, which taste partly like honeycomb and partly like cookies. I spent one New Year's visiting my boyfriend in Sweden, and on New Year's Day we hosted a hang out at his house with everyone we'd been celebrating with the night before. When we needed something quick to serve as an after-dinner snack, I improvised nuts, coconut, natural syrup and spices into what turned out to be one of the best things I've ever made.

8–10 tbsp natural syrup
2 tbsp water
1 tbsp melted coconut oil, plus extra
    for greasing
150g pecans
150g flaked almonds

40g desiccated coconut
1 tsp vanilla powder
generous pinch of sea salt
½ tsp ground cinnamon
1 tbsp maca powder
1 quantity Dark Chocolate (page 194)

Line a baking tray with baking paper and grease the paper lightly with a little coconut oil.

Bring the syrup and water to the boil in a large saucepan over a high heat and continue to boil for 2 minutes, until the mixture forms thick bubbles. Remove from the heat and add all the remaining ingredients apart from the chocolate to the pan. Use a spatula or a wooden spoon to mix together well and ensure everything is evenly coated in the syrup.

Take 1 heaped tablespoon of mixture and drop it onto the prepared baking paper. Use the back of the spoon to press it down and shape into a cookie-like round. Repeat until all of the mixture is used up. Bake for 6–8 minutes, until the edges begin to turn golden brown.

Remove from the oven and place in the fridge to cool for about 10 minutes. Whilst they cool, prepare the chocolate. (If you would prefer to use shop-bought raw or dark chocolate, melt approximately 100g, following the same instructions for homemade chocolate on page 194.)

Dip the bottom of each Florentine into the melted chocolate, then place on a cooling rack. Alternatively, drizzle the chocolate over the top of each biscuit. Leave to set. Store in the fridge for up to 2 weeks.

Evening Time

Evening Time

Evening time should revolve around cooking, gathering, eating and sharing. This time should be dedicated to reconnecting with family or friends at the end of your separate days, and to begin switching off from work and transitioning into downtime. After a long day of doing, this is a chance to reflect, appreciating the positive moments and releasing the more negative parts of each day (which can not only affect you mentally but can also create physical tension, cellular disorder and energy blockages around the body).

The practices in this chapter are about letting go and tuning in whilst you go about your evening activities. The breathing techniques that follow aim to calm wired-up minds that are still in work mode and guidance for creating a comfortable and relaxing space to be in will help to ensure you remain peaceful and present.

Traditionally, food was always something to be celebrated and often enjoyed as a communal feast, but nowadays it is increasingly common to work late into the night and eat on-the-go. We have lost this sense of celebrating food and enjoying it in the company of others, often settling for packaged, precooked options or fast food – all of which are convenient but none of which are nutritionally ideal. Whether you're dining alone, feeding a family or entertaining guests, the recipes in this section are uncomplicated and adaptable, with lots of scope for personal customisation and experimentation. You'll find light and simple options for everyday meals for when you're short of time during the week, as well as more creative ideas for special occasions or lively dinner parties. With the simple introduction of cocktails and fizzy drinks, decadent desserts and after dinner sweets, you can transform everyday dinners into nutritionally functional feasts for all.

Mind

Create

Creativity is a large part of our human make-up and we are all creative in different ways. People generally associate being creative with being artistic or innovative, but we all make small creative choices on a daily basis. Being creative and using your imagination can refer to so many things, including making something, drawing or painting, writing, photographing, gardening, cooking, singing, dancing, studying or learning a new skill. It basically includes anything that requires us to use the creative parts of our brain.

Creating something or being in a creative flow is known to improve problem-solving (which helps overcome challenges), increase energy, improve mood, release stress, improve focus and create a new sense of openness and acceptance to challenges and struggles, seeing them as possibilities and opportunities rather than barriers. It helps clear the mind and gives a sense of control and order. It keeps things interesting, and can be exciting, especially if you are creating something entirely unique, which brings a sense of anticipation and ultimately, fulfilment and contentment.

Many people don't consider themselves to be creative, but give yourself permission to try, even if you don't create anything to your standards of 'good'. Do it in the evening time, whether it's straight after work, just before dinner (or maybe it is dinner), after chores or just before bed. It is freeing and therapeutic to create, and by focusing on something new, you are switching off that part of the mind that is working, worrying or focused on stressful thoughts, which creates more mental space for self-discovery and growth.

Enjoy

Similarly to being creative, we rarely give ourselves permission to do the things we most enjoy on a daily basis. At a recent retreat I attended on with Lululemon (a sportswear company and so much more), we were asked to share, with a stranger, three things that bring us joy. When I did this, I followed it with, 'but I never really make time to do it'. My partner asked me why and I was stuck for an answer. It made me think about making more time and prioritising doing something that brings me joy, rather than, say, working late into the night to finish something off. I vowed to start scheduling time to do the things I enjoy, which, in such a fast-paced society driven by success, is hard to do and almost seems something to feel guilty about. In the evenings, try to schedule time do something that brings you joy, be it a hobby, playing a game, reading a book, watching a movie or something creative.

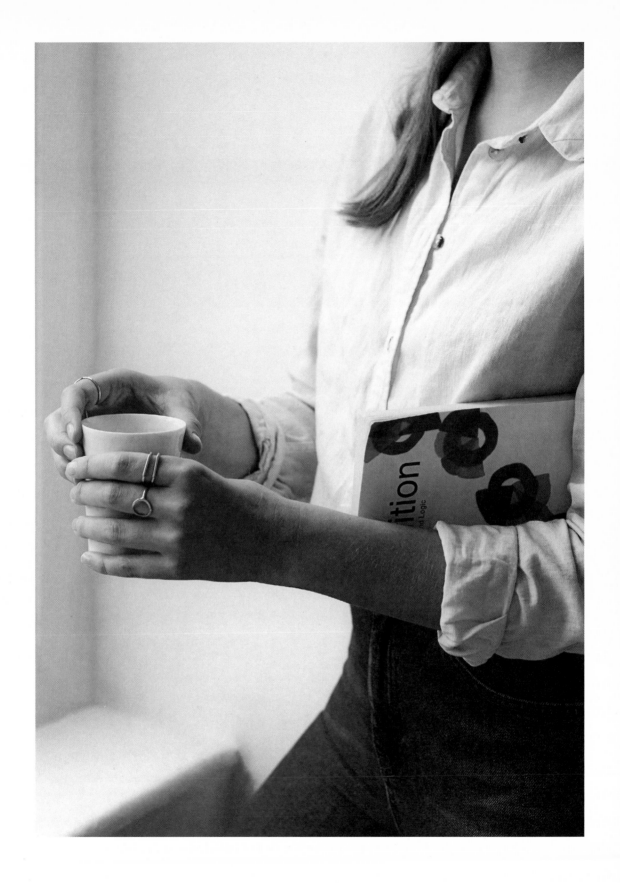

Mind & Breath

Sand Bag Technique

I picked up this technique whilst studying shiatsu and it really helped to ground and reset my body and mind, and to leave the day behind and transition to the evening, helping you to slow down and feel present.

1. Come to a comfortable standing position, somewhere you are not going to be disturbed. Close your eyes and bring your attention to your breath.

2. Breathe slowly and passively through your nose for a few moments then bring your attention to your body. Notice how it feels. Maybe you feel tension or discomfort in some areas or perhaps you feel relaxed and calm.

3. Begin to imagine your entire body is filling up with sand. Visualise each part of your body, starting at the head, and focus on the motions, the feeling and the weight of the sand filling your body. Notice it fill your shoulders, then your arms, your hands and fingers, then your chest, your stomach, then your pelvis, then your legs, and finally your feet. Do this for 2–5 minutes, working at a pace that feels right for you, and end by focusing on the feet. Do they feel full, heavy, anchored?

4. Settle here for a few moments, exploring how your body feels, and then imagine there is an opening in your left foot, maybe a tear or a hole, through which the sand begins to pour out. Bring your attention to your left foot, and watch as the sand spills smoothly and almost silently out until your foot is empty. Explore the weight of your foot and notice any changes in how it feels, as every muscle become weightless. Continue this exercise, working through every part of the left side of the body, and then repeat on the right side.

5. When the sand has emptied out of your body, be still and acknowledge how each part of your body now feels. You should feel physically lighter and more open, relaxed and calm. Bring to a close by opening your eyes and taking a few moments to readjust to your surroundings.

Lion's Breath (Simhasana)

Lion's breath is a pranayama technique known to strengthen the nervous system and create calm. It is used to relieve tension and stress, particularly in the face, by stretching the entire face, including the jaw and tongue. The first time I did it I felt timid, but now I look forward to it in class as it feels like a physical letting-go of any negative vibes that I have collected throughout the day. We often act in certain ways to fit in with society, and having permission to let everything go in a way that looks 'strange' is extremely liberating.

1. You can do this practice in many poses. I like to practise it either sitting on the floor with crossed legs or kneeling.

2. Bring your hands to your knees, keeping your arms straight but relaxed. Take a few deep breaths and then take a more conscious inhale through your nose. Exhale strongly through the mouth, making a 'haaaaah' sound forming from the back of your throat. As you exhale, open your mouth wide and stick your tongue as far out as possible towards your chin, in one quick movement.

3. Inhale and settle back into your starting pose with a neutral breath and relaxed face. Repeat this 2–6 times, or however many times feels natural and necessary.

Movement

In the evenings, if you're still 'on' from a full day of working and have excess energy that needs using up, then aerobic practice, natural movement exercises, home workouts or guided classes are a great way to release the day. This is also a chance for many people who can't exercise in the morning or during lunch breaks to be active. You'll work up an appetite for dinner, and you'll also tire your muscles, increasing the likelihood of physical relaxation and effortless and better-quality sleeping patterns.

1. Take a walk or go on a run locally.

2. If you find it easy to stay motivated, invest in some weights, a jump rope, a resistance band and any other gym equipment you tend to use and create your own bodyweight workout to practise at home. If you need more equipment and inspiration, head to the gym, even if only for 20 minutes.

3. Attend a class, depending on your mood. Classes provide more structure and guidance, enhancing stamina and enthusiasm. Be mindful of what will assist you best each day and accept that some days maybe yoga will be demanding enough, and other days a high-intensity, cardio class might be what you need.

Do-In
Read more about Do-in on pages 47, 115 and 324.

Back exercise

1. Lie on your back with your knees bent and your feet flat on the floor. Keeping the back flat against the floor, engage your abdomen and hug the knees with your arms, tugging them in closely to your chest.

2. Begin to roll to the right and then using your abdominal muscles, roll back to centre and over to the left. Do this a few times and then return to centre.

3. From centre, begin to gently rock forwards and backwards along the length of the spine. Do this a few times and then return to centre.

4. Release the arms and take each knee in each hand. Slowly release the legs away from the chest, stopping when your knees are pointing upwards. From here, begin to move your knees with your hands in slow circular motions away from the body to the left, and back in to the body from the right. This massages the lower part of the spine and is a deeply relaxing and soothing way to open and release the lower back.

Neck exercise

1. Stand tall and relax your shoulders down your back, elongating the neck. Link your hands together behind your head and inhale. As you exhale, drop your chin to your chest and relax the arms and elbows, allowing their weight to increase the stretch down the back of the neck. Hold here for a few moments, breathing fully. Slowly release the hands and roll back up to your starting position.

Chopping, thumbing & self-massage

1. Stand tall and relax your shoulders down your back, elongating the neck.

2. Support your forehead by resting it in the palm of your left hand and then let the head tip slightly forwards. Using the edge of your right hand (along your little finger to where your hand joins the wrist), use a gentle chopping motion to lightly tap up the base of the skull. Stay in this vicinity, working around the base of the skull and top of the neck. If tapping is too much, use sawing motions to release tension at the base of the skull and in the neck. Do this for about 1–2 minutes.

3. Return to standing and slightly tip your head back. Take your hands to your head with thumbs just under the ears, palms on the side of your cheeks and fingers along the sides of your face, fingertips on the temples (as if you were going to lean on a table with your head supported in your hands).

4. Then, use the pads of your thumbs to work around the base of the skull, pressing and massaging the area with however much pressure feels right (you will just know). Move your hands passively, however feels comfortable, and work inwardly with the thumbs from behind the ears towards the spine. Work for about 2 minutes, and feel free to use the thumbs at other points in the skull that feel tight, such as above the ears or the temples.

Lemon*aid* – Many Ways

Lemon juice in hot or cold water is one of the most popular remedies for hydrating and cleansing the body and aiding digestion, and if you add a little sparkling water and some natural sweetness, you've got yourself a deeply refreshing fizzy drink not dissimilar to mainstream, manufactured sodas.
I call this lemonaid, as I use many 'aiding' ingredients in the place of artificial additives and flavourings. Experiment with adding other natural flavours, such as fresh fruit or vegetable juices, fresh herbs and plant powders.

Basic Lemonaid (*Makes approx. 1 litre*)
4–6 tbsp honey or other natural sweetener – to taste, juice of 7 lemons, 1 litre of still or sparkling water

Elevate it: 10g lemongrass stalks or lemon balm

If using lemongrass or lemon balm, place in a jug along with the honey or sweetener, cover with the lemon juice and muddle with a wooden spoon to release the flavour. After a couple of minutes, strain the mixture into a separate jug or bottle and add your still or sparkling water. Serve instantly over ice, or chill in the fridge to enjoy later.

Basic Lemonaid Syrup (*Makes approx. 200ml*)
juice of 6 lemons, 100ml water, 100ml natural syrup

Elevate it: 10g lemongrass stalks or lemon balm

Place a small saucepan over a medium heat and add the lemon juice, water and natural syrup. Bring to the boil for 5–6 minutes, stirring constantly, then reduce the heat and simmer for 5–10 minutes, until it begins to thicken into a syrup.

Pour into a sterilised bottle or jar with a lid and allow to cool before storing in the fridge until ready to use.

To serve, use 1–2 tbsp lemon syrup per 250ml water, coconut water or sparkling water. Serve over ice and garnish with slices of lemon and fresh herbs or spices of your choice.

Green Tea Lemonaid
Brew 1 green tea bag in a mug with 200ml boiling water for 2–3 minutes. Strain into 500ml Basic Lemonaid (see left) and place in the fridge to chill, or serve instantly over ice.

Vanilla Charcoal Lemonaid
Add 1 tsp vanilla powder and ¼ tsp activated charcoal powder to 500ml Basic Lemonaid (see left). Serve instantly over ice.

Rose Coconut Lemonaid
Add 1 tbsp rose water, a few drops of apple cider vinegar and ¼ raw beetroot to 500ml Basic Lemonaid (see left). Leave to infuse for 5 minutes, then remove the beetroot and serve instantly over ice.

Orange Blossom Lemonaid
Add 1 tbsp orange blossom water to 500ml Basic Lemonaid (see left). Serve instantly over ice.

Herbal Cola Cordial

Although I loved cola as a child, I soon grew out of it. My boyfriend, on the other hand, is still very much attached to it and drinks it as I do water, so this recipe, made with natural and botanical ingredients, is dedicated to him (along with anybody else trying to wean themselves off artificial fizzy drinks).

juice of 2 oranges
juice and peel of 2 lemons
juice and peel of 2 limes
12 drops food-grade cinnamon essential oil
    or 2 cinnamon sticks
8 drops food-grade orange essential oil
80–100g natural sweetener
20g dried or fresh orange peel
1 tsp ground ginger or fresh ginger juice
8g coriander seeds or ground coriander

½ tsp ground nutmeg
2 tsp vanilla seeds, powder, paste or extract
2 tbsp chicory powder or 10g chaga bark
2 black tea bags or 2 tsp coffee, optional
4 tbsp filtered water or coconut water

Elevate it: 4 dried apricots, 1 tsp reishi powder, 6 drops food-grade neroli essential oil

Place a large saucepan over a high heat. Add all the ingredients and bring to the boil, lower the heat and simmer for 5–10 minutes, until reduced and thickened slightly. Strain the mixture through a sieve into a sterilised jar, bottle or airtight container. Allow to cool before sealing. When ready to serve, use 1 part cordial to 3 parts sparkling water and serve with ice. Add more or less cordial to suit your taste. Refrigerate the cordial for up to 2 months.

Grape & Coconut Cocktail

Serves 2

Unlike most cocktails, which often rely heavily on sugar syrup, this one uses white grapes to create both a natural and nutritious sweetness. Above that, coconut water (or sparkling water) and citrus fruits make this a highly refreshing and deeply hydrating drink. Enjoy with or without alcohol and garnish with sliced grapes and fresh or dried herbs or edible flowers (such as thyme, rosemary or elderflowers).

400g white grapes
juice of 1 lemon
80ml water
½ teaspoon ginseng powder

8 ice cubes
500ml coconut water or sparkling water
alcohol of choice (optional) – I like gin, vodka,
    rum or Kamm & Sons (a botanical aperitif)

Blend the grapes, lemon juice, water and ginseng powder in a high-speed blender for 2 minutes, until smooth. Strain the juice through a sieve into a jug, saving the pulp for smoothies. Divide the ice between two glasses and pour the juice over the top. Add 250ml coconut water or sparkling water to each glass and stir to combine. If using alcohol, use less coconut water or sparkling water to make room for a single or double measure of your chosen spirit.

If you prefer wine or Prosecco to spirits, replace half of the coconut water or sparkling water with 125ml of either.

Place a lemongrass stalk (ends trimmed) in each glass as a decorative straw.

Evening Time

Hibiscus & Ginger Yin & Tonic

Serves 2

A couple of years ago I spent New Year's Eve with one of my closest friends, Georgia. It was crazy weather out so we had to work with her existing supplies to make something to toast with at midnight. It is often these accidental, of-the-moment improvisations that turn out the best and I've been making this ever since. The bitter citrus fruits and tart hibiscus are tamed by juicy raspberries and blood orange, which bring a subtle sweetness and a gorgeous rosy hue to this refreshing cocktail.

juice of 1 blood orange or orange
juice of 2 limes
juice of 1 pink grapefruit (about 100ml)
handful of raspberries
30g ginger or fresh ginger juice
1 tbsp honey or other natural sweetener
15g dried hibiscus leaves
8 ice cubes
250ml sparkling water (or tonic, soda or coconut water)
alcohol of your choice (optional) – I like vodka, gin or Kamm & Sons (a botanical aperitif)

Elevate it: 5 drops schizandra tincture, 1 tbsp aloe vera juice, 20ml fruit infusion (pages 119–120), 20ml fresh fruit juice of your choice

Place a small saucepan over a medium heat and, once hot, add the orange, lime and grapefruit juices, raspberries, ginger or ginger juice, honey and hibiscus. Bring to the boil for 5 minutes, then reduce the heat and simmer to infuse for 10–15 minutes. Set aside to cool.

Divide the ice cubes between two glasses and strain the syrup over the top. If using alcohol, top each glass up to just over halfway with sparkling water and then add a single or double measure of your chosen spirit. If not using alcohol, fill each glass with sparkling water and stir to combine.

Garnish with hibiscus leaves, smashed raspberries and a wedge of lime.

If you have any leftover syrup, store in a jar or airtight container in the fridge and serve with pancakes, porridge, yogurts or ice cream.

Evening Time

Sweet Potato Gratin

Serves 4–6

Preheat the oven to 180°C / gas mark 4

In my first home away from home, my flatmates, Sam and Charlotte, and I cooked a lot, and when I started experimenting with new and more functional ingredients, they were always willing 'tasters'. This was one of the first things I made them when I began making changes to my diet and subsequently started my blog and, without their approval, it might not have been here today. I've served it on the menu at many of the supper clubs I've hosted in the past and it always goes down a treat.

2 tbsp coconut or extra virgin olive oil
½–1 tsp sea salt
6 tbsp nutritional yeast
½ tsp ground cinnamon
½ tsp ground nutmeg
few sprigs of fresh rosemary, thyme, sage or oregano
1 × 400g can coconut milk
125ml plant-based milk (pages 304–306) or broth or stock
3 sweet potatoes or standard potatoes or a mixture of both, thinly sliced with a sharp knife or mandolin

Elevate it: 1 crushed garlic clove, 1 finely chopped white onion, handful of diced kale or spinach, 2 thinly sliced carrots or beetroots

Put the oil in a saucepan over a medium heat. Once hot, add the salt, nutritional yeast, cinnamon, nutmeg and herbs (along with the garlic, onion, and greens, if using). Sauté for 3–4 minutes, until fragrant. Then add the coconut milk and plant–based milk, and stir to combine. Bring to the boil, then reduce the heat and simmer for 10 minutes. Add your potatoes to the pan and continue to simmer for 5 minutes.

Using a slotted spoon, remove the potatoes from the pan. Arrange one-third of them over the base of a 33 x 22cm baking dish, until it is covered. Press them down firmly with the back of a wooden spoon or spatula (add the carrots or beetroot, if using). Then cover with one-third of the coconut mixture. Repeat this layering process until all the potatoes and the coconut milk mixture are used up. I usually manage 3 layers of each. The sauce should only just cover the top layer of potatoes, but shouldn't be overflowing.

Press down on the mixture a final time, ensuring the potatoes are as compact as possible, then place in the oven and bake for 50–60 minutes until it turns golden on top. (I usually bake mine for 50 minutes, remove from the oven, then sprinkle with extra nutritional yeast or Nut Parmesan (page 313), turn the oven up to 200°C /gas mark 6 and bake for a further 10 minutes, until it turns golden on top.)

Creamed Lentils with Greens

Serves 4–6

This heart-warming dish resembles a creamy risotto and yet calls for no grains at all – ideal if you prefer to avoid them for dietary reasons or simply find them too filling in the evenings. I serve these lentils over plain millet or quinoa, but you could also stir them through pasta or serve them with potatoes or simple vegetable sides. Whatever you do, have some Magic Vegetable 'Bread' Rolls (page 314) to mop up every last bit of the sauce.

140g green or puy lentils
2 tbsp extra virgin olive oil or coconut oil
1 medium white onion, finely chopped
1–2 garlic cloves, crushed
80g cauliflower, finely chopped
450g mixed mushrooms, sliced
6 fresh sage leaves
2 sprigs of thyme
350ml vegetable stock
1 × 400g can coconut milk
2 tsp tamari

1–2 tbsp nutritional yeast, to taste
1 tsp apple cider vinegar
2 handfuls of spinach or kale
sea salt and freshly ground black pepper

To serve
300g cooked millet, quinoa or brown rice
Cider Vinegar Mushroom Crisps (page 177)
organic Dijon mustard

Elevate it: 1 tsp reishi or shilajit powder

Bring a large saucepan of water to the boil, add the lentils and season with salt. Reduce the heat and simmer for 15–20 minutes, until the lentils begin to soften, then drain and set aside.

Set a separate saucepan over a medium heat and add the olive oil, onion, garlic and cauliflower. Cook for 5 minutes, stirring constantly, until the cauliflower becomes tender, then add the mushrooms and season with salt and pepper. Sauté for a further 5 minutes and then add the herbs.

Add the stock, coconut milk, tamari, nutritional yeast and vinegar and stir to combine before adding the lentils. Bring to the boil for 5 minutes and then turn the heat right down.

Transfer half of the mixture to a blender and blend on a high speed until smooth. Return this purée to the pan and stir well. Lastly, add the leafy greens and continue to simmer until they have wilted. Serve immediately.

Roasted Brussels, Broccoli & Red Grapes

Serves 2 as a main, 4 as a side

Preheat the oven to 180°C / gas mark 4

We've all hated Brussels sprouts at some point in our lives, and I probably still would if it wasn't for Hu Kitchen in New York. When I was living in the city a couple of winters ago, I spent a lot of time there inbetween castings or on my way home from shoots. I didn't have a kitchen in my apartment so I stocked up on their pre-cooked ingredients most nights, and became addicted to their roasted Brussels sprouts – soft and caramelised on the inside, crispy on the outside. Roasted grapes add a rich, juicy flavour to this dish and bind the other ingredients together in a subtly sweet sauce.

250g Brussels sprouts
250g red grapes
4 tbsp extra virgin olive oil or coconut oil
½ broccoli head, chopped into florets

60g chard or kale, chopped
1 quantity Basic Tahini Dressing (page 135)
sea salt and freshly ground black pepper

Arrange the Brussels sprouts and grapes in a large baking tray, drizzle with 2 tablespoons of the oil and sprinkle with salt. Use a sharp knife to pierce the grapes slightly and then place in the oven and roast for 45 minutes.

Add the broccoli to the baking tray and roast for a further 15–20 minutes. When the broccoli is tender, the grapes are soft and caramelised and the Brussels are beginning to crisp, heat the remaining olive oil in a frying pan and sauté the chard or kale for 10 minutes, until wilted. Stir the chard or kale into the tray, coating them in the juices of the roasted vegetables. Divide the vegetables among individual bowls or transfer to a larger dish if serving as a side. Drizzle with the tahini dressing and enjoy.

Enjoy as a warm salad or serve with grains or psuedograins or White Bean Cloud Mash (page 228).

Honey & Mustard Portobello Mushrooms with Ancient Grains

Serves 2

My Mum makes the best honey and mustard chicken dish and if you tried it, you wouldn't argue. Just the mention of the words honey and mustard together transports me back to our kitchen table at home, smells of our favourite sweet, creamy dinner lingering in the air. These days, I rarely cook with meat, so I like to make a vegetarian version using portobello mushrooms as they lend a tender texture not dissimilar to chicken. However, if you want to use meat, substitute them for 2–4 chicken breasts or thighs, or use half mushroom half chicken.

1 x 400g can coconut milk
2 tbsp Dijon mustard
2 tbsp wholegrain mustard
½ tsp lemon juice
1 tbsp coconut or extra virgin olive oil
4–6 portobello mushrooms
4 sprigs of fresh thyme or rosemary

2 handfuls of spinach, kale or dandelion greens
1 tsp tamari
2 tbsp honey
sea salt and freshly ground black pepper
250g cooked quinoa, millet or brown rice,
    to serve

For the sauce, whisk the coconut milk, mustards and lemon juice together in a bowl and set aside.

Heat the oil in a griddle pan and, once hot, add the mushrooms, upside down. Fry over a medium heat for 5–10 minutes, until charred. Flip over the mushrooms and fry the other sides for a further 5–10 minutes.

Set a large saucepan over a medium heat and add the mustard sauce. Bring to the boil and then reduce the heat. Transfer the griddled mushrooms to the sauce and cook for 20 minutes. Finally, stir in the thyme or rosemary, spinach, kale or dandelion greens, tamari and honey and season with salt and pepper.

Serve with grains of your choice and/or a warm or cold salad.

Pasta

Serves 4–6

Although it doesn't taste of much on its own, pasta is a popular base for all kinds of sauces and toppings. If you try to avoid gluten and wheat, buckwheat, quinoa and rice pastas are great store-bought substitute but, to me, there is noting like fresh pasta, so I like to make it from scratch when I can. It might seem a laborious process but using the buckwheat and cassava can actually be very easy. As for the sauces you serve them with, shop-bought pasta sauces often contain unnecessary sugars, acidity regulators and emulsifiers. Luckily, there are many natural ways to make your own. 'Carbonara, bolognaise, lasagne?' I hear you ask. Well, obviously.

Buckwheat Pasta

120g buckwheat flour, 20g arrowroot, 1 whole egg and 1 egg yolk (for a vegan option, use 6 tbsp water and a dash of olive oil instead)

Put all the ingredients a in a food processor and blend for 30 seconds. Keeping the machine running, gradually add 2 tbsp water. At first the mixture will be crumbly, but after 30 seconds–1 minute it will form a smooth, doughy ball. Stop blending at this point.

Using a rolling pin, roll the dough out on a lightly floured board, aiming for a thickness of 1–2mm. Next, use a sharp knife to cut the dough into your desired shapes – thin, string-like strips for spaghetti, slightly wider strips for tagliatelle, and even wider strips for pappardelle, or squares or circles for ravioli or large lasagne sheets.

To cook the pasta, bring a large saucepan of water to the boil and add a little salt and olive oil, then turn down the heat until it is just a little livelier than a simmer. Working in batches, drop the pasta into the water and cook for 2–5 minutes, until the pasta becomes a little harder, but is still soft and pliable. Drain, divide among bowls and top with your chosen sauce or return to the saucepan, add your sauce and stir to coat entirely.

Variations

For Olive Pasta, add 10–20g black olives and 1 tsp activated charcoal powder.
For Spinach Pasta, add 10g spinach.
For Beetroot Pasta, add 1 tbsp powder
or 10g raw beetroot, puréed
For Algae Pasta, add 1 tbsp spirulina

Cassava & Almond Pasta

120g cassava flour, 70g ground almonds, 1 egg, plus an additional egg yolk, 1 tbsp olive oil

Put the flour and almonds in a food processor and blend for 30 seconds. Keeping the machine running, gradually add the egg and egg yolk. If the mixture seems very dry, add the olive oil, but if it sticks together well, leave it out. Stop blending when the mixture begins to form into a doughy ball.

Using a rolling pin, roll the dough out on a lightly floured board, aiming for a thickness of 1–2mm. Next, use a sharp knife to cut the dough into your desired shapes – thin, string-like strips for spaghetti, slightly wider strips for tagliatelle, and even wider strips for pappardelle, or squares or circles for ravioli or large lasagne sheets.

To cook the pasta, bring a large saucepan of water to the boil and add a little salt and olive oil, then turn down the heat until it is just a little livelier than a simmer. Working in batches, drop your pasta into the water and cook for 2–4 minutes, until the pasta becomes a little harder, but is still soft and pliable. Keep tasting and you will know when it is ready. Drain, divide among bowls and top with your chosen sauce or return to the saucepan before adding your sauce and stirring to coat entirely.

Evening Time

Carbonara Sauce, Three Ways

Serves 2

White Bean Carbonara Sauce

320g cannellini beans (or other white beans) 80ml extra virgin olive oil, plus extra for drizzling, 250ml filtered water or plant-based milk, 4–5 tbsp nutritional yeast, ½ tsp sea salt, plus extra for sprinkling, freshly ground black pepper, to taste, small handful of fresh basil leaves, 2 egg yolks (optional)

Place the beans, olive oil, water or milk and nutritional yeast together in a blender and blend on the highest speed for 2–3 minutes. Season and pulse for a couple more seconds to combine. Taste and season again until you are happy with the flavour.

Transfer the sauce to a saucepan and place on a medium heat, stirring until heated through. Add your pasta to the pan to coat it in the sauce (with the egg yolks, if using), or divide your pasta between bowls and pour the sauce over the top. Garnish with fresh herbs, a drizzle of extra virgin olive oil and an extra sprinkle of salt and pepper, to taste.

Simple Coconut Milk & Mushroom Carbonara Sauce

4 tbsp extra virgin olive oil, 1 garlic clove, crushed, 150g chestnut mushrooms, sliced, ½ tsp sea salt, freshly ground black pepper, 5 tbsp nutritional yeast, 1 tsp lemon juice 1 × 400g can coconut milk, handful of fresh herbs of your choice, chopped, 2 fresh egg yolks (optional)

Heat 1 tbsp oil in a medium saucepan and once hot, add the garlic. Fry for 2–3 minutes and add the mushrooms, along with the salt, pepper, nutritional yeast, the remaining olive oil and the lemon juice. Sauté for 10 minutes and then add the coconut milk and your herbs of choice. Bring to the boil and then reduce the temperature to a medium to low heat and simmer for 20–30 minutes, until the sauce has thickened. Once you are happy with the taste and consistency, either add your pasta to the pan to coat it in the sauce (and the egg yolks, if using) ,or divide your pasta between bowls and pour the sauce over the top. Garnish with fresh herbs, a drizzle of extra virgin olive oil and extra seasoning, to taste.

Walnut Carbonara Sauce

120g walnuts, 250ml filtered water, 80ml extra virgin olive oil, 3–4 tbsp nutritional yeast, 1 tsp lemon juice, ½ tsp sea salt, freshly ground black pepper, to taste, 2 fresh egg yolks (optional)

Blend the walnuts, water, olive oil, nutritional yeast and lemon juice in a blender for 2–3 minutes, on the highest speed. Add the salt and pepper and then pulse for a couple more seconds to combine. When you are happy with the flavour, transfer the sauce to a saucepan.

Heat the sauce through and either add the cooked pasta to the pan to coat it in the sauce (with the egg yolks, if using), or divide your pasta between bowls and pour the sauce over the top. Garnish with fresh herbs, a drizzle of extra virgin olive oil and an extra sprinkle of salt and pepper.

Add 150–200g sautéed mushrooms, grilled bacon, Coconut 'bacon' (page 313) or Cider Vinegar Mushroom Crisps (page 177).

Roasted Tomato & Red Pepper Passata

Serves 2–4

Preheat the oven to 200°C / gas mark 6

2 red peppers, chopped
4 medium tomatoes, chopped
½ white onion or shallot, chopped
1–2 garlic cloves, finely chopped
3 tbsp extra virgin olive oil
60ml water or stock (or unsweetened plant-based milk)

2 tbsp nutritional yeast
handful of fresh basil leaves
½ red chilli, finely chopped (optional)
sea salt and freshly ground black pepper

Arrange the red peppers, tomatoes, onion and garlic on a baking tray, drizzle with a little olive oil and sprinkle with a pinch of salt. Roast for 25–30 minutes, until the vegetables become soft and the peppers begin to darken at the edges.

Heat 1 tablespoon of the extra virgin olive oil in a saucepan over a medium heat. Once hot, add the chilli, if using, and sauté for 4–5 minutes. Add half the roasted vegetables. Put the remaining vegetables in a blender, add the water or stock and nutritional yeast and blend on a high speed for 20–30 seconds, until smooth. Pour into the pan with the chilli and whole roasted vegetables and heat through. Season to taste.

When you are happy with the flavour, either add the cooked pasta to the pan to coat it in the sauce, or divide your pasta among bowls and pour the sauce over the top. Garnish with basil, a drizzle of the remaining extra virgin olive oil and an extra sprinkle of salt and pepper.

Add black olives, flaked tuna or anchovies and spinach to the sauce for a puttanesca-style pasta dish.

Lasagne

Serves 4–6

Preheat the oven to 200°C / gas mark 6

1 quantity fresh pasta (page 220), cut into lasagne sheet shapes

1 quantity White Bean Carbonara Sauce (page 223)

For the mushroom and lentil 'bolognese'
2 tbsp extra virgin olive oil
1 white onion, finely chopped
2 garlic cloves, crushed
500g tomatoes, chopped
2 long red peppers, chopped
50g green lentils
1 small raw beetroot, cut into tiny cubes
450g button or chestnut mushrooms, finely minced (or pulsed in a food processor)
200ml vegetable stock
2 bay leaves
4 tbsp nutritional yeast
small handful of spinach
sea salt and freshly ground black pepper

Elevate it: 50g cooked grains or psuedograins, 1 tbsp reishi powder, 1 tbsp cacao powder

First make the 'bolognese'. Heat the oil in a saucepan and, once hot, add the onion and garlic. Sauté for 4–5 minutes, then and add the tomatoes, red peppers, lentils, beetroot and mushrooms. Sauté for a further 10 minutes and then add the stock, bay leaves and nutritional yeast and season with salt and pepper. Bring to the boil, reduce to a medium heat and simmer for 30 minutes.

Once the vegetables have softened, transfer 6 large tablespoons of the mixture (avoiding the bay leaves) to a blender. Using a slotted spoon, retrieve the red peppers, or as many of them as you can, and add them to the blender. Blend on a low speed for 20–30 seconds, until smooth, then return to the pan and stir through the remaining mixture.

Taste the sauce and add more nutritional yeast, salt or pepper, as desired, along with any elevational extras (I always add cacao as it adds a real richness to the sauce). Add the spinach and allow it to wilt. Once the sauce has thickened and reduced and you are happy with the flavour, remove it from the heat and discard the bay leaves.

Take a rectangular dish (approx. 33 × 22cm) and fill the base with one-third of the 'bolognese'. Spread one-third of the sauce over the top and cover it with one layer of pasta sheets. Season with a little salt and pepper and then repeat these steps, covering the pasta with half the remaining 'bolognese', followed by half of the remaining sauce and another layer of pasta. Finally, add the remaining 'bolognese', followed by the remaining sauce and season. Bake for 35–40 minutes.

Beetroot, Carrot & Seaweed Laksa-Style Curry

Serves 4

I think it's only right to dedicate this recipe to one of my oldest friends, Esme. She recently moved just down the road from me and when she came round for the first of many 'neighbourly' dinners, this dish marked the occasion. Beetroot may not seem like the most common base for a curry, but it creates a really uniquely sweet and earthy flavour, which really complements the neutral nuttiness of grains and psuedograins. For something a little different, replace the grains with soba or rice noodles.

2 tbsp coconut oil
1 tsp sesame oil (optional)
1–2 garlic cloves, crushed
1 white onion, choppped
1 red chilli, chopped
5g grated fresh turmeric or ½ a tsp
    ground turmeric
10g grated fresh ginger
1 tbsp ground ginger
5g lemongrass (optional)
3 large beetroots, peeled and chopped
4 carrots, peeled and chopped
200g mushrooms (I like button or chestnut),
    sliced thinly or quartered

10g seaweed
1 tbsp lemon juice
1–2 tsp tamari, to taste
500ml vegetable, seaweed or fish stock
3 bay leaves
1 tbsp nutritional yeast
1 × 400g can coconut milk
4 servings of quinoa, millet or brown or
    black rice
2 handfuls of spinach
large handful of coriander leaves
1 lime, cut into wedges
4 portions of chicken, fish, prawns, tofu
    or tempeh (optional)

Heat the oils in a large saucepan over a medium heat and, once hot, add the garlic, onion, chilli, turmeric, gingers and lemongrass, if using. Cook for 2–3 minutes, stirring constantly. (If adding raw meat, fish or prawns, add them to the pan now and sear for 10 minutes before continuing with the following steps. If using pre-cooked prawns, add them to the sauce just 5 minutes before serving).

Add the beetroot, carrots, mushrooms and seaweed and cook for 4–5 minutes, then add the lemon juice, tamari, stock, bay leaves and nutritional yeast. Bring to the boil for 5–10 minutes, cover with a lid, reduce to a medium to low heat and simmer until the beetroot is cooked (about 15–20 minutes).

Once the beetroot has softened, stir through the coconut milk and continue to simmer until warm through. Add the spinach and most of the coriander and season with a little more tamari or lemon juice, to taste. Remove and discard the bay leaves before serving with the grains, garnished with the remaining coriander and slices of lime.

Chanterelle Mushroom, Lentil & Chestnut Casserole with White Bean Cloud Mash

Serves 6

Preheat the oven to 190°C /gas mark 5

This recipe is inspired by a casserole dish I had in Stockholm. Chanterelle mushrooms were everywhere and I immediately took to their earthy, buttery flavour, much richer than the standard mushrooms I was used to. This recipe combines them with many of my favourite autumnal ingredients, creating a nourishing and warming casserole-like dish. For the simplest option, serve it with grains and vegetables or atop a cloud of white bean mash.

For the casserole
2 tbsp extra virgin olive oil or coconut oil
180g chestnuts, chopped (vacuum-packed)
1 garlic clove, crushed
½ white or red onion, chopped
250g chanterelle mushrooms, sliced
200g chestnut mushrooms, sliced
60g raw beetroot, chopped
200g puy or green lentils
6 fresh sage leaves
2 sprigs of rosemary
200ml coconut milk or plant-based milk

1 tsp apple cider vinegar
200ml vegetable or meat stock
3 handfuls of spinach, chopped
2 large handfuls of cavelo nero, chopped
sea salt and freshly ground black pepper

For the white bean cloud mash
4 tbsp extra virgin olive oil
400g tin cannellini / butter beans, rinsed and drained
60ml water or plant-based milk
sea salt and freshly ground black pepper

Heat the oil in a large saucepan and, once hot, add the chestnuts, garlic, onion, mushrooms, beetroot, lentils, sage and rosemary. Sauté for 15 minutes and then add the coconut milk, vinegar and half of the stock. Bring to the boil, then reduce the heat and simmer for 20 minutes. Gradually add the remaining stock to loosen it, but you may not need it all.

Meanwhile, prepare your white bean mash. Put the oil and beans in a saucepan and set over a medium heat. Add half of the water or plant-based milk and then gently begin to break up the beans using a fork or a potato masher. Add the remaining water or plant-based milk and continue to stir and mash until the beans completely loose their shape and the mixture becomes smooth and fluffy. Season to taste and remove from the heat. If you want a smoother result, blitz the mash in a blender for 30 seconds, with a little extra water or plant-based milk, if needed. Set aside.

Add the spinach and cavelo nero to the casserole and season with salt and pepper. Once the greens have wilted and the liquid has reduced, remove from the heat and serve instantly along with the mash.

Variation
Preheat the oven to 200°C . To make a shepherd's pie variation, layer the white bean mash on top of the casserole. Bake for 15–20 minutes until the mash turns a warmer shade of white and the casserole begins to bubble underneath.

Sweet Potato Lentil Dahl

Serves 4

I made this dahl for a tea ceremony I once hosted with The London Tea Club. Cecelia, who sources and sells the most amazing teas, took our guests through a silent tea ceremony and then I led them through some pre-meal breathing exercises before serving up this dahl topped with Savoury Qnola. In Ayurveda and other Eastern healing traditions, dahl is honoured for its anti-inflammatory and immune-boosting abilities. It's satisfying without being too demanding on the digestive system and so makes a great option for dinner.

For the dahl

2 tbsp coconut oil
1 small white onion, finely chopped
2 garlic cloves, crushed
150g red lentils
2 baby aubergines or ½ large aubergine, chopped
100g sweet potato, chopped
120g tomatoes, chopped
1 × 400g tin coconut milk
250ml vegetable or meat stock
2 large handfuls of spinach or kale
handful of fresh coriander leaves

For the spice paste

2 tsp coriander seeds
2 tsp cumin seeds
2 tbsp grated fresh ginger
1 tsp chilli flakes
1 tsp ground turmeric
2 tsp garam masala
2 tsp paprika
pinch of Himalayan pink salt
3 tbsp melted coconut oil
2 tbsp natural tomato purée or chopped tomatoes
handful of fresh coriander leaves
1 tsp natural syrup (optional)

To serve

Coconut Yogurt (page 306) or the solid part of a can of coconut milk or crème fraiche
1 lime, cut into wedges

Start by making the spice paste. Toast the coriander and cumin seeds in a dry frying pan until fragrant. Transfer to a herb blender or small food processor and add the ginger, chilli, turmeric, garam masala, paprika and salt. Blend for 1 minute and then add the coconut oil, tomato purée or chopped tomatoes, coriander leaves and natural syrup, if using. Blend for a further 2 minutes until smooth, then set aside until needed.

For the dahl, heat the coconut oil in a saucepan over a medium heat. Add the onion, garlic, lentils, aubergines and sweet potato and sauté for 10 minutes. Stir in the spice paste and then add the chopped tomatoes, coconut milk and 200ml of the stock. Bring to the boil, then reduce to a medium–low heat and simmer for 25–30 minutes, stirring occasionally.

When the dahl is becoming soft and tender, add the spinach or kale and the coriander and season. Stir for a few minutes so the greens wilt and, if the mixture seems too thick, add the remaining stock. When you are happy with the consistency, divide among the bowls and serve with coconut yogurt and a wedge of lime.

Black Beet Rice with Sweet Potato Purée & Orangey Greens

Serves 4

Black rice is one of my favourite ingredients and it takes on new life in this recipe, simmered and infused with beetroot. I'm always making variations of this recipe as a quick and easy dinner or as a component to keep in the fridge to use in salad bowls or broths. I served this dish to some of my oldest friends and my Qnola girls when we retreated out of London to my friend Betty's beach house in Cornwall. Now every time I make it, I'll think of those times. You could serve it with seared or baked cod, salmon, sea bass or tuna or garlicky king prawns.

For the sweet potato purée
400g sweet potato, peeled and chopped
100ml extra virgin olive oil
1 tsp tamari
½ tsp lemon juice
splash of plant-based milk (optional)

For the black rice
pinch of sea salt
1 tbsp coconut oil
300g black rice
1 large raw beetroot, grated

For the orangey greens
200g green runner beans
1 large broccoli head, broken into florets

1 avocado
sprinkling of chilli flakes or 1 tsp fresh red
    chilli, chopped
juice of 1 large orange (approx. 100ml)
2 tbsp extra virgin olive oil
½ tsp apple cider vinegar
5 tbsp tahini
2g grated fresh or ground ginger
2 tbsp tamari
1 tsp lemon juice
1 tsp honey

Elevate it: 50g sauerkraut, 2 handfuls of chopped Medjool dates or goji berries, 4 tbsp soaked seaweed

First make the sweet potato purée. Bring a small saucepan of water to the boil over a medium heat, add the sweet potato and cook for 10 minutes, until tender but not too soft. Drain and transfer to a blender along with the extra virgin olive oil, tamari and lemon juice. Blend on a high speed for 2–3 minutes, until silky smooth, adding a little more oil or a splash of plant-based milk to loosen it if it seems too thick. Transfer to a serving bowl and cover with foil to keep warm.

Meanwhile, make the rice. Bring 500ml water to the boil in a saucepan and add the salt, coconut oil and black rice. Reduce to a simmer, cover with a lid and cook for 25 minutes, stirring frequently. Add the grated beetroot (along with dates, goji berries or seaweed, if using) and cook for a further 10–15 minutes, leaving the lid off. If the rice is too thick or if it's catching and sticking to the pan, add a splash more water. Keep checking on it and stir occasionally whilst you make the greens.

Fill a separate small saucepan with water and bring to the boil over a medium heat. Add the beans and broccoli and cook for 6–8 minutes, until cooked al dente (you want them soft but with a little bite to them). Transfer to a serving dish and set aside.

Next, for the orange tahini sauce, place all of the remaining ingredients in a jar or other container with a lid. Secure the lid and shake well to combine. Pour the dressing over the cooked greens, cover the dish with foil and leave the sauce to soak in.

Once the rice is cooked through, drain and rinse and transfer it to a serving dish. Stir in the sauerkraut now, if using, and place the rice on the table along with the greens and the sweet potato purée for people to help themselves.

Serve with Pickled Ginger (page 316), a wedge of lime, Caramelised Onions (page 234) and a raw egg yolk – bibimbap-style.

Jo Jo's Sticky Miso-Glazed Aubergines with Millet & Caramelised Onions

Serves 4

Preheat the oven to 180°C /gas mark 4

I first made this for my sister Jo Jo and, although she doesn't enjoy cooking, she enjoys making this. It's simple to make yet full of flavour. You can serve with millet like I have done here, or as a side to other mains. If you have some leftover, enjoy it cold the next day, either for breakfast with a poached egg, or stirred through salad for lunch.

2 large aubergines or 500g mini aubergines
8 whole garlic cloves
8 tbsp extra virgin olive oil
200g chestnut or portobello mushrooms, sliced
300g millet, quinoa or brown rice
2 tbsp tamari
2 tsp brown miso paste
½ tsp apple cider vinegar or rice vinegar
2 tbsp natural syrup
juice of ½ lemon

2 tsp sesame oil
2 tbsp sesame seeds, to serve

For the caramelised onions
1 tbsp extra virgin olive oil
1 red onion, finely chopped
1 tbsp natural syrup
½ tsp lemon juice
1 tsp apple cider vinegar
a pinch of sea salt

Slice the aubergines into strips, lengthways, and arrange them in a large ovenproof dish along with the whole garlic cloves. Drizzle with 4 tbsp extra virgin olive oil and roast for 20 minutes, then add the mushrooms and roast for a further 10 minutes.

Meanwhile, cook the millet, quinoa or brown rice as per packet instructions.

Whilst the millet and vegetables cook, put the remaining olive oil, tamari, miso paste, vinegar, natural syrup, lemon juice and sesame oil in a small bowl and whisk to combine.

For the caramelised onions, place the olive oil in a saucepan over a medium heat and, once hot, add the onion, natural syrup, lemon juice, cider vinegar, 2 tablespoons water and a pinch of salt. Stir for 5 minutes, then reduce the heat and cook for 15–20 minutes, until the onions are soft and the sauce becomes sticky. Transfer to a serving dish and set aside.

Remove the cooked vegetables from the oven and pour the marinade over the top, ensuring the aubergines and mushrooms soak up as much as possible. Stir gently and then return to the oven to roast for a final 10 minutes.

Divide the millet, quinoa or brown rice among individual plates. Top each one with a generous serving of the miso vegetables, a spoonful of caramelised onions and a sprinkle of sesame seeds.

Evening Time

Indian Bowl with Tandoori Tikka Mushrooms, Cauliflower Curry & Sunflower Chutney

Serves 4

Preheat the oven to 180°C · /gas mark 4

This dish is inspired by one of my favourite eateries in New York. Inday is a restaurant rooted in the traditional Indian belief that food should provide nourishment for your body and bring balance to your life. It combines ancient traditions with modern flavours and serves simple bowls, designed to fit easily into busy lives. Although there are a lot of separate components to handle in this recipe, they all work so well together and, once you've made them all, you'll have a supply of leftovers for days.

1 large sweet potato, peeled and cubed
4 carrots, cut into thin sticks
2 tbsp virgin olive oil
100g leafy greens, such as kale or spinach
300g millet, brown rice or quinoa
Mango Chutney (page 310)
1 quantity Quickled Cucumber (page 316)
Herbal Sunflower Chutney (page 310)
black onion seeds
fresh coriander leaves
1 lime, cut into wedge

For the cauliflower curry
1 tbsp extra virgin olive oil
250g cauliflower, chopped
1 red onion, chopped
1 garlic clove
1 tsp ground cumin
1 tsp ground coriander
½ tsp cayenne pepper
1 tsp paprika
1 tsp garam masala
1 tsp ground turmeric

2.5cm piece of fresh ginger, finely chopped
1 fresh red chilli
handful of fresh coriander leaves
2 tbsp coconut oil
1 × 400g can chickpeas, drained
1 × 400g can coconut milk
1 tsp natural syrup
sea salt

For the tandoori tikka mushrooms
2 tbsp coconut oil
100g mushrooms, cut into 1–2cm cubes
1 tsp ground cumin
1 tsp ground coriander
½ tsp cayenne pepper
½ tsp ground paprika
1 tsp garam masala
½ tsp ground turmeric
1 tsp ground ginger
1 tsp chilli powder
½ tsp lemon juice
pinch of sea salt

Place the sweet potato and carrots in a baking tray, drizzle with the olive oil and roast in the oven for 45 minutes. Transfer to a bowl and set aside. Leave the oven on for the cauliflower, and reuse the baking tray.

Meanwhile, bring a saucepan of water to the boil, add the leafy greens and cook for 5–8 minutes, until wilted. Drain and set aside in a small bowl.

Put the cauliflower in the baking tray, drizzle with the olive oil, sprinkle with salt and roast in the oven for 15 minutes.

Meanwhile, blend the onion, garlic, ground spices, ginger, chilli and fresh coriander in a herb blender or small food processor for 2 minutes, until smooth. Heat the coconut oil in a saucepan, add the spice mixture and sauté

Evening Time

for 5 minutes. Add the cauliflower and chickpeas, sauté for 5 minutes, then add the coconut milk and bring to the boil. Reduce the heat to a simmer and cook for 20–25 minutes, until the mixture begins to thicken.

Meanwhile, cook the millet, brown rice or quinoa as per the packet instructions.

Finally, make the tikka mushrooms. Heat the coconut oil in a frying pan and, once hot, add the mushrooms and sear over a high heat for 5 minutes. Stir in the spices, lemon juice and salt and continue to cook for 10–15 minutes, until the mushrooms are tender, fully infused, dried out and flavoursome.

Once everything is cooked, fill each bowl with a layer of millet, brown rice or quinoa. Then assemble the sweet potato and carrots at the edge of the bowl. Do the same with the leafy greens, the cauliflower curry and the tikka mushrooms until all the rice is covered. Serve the mango chutney and pickled cucumber in a pot on the side and place a large spoonful of the sunflower chutney in the middle of each bowl. Top with black onion seeds, fresh coriander and slices of lime.

Evening Time

Creams, Frostings & Sauces

There is little meaning to a dessert without cream, crumble without custard, cake without frosting or life without caramel or chocolate spread for that matter. However, such sauces and spreads tend to be highly processed, unhealthy and addictive, especially when shop-bought. Enjoy the following variations with healthy homemade desserts, or use them to steer shop-bought desserts in a better direction, one layer of avocado frosting at a time. Also try them in drinks or as a topping for breakfast pots, birchers, porridge, toast or pancakes.

Coconut Cream

In a blender, blend 400g can coconut cream with a splash of boiling water for 2–3 minutes, until silky smooth. To add flavour or sweetness, add 1 tsp vanilla powder and ½ tsp natural syrup and blend for another 30 seconds, until combined. Transfer to a jug or a pot and serve instantly or store in the fridge. You will need to blend it each time before serving as it will solidify once chilled. For a thicker cream, don't add the splash of water and place in the fridge for 30–40 minutes, then remove from the fridge and stir vigorously using a small whisk or a fork.

For a whipped cream, refrigerate a can of coconut milk for a minimum of 6 hours, or overnight. Scrape the solid part of the cream into a bowl (reserve the liquid for use in other recipes), then use an electric whisk to whip the coconut cream into soft peaks. To add flavour or sweetness, add 1 tsp vanilla powder and ½ tsp natural syrup of your choice.

Cashew Cream

Put 100g cashews (soaked for a minimum of 2–4 hours), 50ml plant-based milk, 1 tbsp melted coconut oil, 1 Medjool date or 1 tsp natural sweetener, ½ tsp lemon juice and a pinch of salt in a blender and blend for 2–3 minutes, until smooth. For extra flavour, add 1 tsp vanilla powder or spices of your choice. Blend for a further 30 seconds to combine. Transfer to a jug and store in the fridge. You can add a dash of extra plant-based milk and use a whisk or fork to loosen it up if the mixture needs thinning. For a thicker cream, use the buttercream recipe .

Cashew Buttercream

Put 200g cashews (soaked for 2–4 hours), 6 tbsp melted coconut oil, 30ml plant-based milk, 1 tsp lemon juice, 4 tbsp natural sweetener, a few drops of apple cider vinegar and a pinch of salt in a blender and blend for 2–3 minutes, until smooth. To add more of an icing flavour, add 2–4 tbsp creamed coconut or melted coconut butter. Transfer to a small bowl; add colours and flavourings (page 241), if using, and place in the fridge to set for 20–30 seconds.

Avocado Chocolate Frosting

Put 200ml melted coconut oil, 1½ avocados (as ripe and soft as possible), 15 tbsp raw cacao powder, 5 tbsp natural sweetener and a pinch of salt in a blender and blend for 2–3 minutes, until smooth. Add a little more cacao, natural sweetener or salt, to taste, and then transfer to a small bowl and place in the fridge to set for about 20–30 minutes. Ensure your cake has entirely cooled before topping it with a generous layer of this frosting.

Creamed Coconut Fondant Icing

Fill a small bowl with boiling water. Take 1 bar of creamed coconut (or 200g of coconut butter) and place it in the water (do not cut the plastic film). Let it melt for 10 minutes, then massage it a little to help it melt and, if it needs a little longer, place it back in the water for a further 5 minutes. When it has fully melted, cut the end of the plastic film and pour the mixture into a bowl. If you choose to add some colour, add your choice of natural colourings now (page 240). If not, place in the fridge to harden for 10–20 minutes. Ensure your cake has entirely cooled before applying a generous layer of the frosting on top, using a knife of another flat tool to spread it evenly.

Colourings for Frosting

Mix the following one of these colourings into a batch of Cashew Buttercream or Creamed Coconut Fondant Icing (see previous page), in a small bowl, using a small spatula.

Beetroot Pink: 2 tsp beetroot powder or 1 tbsp beetroot juice and a pinch of maca powder.

Golden Turmeric: 1 tsp ground turmeric/fresh turmeric juice and 1 tsp ground ginger or ½ tsp fresh ginger juice with a pinch of bee pollen.

Matcha Green: ½ tsp matcha powder and ½ tsp wheatgrass powder. For a darker green, add ½ tsp spirulina or a pinch of activated charcoal powder.

Berry Purple: 1 tbsp acai powder, 1 tsp beetroot powder, 1 tsp maca powder and 4 tbsp frozen blueberries or blackberries.

Brown Mocha chocolate: 1 tsp espresso or 1 tsp instant ground coffee or chicory powder, 2 tbsp cacao powder, ½ tsp reishi, shilajit or he shou wu and 1 tsp maca powder or mesquite.

Mint green: 2–4 drops of food-grade spearmint or peppermint food-grade essential oil, 5–6 fresh mint leaves and a pinch of wheatgrass powder.

Cashew Custard

Put 120g cashews (soaked), 40g melted coconut oil, 125ml plant-based milk, 1 tsp vanilla powder, 1 tsp natural sweetener and a pinch of salt in a blender and blend for 2–3 minutes, until smooth. Elevate it by adding 20g creamed coconut or coconut butter or, if you have access to one, the flesh of a young thai coconut and blend for a further 30 seconds to combine. Transfer to a saucepan and cook over a medium heat for 1–2 minutes, then serve immediately. For a rich and nutty flavour, use the toasted coconut milk (page 306) instead of other plant-based milks.

Macadamia Chocolate Spread

Put 150g coconut milk solids, 25g cacao powder, 40g Medjool dates, 5g coconut sugar or natural syrup, 5g vanilla powder, a pinch of sea salt, 5g maca powder and 40ml coconut milk liquid in a blender and blend on a high speed for 2–3 minutes, until smooth. Add 30g raw macadamia nuts (or cashews, pecans, hazelnuts or Brazil nuts) and 60g soft coconut oil and blend for a further 1–2 minutes, until smooth. Transfer to a pot, jar or airtight container and place in the fridge to set. Store in the fridge for up to 1 week.

Almond & Date Salted Caramel

Put 8 Medjool dates, 5 tbsp nut butter (I like almond or cashew), 1 tsp vanilla seeds, powder, paste or extracts, ¼ – ½ tsp sea salt or himalayan pink salt, 3 tbsp melted coconut oil, 1 tbsp coconut sugar or natural syrup, 2 tbsp plant-based milk in a blender and blend on a high speed for 2–3 minutes, until smooth. The mixture should form a sticky ball of dough. Transfer the doughy caramel to a small bowl or container and set in the fridge for at least 20 minutes or until ready to use.

To make this into a caramel sauce, follow the recipe but add an extra 4 tbsp melted coconut oil and 4 tbsp plant-based milk to the blender. Heat through in a saucepan and pour over ice cream, Soul-soothing Chocolate Molten Cakes (page 242) or other desserts.

Chocolate Dipping Sauce

Put 2 tbsp coconut oil in a saucepan over a medium heat and, once melted, gently whisk in 6 tbsp cacao powder. When the cacao has dissolved, remove from the heat and stir in 2 tbsp coconut milk (solid part only), ½ tsp vanilla powder and 1 tsp sweetener of your choice. When the sauce is smooth and beginning to thicken, pour into a small bowl or jug to serve instantly.

Soul-Soothing Chocolate Molten Cakes with Chaga Lava Eruption

Serves 2

Preheat the oven to 200°C /gas mark 6

This chocolate molten cake is dedicated to Jada who challenged me to make a functional version of her favourite dessert. The chocolate sponge is magically light and airy and, when sliced, releases an indulgent, adaptogenic eruption of chocolatey, chaga-infused goodness. You can double the recipe as two might not be enough. If you like, you can serve with fresh herbs, cacao nibs, cruhsed nuts or Cacao and Cashew Qnola.

For the sponge
40g cacao butter
30g coconut oil, plus extra for greasing
1 tbsp natural syrup
a pinch of sea salt
30g cacao powder, plus extra for dusting
1 tsp reishi powder
1 egg and 1 egg yolk

30g coconut sugar
2g vanilla powder
10g ground almonds
¼ tsp bicarbonate of soda

For the filling
2 tbsp almond butter (page 308)
1 tsp chaga powder

Grease two glass or metal ramekins or 2 cups of a muffin tin with a thin layer of coconut oil and dust with cacao powder.

Fill a small saucepan with water and bring to the boil. Place a heatproof bowl on top of the saucepan (creating a double boiler), then add the cacao butter, coconut oil, natural syrup and salt. Stir with a spatula until combined. When melted, remove from the heat and whisk in the cacao and reishi powders. Leave to cool.

For the filling, mix the almond butter and chaga powder together in a small bowl, then place in the fridge until required.

Put the eggs, coconut sugar and vanilla in a small bowl or jug, and beat with a whisk until light and frothy. Gradually pour the egg mixture into the cooled chocolate mixture and whisk vigorously. Continue to whisk as you add the ground almonds and bicarbonate of soda. The mixture should develop into a thick, custard-like consistency.

Divide most of the mixture between the prepared ramekins, filling each just about half full. Drop a teaspoon of filling into the centre of each and do your best to tuck it in and avoid it spreading too close to the edges. Use the remaining sponge mixture to cover the filling, then place the ramekins in the oven and cook for 10 minutes.

Leave the cakes to cool for 2 minutes, then carefully run a knife around the inside of each ramekin. Lay a small plate over the top of each one and then tip the ramekin upside down to release the cake onto the plate. Serve instantly, topped with any remaining filling mixture.

If you can't get hold of cacao butter or cacao powder, use 60g of a bar of raw or dark chocolate instead.

Serve with Chocolate Dipping Sauce (page 240), whipped or runny Coconut Cream (page 239) or Almond & Date Salted Caramel (page 240).

Sweet Potato Ice Cream & Choc-ices

Serves 4-6

Preheat the oven to 200°C / gas mark 6

I inherited an ice cream addiction from my grandma Don Don. My childhood dinner times ended with Mini Milks, Vienetta or Mars Bar ice creams as often as we could persuade our mum (or more likely, our dad) to buy them for us. This ice cream (or 'nice cream' as dairy- and sugar-free ice creams are increasingly known) is naturally sweetened by sweet potato. Make a large tub or spoon it into ice cream moulds (or a loaf tin to cut into triangles) to form choc-ices and coat them with Dark or White Chocolate (page 194) to coat them. They take me back to long-ago summers, choc-ices melting and half tasting of their flimsy paper wrapping ...

1 large sweet potato (approx. 300g)
200g cashews, soaked
1 × 400ml can coconut milk
1 tsp ground cinnamon
2 tsp vanilla powder
1 tbsp coconut oil
8 Medjool dates

2 tbsp natural syrup, optional
1 quantity Dark Chocolate (page 194)

Elevate it: 1 tbsp maca powder, 1 tsp bee pollen, 1 tbsp tocotrienols, 5 tbsp cacao powder (for a chocolate version), a handful of cookie dough pieces (page 191)

Prick the sweet potato with a fork or knife and then bake for 50–60 minutes, until soft and beginning to caramelise. Scrape the flesh (not exceeding 300g) into a blender, add the remaining ingredients apart from the chocolate, and blend on a high speed for 2–4 minutes, until smooth.

For a tub of ice cream, pour the mixture into a dish or freezerproof container, cover with clingfilm and place in the freezer to set.

For choc ices, pour the mixture into rectangular moulds or ice-lolly moulds and place in the freezer for 2–4 hours to set. When fully frozen, remove them from the freezer and carefully release them from their moulds. Place them on a cooling rack and coat in the liquid Dar Chocolate or shop-bought raw or dark chocolate. I coat them twice for extra crunch. Return to the freezer after each coat to allow the chocolate to harden.

Store both the tub and the choc ices in the freezer and remove 5 minutes before serving to allow them to thaw slightly.

If your ice cream sets too icy, carefully break it into smaller pieces using a knife and place in a food processor. Blend on the highest speed for 2–3 minutes, until smooth and thick, and serve as a soft-scoop ice cream. Alternatively, you can freeze the ice cream in muffin tin moulds and blitz them in the food processor before serving.

Serve with Chocolate Dipping Sauce (page 240), Almond & Date Salted Caramel (page 240), Coconut Cream (page 239), natural botanical cordials (page 322) or nut butter.

Top with Qnola or Freezer Granola (page 82), a handful of Dark Chocolate chunks (page 194), hemp seeds or chopped nuts and seeds. For the choc-ices, dip the ends in crushed nuts, Qnola or cacao nibs to decorate.

Roasted Grape Crumble

Serves 6–8

Preheat the oven to 200°C /gas mark 6

This dessert is for Eva, who somehow doesn't like grapes but loves this crumble. I made this for a winter equinox party that we hosted together and every time I make it I remember that dreamy night. We huddled into the studio, where I was then operating my business, and my good friend Poppy guided us through a beautiful meditation. We spent the evening washing this life-affirming crumble down with a few rounds of reishi root tea. Serve with cashew custard (page 241).

For the fruit layer
500g red grapes (or cherries)
2 oranges
80g Medjool dates, stoned and chopped
1 tsp ground ginger
1 tsp vanilla powder
juice of ½ lemon
40ml water
1 tbsp milled chia seeds or milled flaxseeds

For the topping
60g walnuts
20g desiccated coconut
80g buckwheat flour
100g ground almonds
5 tbsp coconut sugar or natural syrup
generous pinch of sea salt
1 tsp ground cinnamon
¼ tsp ground cardamom
50g flaked almonds or other chopped nuts
2 tbsp cacao powder (optional)
4 tbsp coconut oil at room temperature

Elevate it: 1 tsp acai powder, ½ tsp beetroot powder, 40ml coconut milk (instead of the water), 2 tbsp raw cacao powder, a handful of dark chocolate chunks (page 194)

Arrange the grapes, oranges and dates, if using, in an ovenproof dish. Add the ginger and vanilla and drizzle with the lemon juice and water. Pierce and roughly mash the grapes with a fork, then place the fruits in the oven and cook for 40 minutes. Stir occasionally to ensure the fruits cook evenly. Remove from the oven (leave the oven on) and strain the juices into a jug. Store the juice in the fridge – it makes a delicious sauce to serve with the crumble and/or other desserts.

Add the chia seeds or flaxseeds to the fruit mixture, along with any other elevational extras. (Adding cacao will make for a 'black forest' kind of vibe. Stir to combine then set aside until ready to use).

For the topping, blend the walnuts and dessicated coconut together in a food processor for 20–30 seconds until coarsely chopped and crumbly. Transfer to a bowl and add the buckwheat flour, ground almonds (or oats/buckwheat flakes), coconut palm sugar (or other natural sweetener), salt, cinnamon, cardamom, flaked almonds or chopped nuts and cacao powder (or dark chocolate chunks, if using). Stir, then add the coconut oil, breaking it up into small pieces and rubbing it into the dry ingredients with your hands. Massage until the mixture resembles dough-like breadcrumbs.

Arrange the crumble layer on top of the fruit, evenly spreading the mixture to completely cover the surface. Press down gently with the back of a spoon or a spatula to make the crumble compact, as this will encourage it to bind and crisp up in the oven. Return the crumble to the oven and cook for a further 30 minutes, until the topping turns a golden brown and the fruit layer is bubbling underneath. Serve with Cashew Custard (page 241).

Mango & Lemon Posset

Serves 2

A nutritional upgrade of the lemon posset, this recipe turns to nuts and natural fruits to form its vibrant flavours. You can make it in the time it takes to make a smoothie, so if you have guests arriving and are still stuck for dessert inspiration, this is your girl.

150g mango flesh, plus a few slices to serve
1 tsp vanilla powder
60ml coconut water or plant-based milk
160g cashews, soaked (or macadamia nuts)
40g coconut oil, melted
juice of 2 lemons (add the zest, if desired,
  or reserve to decorate)

2 Medjool dates
1 tsp natural sweetener
sprinkling of bee pollen, to decorate

Elevate it: 5g chopped lemon grass, 1 probiotic capsule or 1 tsp liquid probiotics, 1 tbsp tocotrienols, 20g young Thai coconut flesh

Put all the ingredients in a high-speed blender and blend for 2–3 minutes, until completely smooth. Add any elevational extras of your choice, then blend again to combine.

Pour into individual pots or one large serving bowl and refrigerate 2 hours, or until set. Decorate with a sprinkling of bee pollen, mango slices and lemon zest, if using.

Serve with fresh or preserved lemon wedges, seasonal fruits, Botanical Granola (page 70) or Cacao & Hemp Seed Freezer Granola (page 82), Mango Chutney (page 310) or other toppings of your choice.

Fantasy Ganache Cake with Hazelnut Frosting

Makes 1 cake

I made this cake as a gift for my eldest sister, Jules, on her first birthday as a vegan. As one of her guests took his first bite of the cake, his exact words were, 'Sweet Jesus... this cake'. There are no other words to describe it, so instead of typing, I'll let you see for yourself!

For the cake
60g hazelnuts (or cashews)
50g flaked or whole almonds
50g ground almonds
80g cacao nibs
½ tsp sea salt or tamari
1 tbsp vanilla powder
45g raw cacao powder
10g maca powder
10 Medjool dates, halved and stoned
50g coconut milk powder (or 4 tbsp melted creamed coconut or coconut butter)
8 tbsp natural syrup
2 tbsp almond butter
2 tbsp coconut sugar
2 tbsp melted coconut oil
chopped nuts or seeds or cacao nibs or chocolate chunks, to decorate

For the frosting
1 tbsp melted coconut oil
3 tbsp tinned coconut milk (solid part only)
3 tbsp tinned coconut milk (liquid part)
2 tbsp almond butter
4 tbsp coconut milk powder (or 4 tbsp melted creamed coconut or coconut butter)
pinch of sea salt
1 tsp vanilla powder
2 tbsp natural syrup
120g hazelnuts

Elevate it: 1 tsp reishi powder, 1 tsp cordyceps powder, 1 tsp mucuna pruriens powder, 2 tbsp tocotrienols

First, make the cake. Put the hazelnuts, almonds and cacao nibs in a food processor and blend on a high speed for 2 minutes, until they form a fine flour-like consistency. Add the salt or tamari, vanilla, cacao powder, maca and any elevational extras and blend for a further minute to combine.

In a separate bowl, cover the dates with boiling water. Leave to soak for 1–2 minutes.

Add the coconut milk powder, natural syrup, almond butter, coconut oil and coconut sugar to the food processor and blend for a minute. Drain the dates, squeezing them to release as much of the liquid as possible, then add them to the food processor and blend for a further 2 minutes, until the mixture becomes smooth and begins to form a doughy ball.

Press the dough into a standard round cake tin (preferably with a removable base) or smaller cake moulds, making sure it is even and compact. Place in the freezer to set whilst you prepare the frosting.

To make the frosting, place the coconut oil, coconut milk, almond butter, coconut milk powder, salt, vanilla and natural syrup in a blender and blend

Evening Time

for 1–2 minutes. Add the hazelnuts and then blend on the highest speed for a further 1–2 minutes, until smooth, thick and creamy.

Remove the cake from the freezer and pour the frosting over the top, smoothing it out with a spoon. Decorate with chopped nuts or seeds, cacao nibs or dark chocolate chunks (page 194) or other toppings of choice. Return to the freezer to set for at least 30 minutes before enjoying.

Store in the freezer and remove 5 minutes before serving to allow the cake to soften slightly. Run a sharp knife under hot water to slice into neat pieces.

If you're not making this cake for a special occasion, cut it into small portions or use small moulds to create lots of small cheesecakes to keep in the freezer.

Pistachio & Courgette Cake with Avocado & Lime Frosting

Makes 1 cake

Preheat the oven to 140°C / gas mark 1

Last year, I made my own birthday cake. It sounds sad, but I didn't have to make breakfast, so it's okay. I wanted something a little different to (and a little healthier than) the usual vanilla or chocolate sponge, and what transpired was this plant-powered masterpiece, containing more greens than a green juice! You may have some leftover frosting, so you could halve the cake horizontally and add a layer of filling or serve extra on the side.

For the cake
100g pistachios, plus an extra handful, to decorate
50g ground almonds
150g buckwheat flour
50g coconut oil, softened, plus extra for greasing
100g coconut sugar
3 eggs
juice of 1 lime
50g coconut yogurt or 50g tinned coconut milk (solid part only)
1 tsp vanilla extract
200g courgette, grated
zest of 3 limes
1½ tsp bicarbonate of soda
2 tsp baking powder

For the frosting
flesh of 1 large avocado (approx. 220g)
150g coconut yogurt (or tinned coconut milk – solid part only, or coconut cream)
60g natural syrup
50g coconut oil, softened
zest of 1 lime
juice of 2 limes

Spread the pistachios out on to a baking tray and roast for 10 minutes, until golden brown, then remove from the oven and leave to cool. Increase the temperature of the oven to 180°C/gas mark 4. Grease a 20cm cake tin with a little coconut oil, then line with a sheet of baking paper.

Place the roasted pistachios in a high-powered food processor and blend into a fine flour. Add the ground almonds and buckwheat flour and pulse for 30 seconds, until combined. Add the oil, sugar, eggs, lime juice, coconut yogurt (or coconut milk) and vanilla and blend for a further minute.

Transfer the mixture to a bowl and fold in the grated courgette, lime zest, bicarbonate of soda and baking powder and stir to combine. Scrape the mixture into the prepared cake tin, smoothing the top with the back of a spoon or spatula, and bake for 40–45 minutes. Test to see if the cake is cooked by inserting a skewer into the centre – if it comes out clean, remove the cake from the oven. If the skewer brings a little cake mixture with it, continue to cook for a further 5–10 minutes, testing again before removing from the oven and setting aside to cool.

Whilst the cake is cooling, prepare the frosting. Put the avocado, coconut yogurt, natural syrup, coconut oil, lime juice and lime zest in a food processor.

Evening Time

Blend on a high speed for 2 minutes, until smooth. Scrape down the sides of the bowl of the food processor if needed. Refrigerate for 15–20 minutes.

Once the cake is completely cool, spread the avocado lime frosting on top of the cake and decorate with the additional crushed pistachio nuts. Serve immediately or store in the fridge or at room temperature for 4–5 days.

Herbal Hair Rinse

Lasts about 4–5 rinses

Equipment: sterilised jar (250-300ml)

This simple water-based hair treatment uses the nourishing and cleansing power of fresh herbs to heal and hone dry or damaged hair. Whilst honey-based hair masks have many benefits, this is a less messy alternative that I find much more user-friendly.

20g fresh rosemary, nettle, mint or coriander – or a mixture of each
250ml filtered water
5 drops of your chosen essential oil (page 303)
1 tsp coconut oil, argan oil or olive oil

20ml apple cider vinegar

Elevate it: 1 tbsp bentonite or green clay or ½ tsp arrowroot or baking soda (for oily hair)

Put the herbs and water in a small saucepan and bring to the boil over a medium–high heat. Boil for 5 minutes, then remove from the heat and strain into a jug. Add the oils, apple cider vinegar and any elevational extras, if using, and stir to combine. Transfer to a sterilised jar or container with a lid.

Allow the mixture to cool to body or room temperature before using, or place in the fridge to cool fully.

To use, apply to dry hair, before showering. Leave the solution to soak in for 5–10 minutes and then rinse off with hot water.

You could also use this as a natural toner for your face, but refrain from adding essential oils or reduce the amount by half, as the strength can sometimes irritate certain skin types.

Cleansing Atmosphere Spray

Lasts about 30 uses

Equipment: 1 × 50ml bottle with a spray-top lid

Whether you've been at home or out all day, by the evening it's important to refresh the scent of your space in order to find comfort. If the air is heavy or the vibe is low, this spray will both freshen and cleanse the atmosphere, lifting stagnant energy whilst simultaneously working its aromatherapy charms on you through inhalation. You can choose calming essential oils to wind down after work, awakening ones if you've got a lot to do, sensual ones to set the mood or purely pleasant-smelling ones if you're entertaining guests.

20 drops of jasmine essential oil
4 drops of eucalyptus essential oil
4 drops of lavender essential oil
10 drops of amber essential oil
2 drops of cinnamon essential oil
4 drops of lemon or orange essential oil

4 drops of spearmint or peppermint essential oil
5 drops of frankincense essential
10 drops of rose geranium essential oil
30ml filtered water

Put all the ingredients into a bottle, screw the lid tight and shake well to combine.

To use, spray 6–8 times around one room and allow to diffuse. Use throughout the day, as and when needed. Shake well before use. You can also apply to wrists, arms, legs, feet and neck.

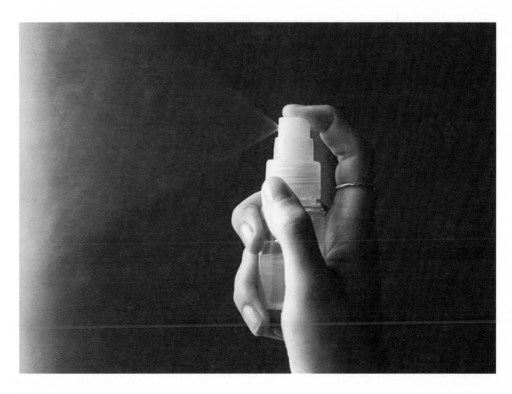

The Sun Worshipper's Cooling After-sun Remedy

Lasts about 10 uses

Equipment: airtight container

The sun drives all life and energy on Earth, its natural phases dictating how we live. It nourishes the body, mind and soul and, rich in vitamin D, has major influences on mental and physical health. If you're a sun baby like me, the sun is your calling and you'll likely spend as much time in the sun as you possibly can. However, basking in it too long has its consequences and can increase the risk of skin disease, skin cancer and premature ageing. In the short term, too much sun exposure can leave you burnt and basted, and it's times like these that you'll want this remedy close by.

10g coconut oil, softened (not melted)
40g pure aloe vera gel, scraped from the plant or shop-bought

5 drops of rose geranium essential oil
2 drops of lavender essential oil
2 drops of peppermint essential oil

Put all the ingredients in a bowl and, using a small whisk, whip together until light, white and creamy. Store in an airtight container in the fridge until required.

To use, apply to burnt areas of skin as you would a lotion, rubbing the treatment in to the skin for optimal absorption. Apply 2–3 times daily.

Natural Bug Repellent

Lasts about 20 uses

Equipment: 1 × 80ml cosmetics bottle with a spray-top lid

This aromatherapy bug repellent smells amazing and can be worn as a fragrance oil or used as an atmosphere spray whether you're being bothered by bugs or not. Whilst manufactured products are supposed to be potent, many of them are also toxic, and not only for bugs but for humans too. The skin is incredibly absorbent so the chemicals used to repel bugs could end up inside your body, repelling your cells, and causing disorder.

20 drops rose geranium essential oil
20 drops citronella essential oil
10 drops orange essential oil

6 drops rosemary essential oil
10 drops jasmine essential oil
50ml filtered water

Put all the ingredients in a bottle, apply the lid and shake well to combine.

To use, shake well and apply to wrists, arms, legs, feet and neck.

Multi-Functional Cleaning Solution

Lasts about 30 uses

Equipment: spray-top bottle (250–300ml)

This natural cleaning solution puts up a tough fight against dirt, germs, mould and lingering bacteria, without depending on any harsh or toxic ingredients. The essential oils used contain a range of antibacterial, antiviral, antifungal and antimicrobial properties, serving as natural detergents that are both safe and effective. I use this to wipe down my windows, attack mould and clean the kitchen floor. To use as polish, add a little olive oil or coconut oil, and a dash of lemon juice.

200ml filtered water
2 tbsp apple cider vinegar
10 drops of your chosen essential oils (I like
　　spearmint, rosemary, citronella, eucalyptus,
　　lavender, lemon, bergamot and cedarwood)

Elevate it: Add 1 tbsp lemon juice to treat mould, add 60g baking soda to clean grease, add 2 tbsp salt to treat carpet stains

Put all the ingredients in a small bowl and whisk to combine. Pour into a jar or airtight container and store in the fridge.

To use, dip a sponge or cloth into the solution and apply to target areas. Alternatively, if using spray bottles, spray directly onto surfaces and rub with a sponge or cloth. Once you've worked on an area, rinse with a little water to remove any residual dirt.

Night Time

Night Time

This chapter focuses on helping you ease out of each day, taking time to acknowledge the things you are grateful for, and to let go of anything that no longer serves you, either from the day or on a more general level. As we transition out of the day and begin to slowly wind down and prepare for sleep, so silencing the mind and freeing it of thoughts about the past and the future should be a crucial practice. Many of us will operate right up until lights out, surrounded by stimulants such as artificial light, sound pollution or transmissions from our screens, and yet we expect to fall asleep, effortlessly and instantly, as soon as we shut our laptops and put down our smartphones. Well, that just ain't gonna happen.

This chapter encourages you to start introducing more wholesome and sleep-supporting rituals into your evening routine. The practices require little effort, as the idea is to slow down the body and enhance its internal operation rather than its physical output. Meditative practices, calming breathing techniques and aromatherapy will help to calm the body and quiet the mind, whilst more active practices such as deep stretches and restorative yin-style yoga poses will help to release both physical and mental tension. Some evenings you might simply think or write about things you are grateful for, or find meditation in taking a moonlit walk. On others, say when there is a new or full moon, you might invite friends over to set intentions or simply gaze up at the night sky and take it all in, feeling grounded by the fact there is so much more out there beyond our own (somewhat insignificant) daily stresses and struggles.

The recipes in this chapter have been devised to reduce stress, encourage sleep and aid digestion; whilst energising and supporting our bodies' overnight processes, which operate whilst we sleep. In order to give your digestive system a chance to rest, and to free up energy required around the body for repair, recovery and restoration, solid food is not included here. Heavy meals before bed and stimulants such as sugar, caffeine and alcohol can impede your body's ability to sleep, but there are many powerful, natural ingredients that can be prepared and enjoyed in liquid form. The recipes you'll find here work to cleanse the system and detoxify the body whilst also slowing down the physiological processes that have been active throughout the day.

Mind

Body Scan

Body scanning is an easy mindfulness exercise to relax the body, calm the mind and shift attention away from overpowering thoughts. It involves spot relaxing each part of the body by focusing on it for a few moments. Practising this meditation in the evening is ideal as it is best performed lying down. It will encourage the body and mind to fully transition from 'doing' to 'being'.

1. Lie on your back on a comfortable surface, with your legs slightly apart and your arms by your sides. If you are not in bed, place a blanket over your body if you tend to get cold easily.

2. Bring your attention to focus on the breath and notice any thoughts or feelings that arise. When they do, try to turn your attention back to the breath, noticing any patterns in it and how it feels moving through the body.

3. Focus your attention on your right toes. Notice any sensations and become aware of the formation and feeling of your toes. Then gradually move your attention up the body, through the right foot, ankle, lower leg, upper leg, right side of the pelvic area, right side of the lower torso, right side of the upper torso, right side of the chest and collarbone, right shoulder, upper arm, lower arm, hand, fingers and then the neck, face, back of the head, back of the neck and back of the shoulders. Then follow the body back down the left side of the body, focusing on the same points in reverse order, starting with the back of the left shoulder, and finishing with the toes.

4. Settle here and notice how your body feels, both part by part and as a whole, and notice how your mind now feels.

* *You can practise this working up the body parts on both sides of the body at the same time, or working up the left and then up the right from the toes.*

Mudras

These are a few of my favourites to use at night time to encourage deep relaxation, digestion, elimination of toxins and sound sleep. Hold each mudra for 3–15 minutes – the longer you hold it the more effective the practice.

Apana Mudra is known for detoxifying the body by stimulating digestion and elimination.

1. Come to a comfortable seated position, either on the floor with your legs crossed, however is comfortable, or on a chair with your feet flat on the floor.

2. Lengthen your spine and extend the back of your neck up, so your head is facing forwards, ensuring your neck is soft, not strained. Decide whether to practise with your eyes open or closed.

3. Place the backs of your hands on your knees and bring the tips of the middle and ring fingers to touch the tip of the thumb. The index finger and little finger should remain outstretched. Settle here for a few minutes or for as long as feels comfortable.

Shakti Mudra is known to induce sound sleep and deep relaxation.

1. Follow steps 1–2 of Apana Mudra, and come to rest your hands on your knees, palms facing up.

2. Bring both hands in front of you and join the little fingers and the ring fingers of each hand so they are touching at the tips, almost in an arch shape. Then fold the index and middle fingers loosely over the thumbs, bending the thumbs under the fingers and in towards the palms. Let the front parts of the index and middle fingers rest on each other. Settle here for a few minutes or for as long as feels comfortable.

Ksepana Mudra helps to remove negativity by encouraging the mind to let go of all that is not needed.

1. Follow steps 1–2 of Apana Mudra, and come to rest your hands on your knees, palms facing up.

2. Bring your hands in front of you and place your index fingers against each other, pointing up. Interlace the other fingers of each hand, including the thumb.

3. Now, begin to point your hands, led by the index fingers, towards the ground and slightly in front of you. You can come to lie down here, gradually, and point the index fingers towards your feet. Settle here for a few minutes or for as long as feels comfortable and then return to a seated position.

Gratitude & journaling

As explored in the Morntime section (page 36), journaling is a powerful way to release any negative thoughts and feelings. The end of the day is the ideal time to write down any or all of your thoughts or feelings about certain things that may have happened during the day. Rather than holding onto negative thoughts or feelings internally, write them down to let them out and let them go. It may sounds futile, but this can be a really cleansing process, and doing this before bed can help remove the mind of active thoughts, allowing for swifter and sounder sleep.

Setting intentions & manifesting

Setting intentions at night is a wonderful way to prepare for the following day, or the future in general. You might have intentions you want to manifest or achieve instantly, or you might simply want to plant seeds of ideas and desires you have for the future, letting them out and honoring them with faith that they will come to fruition as and when they are meant to. See page 34 for instructions and examples.

*   *I like setting intentions in line with the new moon – a powerful time at the beginning of a new cycle that carries hope, opportunity and fresh energy. See page 290.*

Mantras

Mantras are not specifically time-sensitive and can be used at any time during the day, but I wanted to include them as a night time practice as they are a nice way to end the day, helping to quiet the mind and promote better quality sleep. See pages 325–326 to discover more about mantras and how to find one that resonates with you.

Breath

Breath counting

Counting the breath is a powerful pranayama technique that can be practised in various ways, each with different benefits and outcomes. This exercise involves a breathing pattern of 4:7:8 and is considered a natural tranquiliser, helping to induce sleep, support digestion and reduce stress.

1. Sit comfortably with a straight back, either on the floor with crossed legs, or on a chair with your feet flat on the floor. Decide whether you want to practise with your eyes open or closed.

2. Bring the tip of your tongue to the space behind your front teeth and rest it there.

3. Breath naturally for a few moments and then exhale completely through your mouth, keeping the tongue tucked up behind your teeth, which will make a sort of 'whoosh' sound.

4. Close your mouth as you inhale quietly through the nose. As you do so, count to four. At the top of your inhale, hold your breath for seven counts.

5. Exhale fully through the mouth in the same way as before, for eight breaths. This is one cycle. Repeat the cycle 3 or 4 times.

Left-nostril breath

Left-nostril breathing is an easy technique used to activate the para-sympathetic nervous system. In kundalini teachings, the body has two energy channels, one on each side of the body. The energy on the left (ida) is calming, cooling and reflective, whilst the energy on the right (pingala) is fiery, awakening and active. Each is associated with our sympathetic nervous system (responsible for the fight or flight system and handling stress) and the parasympathetic nervous system (responsible for slowing the body down and running its daily functions almost passively). By shutting off the right nostril, we stimulate the more calming, cooling and slow side of the body and mind, switching off the more alert side, which can inhibit sleep.

1. Sit comfortably with a straight back, either with crossed legs or on a chair. Decide whether you want to practise with your eyes open or closed.

2. Breathe naturally for a few moments and then gently place your right thumb on your right nostril, closing the airway and obstructing the breath.

3. Inhale fully through your left nostril and exhale through the left too, keeping the right closed off.

4. Stay focused on your breath and continue breathing in this pattern for a few moments, breathing fully but softly, without strain, and relaxing your body into each exhale.

* If your mind wanders or thoughts intrude, you can add counts to each inhale and exhale, in the pattern 1:1, inhaling for two and exhaling for two. If you want to add breath retention, use the pattern 1:1:1, inhaling for two, holding the breath for two and exhaling for two.

Humming Bee Breath (Brahmari)

Brahmari is the Sanskrit word for 'bee' and this breathing exercise is based on the steady, monotonous and continuous act of humming, which mimics the sound of a bee buzzing. This practice is incredibly soothing and calming, working on a deep energetic level with the vibrations of the body, and it can help encourage sleep if you struggle to drift off.

1. Sit comfortably with a straight back, either on the floor with crossed legs or on a chair with your feet flat on the floor. Decide whether you want to practise with your eyes open or closed.

2. Breathe naturally for a few moments and then take a long inhalation through your nose. As you exhale, create a humming sound from the back of the throat.

3. Continue to breathe, ensuring the inhalation and exhalation are steady and slow, and try to keep the tone of the hum the same throughout the practice.

4. After a few rounds, on your next exhale, close off both ears (you can use your index fingers, which will intensify the practice). Practise for a few minutes, until you begin to feel a calmer shift in your body and mind.

Movement

Self-Massage Treatments

Traditional therapies, including massage, acupressure and reflexology, work on the principle that applying pressure to certain points of the body produces a neurological response in other parts and can relieve pain and induce relaxation. Self-massage is also an effective tool to learn to achieve better sleep. Whilst training in shiatsu I learnt that there are sleep pressure points all over the body, particularly in the hands, wrists, head, ears and feet.

Face

We hold tension and show emotion in our faces, and even if we try to cover our feelings by 'putting on a brave face' it is often ineffective. A face massage may sound indulgent but can be deeply relaxing. It can help soothe headaches, tired eyes, sinus congestion and general muscle fatigue and can help to prevent the signs of ageing by improving muscle tone and circulation.

1. Begin with the top of the head, working around the hairline. Bring your fingers together and using the soft pads of two or three fingertips, begin to stroke outwards from the centre of the forehead to the temples. Rest at the temples for a few breaths if you feel particularly tight or irritated there.

2. Work down the eyebrows in the same way and then, using the index and middle fingertips of one or both hands, hold some pressure on the point between the eyebrows (the so-called third eye). Take away one hand, keeping the other as it is, then use the index finger and the thumb to smooth the eyebrows from the centre out to the temples, allowing the finger and thumb to go in different directions away from one another.

3. Pinch the top of the bridge of the nose with the index finger, middle finger and thumb of one hand.

4. Bring the fingertips to just below the eyes, and, using both hands, run your fingers along the line of the eye sockets a few times and then apply a still and gentle pressure at the corner of the eyes.

5. Now, move further down the face to the cheeks. Use circular motions with the fingertips to massage the cheeks, starting at the nose and working out towards the ears. Hold some pressure just beneath the eyes on the cheekbones with index and middle finger of both hands. Then, do the same at the point where the cheekbone meets the middle of the ears. Work here and also slightly above and below the cheekbone if it feels good.

6. Come to the mouth and jaw area next, massaging the space below the nose and above the top lips. Use circular motions with the index and middle fingers and work along the upper lip out across the cheeks. Repeat this below the bottom lip too, working along the line of the jaw to just under the ears. Hold extra pressure at the edge of the jaw where you feel the hinge of the upper and lower gums. Then, use the thumbs to get into the soft area beneath the chin. Work again along the line of the jaw to the ears. Spend a moment focusing on the ears too, pulling and massaging the lobes, the outer edges and the space behind them that joins the skull.

7. Bring the practice to a close by using the full palms of your hands to smooth and massage the entire face, rubbing gently up and down or in circular motions, focusing extra pressure wherever you notice more severe tension.

Feet

We demand a lot from our feet to support us, yet we rarely consider taking special care of them. The following massage technique helps to invigorate the flow of energy and relieve tension within the feet. Through working on the major muscles and pressure points in the feet we can aid many other organs and ailments in the body, including aches, digestion and inflammation.

Massaging the pressure point just beneath the ball of the big toe, in line with the space between the big toe and the second toe, is particularly calming as this point is associated with the kidney meridian.

1. Sitting on a chair or on the floor, use both hands to massage the arch of your right foot. Work from the ankle and heel towards the toes, using your thumbs to work the top of the foot and your fingers to work the sole. Start with the thumbs at the centre of the foot and massage towards the sides of the foot. Then use your fingers to work on the sole, keeping the thumbs still, and again massage from the centre out towards the side.

2. Roll your foot over onto its outer edge, and then work in circular motions from the body of the big toe to the base where it meets the ball of the foot (underside). Then, use both index fingers to massage the big toe (on top). Keep your fingers straight and bring one either side of the big toe. Roll and rub the toe between your fingers for a few moments.

3. Use your fingertips to massage gently into the ball of the foot, focusing on the pads of each toe. Then firmly hold each toe in turn, with the thumb on top and the index and middle fingers beneath it, and gently rotate and move it from left to right a few times. Gently tug on each toe, pulling it away from you, and allow your fingers to slip off the end of the toe, applying consistent pressure until the contact is broken.

4. Next, use both thumbs to 'thumb' the sole of the foot, from the toes to the heel.

5. At the ankle, use the thumb and index and middle fingers to squeeze and massage the back and sides of the ankle and the heel, then use all of your fingertips to gently massage around the sides and the top of the ankle joint. To release, lift the foot slightly and shake it gently using both hands to support it.

6. Finish by tapping the sole of the foot with your knuckles. Clench your fist and gently hit along the underside if the foot, working from the heel to the toes. You can also apply a still pressure with your fist to the foot (such as the base of the big toe, beneath its 'knuckle' where the foot begins to bridge and wherever else feels good) using a twisting motion to work really deeply into each area.

7. Repeat on the left foot and bring the practice to a close by gently shaking both the feet together, either from sitting or standing.

Yoga poses

Yoga in the evening is an ideal way to stretch out and release any tension you have collected and carried throughout the day. Whilst many yoga classes are energising and challenging, night time, just before bed, is the best time for a deeper practice. Yin and restorative yoga are slow-paced practices that involve gentle movements and the holding postures for longer periods of time than usual. These styles of yoga centre the breath and are deeply relaxing, allowing time for reflection and for tension and negativity to be released.

The following postures are deep, and if you are new to yoga, I would suggest practising with a teacher or in a guided group class before trying these unassisted. Try to hold these postures for a minimum of 45 seconds, provided you are not in pain. Some postures may feel uncomfortable, but working with your pain threshold is a powerful part of growing, expanding and coping with things in other areas of your life.

Lizard Pose (Utthan Pristhasana) is an intense opener for the hips. As well as increasing flexibility and stretching the hamstrings, buttocks and hips, it can also indirectly boost your metabolism and reduce anxiety.

1. Start in Downward Dog (page 54), and from here, step your right foot in between your hands, into a low lunge. Walk your right foot to the outside of your right hand.

2. Begin to release the hips, lowering them towards the ground (but not completely onto the ground) with ease and without force. Walk your hands forwards, and if it is possible for you, come down onto your forearms. Otherwise, stay upright on your hands.

3. Lengthen the spine and neck, and keep the crown of the head facing forwards. Open the chest and draw the shoulder blades down the back towards one another.

4. Keep your right knee drawing in towards your body, and your left leg active and straight, with the knee hovering above the ground. (For a more restorative option, release the left knee, letting it rest on the ground, but maintain the length in the left leg).

5. Breathe deeply and fully in this pose, and with each exhale, go deeper into the right hip and feeling a stretch in the left hip. Settle here for about 1 minute (adjust to suit you).

6. To explore even further, begin to flex the right foot and roll over the outer edge of it, letting the right knee fall gently outwards towards the right.

7. Come out of the pose by bringing the right knee back into the midline and making your way gently back up onto your hands. Return to Downward Dog for a few breaths and repeat on the left side.

Pigeon Pose (Eka Pada Rajakapotasana) is an intense posture and may be difficult and uncomfortable for beginners. It works at opening the hips and calming the mind. It is a natural reaction for us to store stress, fear and anxiety in the hips, which creates tension and tightness and imbalance in the flow of energy. By opening the hips, this posture helps to release negative energy and emotions.

1. Come to the ground and make your way to all fours, with your hips above your knees and your shoulders directly above your wrists.

2. Bring your right knee forwards and place it gently behind your right wrist. Place your ankle

somewhere in front of your left hip, ideally aiming for your shin to be horizontal to your body (or parallel to the front of your mat if using one).

3. Slide your left leg back slowly, straightening the knee and pointing the toes so the front of the foot is flat against the ground, heel pointing up. Ensure that your left leg is in line with the left side of your body, not splaying outwards or inwards, and the hips are square to the ground.

4. Inhale here, opening the chest towards the sky, using your fingertips or the palms of your hands for support. Relax the shoulders down the back and breathe here for a few moments.

5. This may be enough for you, but if you want to go deeper, intensify the stretch by gently walking your hands forward to lower your upper body over your right leg to the ground. Rest on your forearms, or fold completely over the leg, placing your hands under your forehead or stretching the arms out above your head and resting your forehead on the ground, if this is comfortable. You might like to rest your head on your hands and gently rock your head from side to side, massaging the forehead and aligning the spine. Breathe deeply and settle here for about 1 minute (adjust to suit you).

6. On an exhale, replace your hands to the ground and push back on your left leg to release the right knee. Lift the hips and come back to all fours for a few breaths and then repeat on the left side.

Reclining Goddess Pose (Supta Baddha Konasana) is another calming posture to open and release tension in the hips. It is also thought to stimulate circulation and help to reduce stress and anxiety. It is a good idea to have a blanket, bolsters or cushions to hand for this pose.

1. Sit on the floor with your knees out to each side and the soles of your feet together. Bring the heels of your feet in towards your pelvis and relax the knees, dropping them towards the ground. This pose is known as Baddha Konasana.

2. From here, as you exhale, lower your back towards the ground, leaning on your hands for support if needed. Bring your back all the way down to the floor, and use a blanket or bolster, if you have one, either to support your head and neck or to place under the upper back and shoulders to open across the chest more.

3. Ensure your feet are still together and as close to the pelvic area as possible. Use your hands to direct the thighs away from the midline of the body, and to ensure the knees are relaxed. Don't put pressure on the knees to force them to the ground, but instead keep them light, and let them release closer to the ground naturally with the breath.

4. Settle in this posture for a few minutes if you are comfortable (try starting with 2–5 minutes and extending this as your practice develops). If your knees are straining and there is tension in the lower back or groin area, place blankets, cushions or blocks under each knee for support. To come out of the posture, use your hands to bring your knees together and feet flat on the floor. Roll gently to one side then use your hands to unfold and come to a seated position.

Seated Forward Bend (Paschimottanasana) is a great posture to calm a busy and distracted mind, and to help you unwind both physically and mentally. Again, a blanket or cushion is useful for additional support.

1. Sit on the floor with your legs extended in front of you, feet and knees together. Sit tall, lengthening through the neck and crown of the head and drawing the shoulders down the back and away from the ears. If you need extra support or to release the tension in your hips a little, elevate the seat by sitting on a blanket or small cushion.

2. Inhale fully and as you exhale, keeping a long spine, begin to fold forwards, guided by your open chest. Keep the chest reaching forwards and keep the spine straight, avoiding any rounding in the spine and ensuring the head is lifted and neutral and doesn't drop or hang loosly.

3. Hold onto your feet or shins with your hands, however feels comfortable without straining, bending the elbows and relaxing the arms. If possible, bring your forehead to rest on your knees, and if you can't quite reach that far, either keep the head extending towards the feet, or use a block in between your knees or some cushions on top of them, and rest your head comfortably there, releasing any tension in the neck.

4. To come out of the pose, slowly roll back up to a seated position, one vertebra at a time, allowing your head to lift up last.

Inversions

Happy Baby (Ananda Balasana) is a liberating pose that helps to relieve stress, calm the mind, release tension in the hips and realign the back and spine.

1. Lie on your back. Bend your knees into your chest, keeping the feet and knees wide. Bring your hands to the feet and hold the outer edges of the foot, or wrap your index and middle fingers (peace fingers) around your big toes.

2. Keep your ankles over your knees and the shins upright, soles of the feet facing the sky. Gently begin to pull down on the feet, bringing the knees closer to the armpits to deepen the posture. Lengthen the tailbone down towards the ground and draw your shoulders down your back, away from your ears.

3. Stay here and breathe deeply for a few full breaths, or gently rock from side to side to massage the back. You can experiment with extending the legs, either separately or together.

4. To come out of the pose, release your hands or fingers and bring the knees into the chest. Hug your arms around the knees and gently tug them towards you to release the back, and then gently let your feet find the ground, or release the legs fully to return to your starting position.

Leg-up-the-wall (Viparita Karani) is an inverted pose (page 53) that helps to physically rejuvenate tired or overworked legs and feet as well as the spine. It also helps to calm and balance the nervous system. It is a simple way to relax the body and can relieve lymphatic congestion within the body and also boost blood circulation, refreshing and rebalancing the system if you spend most of your day sitting or standing. This pose is known to reduce digestive issues, soothe headaches, improve respiratory ailments, relieve stress and depression and encourage sounder sleep, tapping into the 'rest and digest' nervous system.

1. Find a bare wall to work against and sit beside it with your feet on the floor in front of you and the left side of your body in contact with the wall.

2. As you exhale, slowly lie down on your back and pivot yourself, swivelling the hips, so that the backs of your legs are pressing against the wall and the soles of your feet are facing up. Ensure your buttocks are resting against the base of the wall. You may need to move a little to find your way into this position comfortably.

3. Let your arms rest open at your sides, with palms facing up. Close your eyes and hold for 5–10 minutes, or however long feels comfortable.

4. To release, slowly push yourself away from the wall and slide your legs down and away from it, to the right. Come back to a seated position and settle here, breathing naturally to readjust.

Do-In / Bodywork

I picked up this technique whilst studying shiatsu and it is an incredible way to instantly relax the body and mind. Studies have shown that it slows certain brain waves, and increases those associated with restful and consistent sleep. Rocking is one of the most effective ways to get a baby to sleep, so it makes sense that it is relaxing for adults. Many people find they drift off on long coach journeys or on a boat, and it is the same rhythmic rocking motion that instils that sense of calm and deep relaxation. This motion is incredibly accessible and is something we can either do to ourselves, or with a partner.

Rocking yourself

1. Lie on your front with your legs extended and arms alongside your body. Either place one side of your face on the ground with arms by your sides, or bring your arms up, elbows pointing out to the side, and rest your forehead on your hands.

2. Gently begin rocking from your pelvic area, using small, rhythmic movements from side to side. There is no right or wrong way to do this, just move however comes naturally to you and allow other parts of your body to move in rhythm with the rocking. In shiatsu, the central energy field of the body is known as the *hara* (located just below the navel) so moving from the pelvic or abdominal area will feel much more supportive, natural and controlled than if you began rocking from, say, the feet or the shoulders.

3. The intention is to release the spine, and to rock the body in smooth motions to get the energy flowing. The brain will consequently begin to slow, as you focus on the movements and the sensations, rather than on your thoughts. When thoughts do intrude, accept and acknowledge them and then let them go. Do this for however long feels comfortable. I would suggest 2–5 minutes, but even 30 seconds can help to instil calm and relaxation in the body.

* *You can also practise this in the Reclining Goddess pose (page 272). Simply find your way into the posture and begin rocking from side to side from the hips.*

* *Another way to practise this is lying on your back, with your legs straight and arms beside your body. Simply rock in the same way as outlined above, leading with the hips, working very gently and smoothly to find a satisfying and sustainable rhythm.*

* *You could combine this practice with body scanning (page 262), focusing on each part of the body as it rocks.*

Rocking with a partner

1. Ask a partner or friend to practise rocking with you. Follow step 1 above.

2. Ask your partner to gently place the palm of their hands on your back, with their right hand resting motionless on your sacrum (where the spine ends) and their left hand on your right shoulder. They should begin gently rocking you with their right hand, keeping it in one place on your sacrum. With their left hand, they can move the palm of their hand gently around your back, applying a little pressure, and being sure to avoid the spinal area.

Visualisation

You can also use a visualisation technique here to visualise a situation in which you would be rocking.

1. Sit or lie comfortably with your eyes closed. Imagine you are on a swing, on a small, stationary or slow boat, lying in a hammock or floating in the ocean, either unsupported or on an inflatable. Notice the rhythm of wherever you are and how your environment moves you and acknowledge any sounds, smells or other sensations around you. Settle here for a few minutes, until you feel relaxed, or perhaps until you fall asleep.

Hot Palming

This is something I've only occasionally been guided through in yoga practices, but when I am, I love it. Such a simple action is really soothing and relaxing for the eyes, especially after a long day. With so much 'screen time' these days, our eyes are not only very active but are also dazzled by the artificial light of our devices. Do this after a practice or simply before bed.

1. Sit or lie in a comfortable position, either on the bed, the floor or on a chair. Bring the palms of your hands together in front of you and begin to rub them together rapidly, creating friction and heat. Quickly cup your hands slightly and then gently place the heated palms over closed eyes. Breathe deeply and enjoy the heat spreading across your eyes, the darkness offering a welcome break from the light. Stay in this position for a few moments and then release the hands and gently blink your eyes open again, or head straight to sleep.

Brazil Nut, Almond & Coconut Water Moonmilk with Valerian

Serves 2–4

This restorative recipe contains valerian and chamomile, both of which have been used in remedies for centuries to induce relaxing sleep and to cure insomnia. Coconut water is high in electrolytes, which help to rehydrate the body, and magnesium, which supports muscle and nerve function and the immune system. Enjoy hot or cold, ideally at least 1 hour before you go to bed.

150g raw almonds (preferably soaked for a minimum of 6 hours)
20g Brazil nuts (preferably soaked for a minimum of 6 hours) or hemp seeds
200ml filtered water
pinch of Himalayan pink salt
500ml coconut water
1 tsp vanilla powder
½ –1 Medjool date

2 drops of valerian extract
200ml chamomile tea (from teabags or by steeping 1 tbsp dried chamomile flowers with 200ml boiling water)
1 tsp magnesium powder

Elevate it: ½ tsp ashwagandha powder, ½ tsp rhodiola powder, ½ tsp ground cardamom

Put the nuts and filtered water in a blender and blend on the highest speed for 3–4 minutes, until smooth. Strain through a nut-milk bag, jelly bag, cheesecloth or fine sieve and then return the liquid to the blender. Add all the remaining ingredients and blend on the highest speed for a further minute. For an iced drink, add a handful of ice cubes and blend on the highest speed for a further 30 seconds, until combined. For a hot drink, transfer to a small saucepan and heat through.

Banana, Cherry & Grapefruit Smoothie

Serves 1

On evenings when you're especially hungry, a smoothie is a great way to fill a gap whilst simultaneously flooding the body with vitamins and minerals that it can use to carry out autonomic functions whilst you sleep. Bananas are naturally high in magnesium and fruits such as cherries, grapefruit and watermelons contain other sleep-inducing ingredients, such as lycopene and selenium. Psyllium husk and chia seeds are extremely high in fibre and also play an important part in cleansing the system and regulating elimination of waste and toxins.

½ frozen banana
handful of almonds or Brazil nuts
handful of cherries, pitted
2 tbsp grapefruit juice
250ml filtered water or coconut water
1 tbsp chia seeds

¼ tsp psyllium husk
4–6 ice cubes

Elevate it: 20g chopped watermelon, 2 drops of valerian root extract

Put all the ingredients, apart from the ice, in a high-speed blender and blend until smooth. (If you prefer, soak your chia seeds and psyllium in 2 tablespoons water before blending.)

Add the ice and blend on the highest speed for a further 30 seconds, until combined. Serve instantly.

Sleep-easy Maca Malt

*Makes enough for
10 servings*

Cacao is known for enlivening the body and mind and I often take it in the morning. However, it is also one of the highest plant sources of magnesium and has the ability to reduce stress and anxiety and, subsequently, encourage sounder sleep. Maca encourages the natural production and regulation of melatonin – a hormone that controls your sleeping and waking cycles and your body's internal clock – and so can help if your melatonin levels are out of whack (common if you are stressed or using devices that emit too much light in the lead up to sleeping). Ideally, make this drink 1 hour before you go to bed and you'll be out like a light.

2 tsp cacao powder
10 tbsp coconut milk powder
2 tsp maca powder
2 tsp vanilla powder

pinch of Himalayan pink salt (optional)

Elevate it: pinch of magnesium power, pinch of ground cardamom or cinnamon

In a jar or airtight container, combine all the ingredients, along with any elevational extras. Stir or secure the lid and shake to combine. Store at room temperature until ready to use. To serve, mix 1–2 tablespoons of the malt powder with hot water or hot nut milk and enjoy.

After-dinner Spearmint Tonic

Makes 4 shots

This is a simple tonic to help cleanse the system after a long or heavy meal. It is especially useful if you've eaten later than usual as it helps the body digest efficiently. It's also a nice offering if you're entertaining guests, served as a palate cleanser between courses or as a ritual at the end of the evening.

½ tsp raw or manuka honey or other natural
    sweetener of your choice
4 drops of food-grade spearmint essential oil

5g fresh mint leaves
200ml sparkling water

Put the honey, essential oil and mint leaves in a jug and muddle with a wooden spoon or spatula to release the minty flavour.

Add the sparkling water and stir to combine, then strain and divide among 4 small glasses.

Hot Chamomile Milk

Serves 2

Whenever my sisters and I felt sick or low and needed soothing, my mum would make us a glass of hot milk and honey and it always came with an unbeatable mum-hug which would instantly ease whatever was ailing us. This drink is designed to achieve the same effect, with a few nutritional benefits. If you can't find dried chamomile flowers, use 2 chamomile teabags or 2 tablespoons of loose chamomile tea.

400ml almond milk
100ml filtered water
1 tbsp dried chamomile flowers
½ tsp vanilla powder
1 tsp raw or manuka honey or bee pollen
1 tbsp milled golden linseeds

Elevate it: ½ tsp apple cider vinegar, ½ tsp chaga powder, 1 tbsp tocotrienols

Set a saucepan over a medium heat and add the almond milk, water, chamomile flowers (or tea), vanilla, honey (if using bee pollen, add later) and any elevational extras. Bring to the boil and then simmer for 5–10 minutes. Strain into a blender, add the linseeds and bee pollen, if using, and blend on a high speed for 30 seconds. Strain and serve hot.

Deep Sleep Fennel, Aniseed & Valerian Tea

Makes 1 medium pot

By now you'll know I love a good infusion. With this recipe, in just a few moments, you can create a deeply healing concoction that will not only provide for you physically and mentally, but also stimulate your senses and, through inhalation, relax and calm the mind. These ingredients are soothing and known to induce sleep and detoxify the system. Invest in some DIY tea bags and make up a few batches of this recipe, then divide it between your teabags to have on hand whenever you feel you need it.

2 tbsp fennel seeds
1 tbsp milk thistle
1 tbsp liquorice root, chopped
1 tbsp cardamom seeds, crushed
1 tbsp celery seeds
1 tbsp aniseed
1 tbsp coriander seeds

Elevate it: 2 drops of St. John's wort extract, ½ tbsp dandelion root or 2 drops of dandelion root extract, 2 drops of valerian root extract

Simply measure your dried ingredients in a tea strainer or a teapot with a built-in strainer (if your don't have either, use a cafetiére). Cover with boiling water and leave to infuse for at least 3 minutes; the longer the better.

Night Owl Smoothie

Serves 1–2

I enjoy this smoothie at any time of the day, but particularly in the evening as a fruit–free liquid snack that doesn't threaten my blood sugar levels too much. The coconut water provides a hydrating base and the greens, chia seeds and linseeds are deeply cleansing. Triphala is a digestive-boosting tonic herb and pine pollen is a jing tonic known to promote longevity, growth, deep cellular rejuvenation and healing. If you can't get hold of these tonic herbs, this recipe will work just fine, but I really value the extra support of these miraculous ingredients, noticing differences in my skin, hair and energy.

500ml coconut water
large handful of spinach or kale
¼ ripe avocado
1 tsp maca powder
1 tsp pine pollen
½ tsp triphala
½ tsp cinnamon

1 tbsp chia seeds
1 tbsp milled golden linseeds
4–6 ice cubes

Elevate it: pinch of activated charcoal powder, ½ tsp spirulina or e3 live algae

Place all the ingredients in a blender, apart from the ice, and blend on the highest speed for 1–2 minutes, until smooth. Pause the machine to add your ice and then blend on the highest speed for a further 30–60 seconds, until all the ice has broken down. Serve instantly.

Clean & Green Probiotic Shot

Serves 1

I admit that this is not the most delicious recipe of mine, but it is full of revitalising and restorative ingredients that will quietly work their magic whilst you sleep. I up my intake if my skin is particularly bad or when I'm travelling a lot, and sleeping a lot less.

½ tsp spirulina powder
½ tsp ginko powder
½ tsp wheatgrass powder
pinch of moringa powder
1 probiotic powder capsule
    or 1 tsp liquid probiotics

pinch of mucuna pruriens powder
1 tsp magnesium powder
100ml coconut water or water

Elevate it: ¼ tsp activated charcoal powder

Mix all the ingredients together in a jug or glass. Drink instantly and chase with water if you don't enjoy the flavour.

Coconut Oil & Essential Oil Make-up Remover

Equipment: glass jar or container

Not only is coconut oil incredibly nutritious, when applied externally, it can also treat skin conditions, irritations and infections, soothe sunburn and even heal cuts and scars. It deeply cleanses the skin, preventing breakouts, and it increases softness and smoothness across the surface. To this day, coconut oil is by far the most effective make-up remover I have ever used. It eases the make-up away from around my eyes and doubles up as a natural all-over moisturiser as I remove the make-up from the rest of my face.

100g coconut oil
2 drops of essential oil (choose soothing, relaxing and antibacterial oils from page 303), but avoid using essential oils around the eye area as they can iritate the skin

Fill a small saucepan with water and bring to the boil. Place a heatproof bowl on top of the saucepan (creating a double boiler), and add the coconut oil. Once melted, add the essential oils and mix to combine. Transfer to a glass jar or a container with a lid and place in the fridge to set. To use, scoop up a tablespoonful of the mixture and warm between your fingers, or apply directly to cotton wool pads and use to remove make-up accordingly.

If you prefer, melt the oil by sitting it in a bowl of boiling water, and use it in liquid form. Use a hot muslin cloth/flannel to remove any residual greasiness.

Night Time

Pillow Sprays & Pillow Rubs

These remedies changed my life when I began modelling full time and found myself travelling a lot. I remember one time in particular where I was working for 15 days straight, passing through five cities, from Liverpool to LA, and I hardly remember any of it. My sleep was disrupted and I was running on autopilot. Now, when I find myself in transit, I always arm myself with a pillow spray or rub to use either on long-haul flights or to help me handle hopping between different time zones and hotel rooms.

Aloe Vera, Ylang Ylang & Chamomile Pillow Spray

Makes approx. 40ml

Equipment: a 50ml bottle with a spray-top lid

20ml pure chamomile flower water
10ml orange blossom water
4 drops of ylang ylang essential oil

4 drops of frankincense or jasmine essential oil
4 drops of vanilla essential oil

Simply measure the ingredients into a bottle, secure the lid and shake to combine.

To use, spray a few times around your bed or around the edges or corners of your pillow, just before you plan to sleep. Store at room temperature.

Shea Butter, Chamomile & Clary Sage Pillow Rub

Makes approx. 40ml

2 tbsp shea butter
4 drops of clary sage essential oil

6 drops of chamomile essential oil

Fill a small saucepan with water and bring to the boil. Place a heatproof bowl on top of the saucepan (creating a double boiler) and then add the shea butter. Stir with a spatula and, once melted, whisk in the essential oils. Pour into a small container or jar and place in the fridge to set.

To use, apply to the edges of your pillow or bed or rub onto your sleepwear, or even your wrists and temples.

Mocha Coffee, Cacao, Almond & Macadamia Body Scrub

Lasts about 10 uses

Equipment: airtight container

Exfoliation has always been a constant in my day-to-day beauty regime. It is the most refreshing and invigorating ritual, and, due to the sensation of the rough, grainy texture and the motions involved in application, it has been proven to increase blood circulation and promote lymphatic circulation. If you exfoliate at least twice a week, you will help to encourage the growth of new skin cells, whilst breaking down fatty tissues (bye, cellulite!). In this scrub, caffeine-rich coffee and cacao wake up the skin and serve as the main exfoliants of this scrub (use sand if you live by a beach or collect some next time you visit one), and almond and macadamia oil, add a rich aroma and leave the skin feeling soft and naturally moisturised. This might be my favourite recipe in this book and it is the one I make most often. Luckily, it's one of the easiest too.

100g organic coffee beans, ground
10g cacao or cocoa powder
20g coconut sugar or salts
2 tbsp almond oil
2 tbsp macadamia oil (or olive, coconut or walnut oil)
6–8 drops of your chosen essential oils (I like vanilla, bergamot, ylang ylang, but choose yours depending on how you are feeling at the time (page 303).

Elevate it: 1 tsp chilli oil, powder or flakes, 1 tsp vitamin E oil, 1 tsp pink clay, 1 tsp vanilla powder

Mix all the ingredients in a bowl until combined. Transfer to a jar with a lid and store in your shower (you're more likely to use it if it's there in front of you).

To use, apply to damp skin whilst you are in the shower (preferably once you've finished your hair regime) and leave on for 5–10 minutes, if you have the time. If not, rinse off immediately, rub dry and follow with moisturiser.

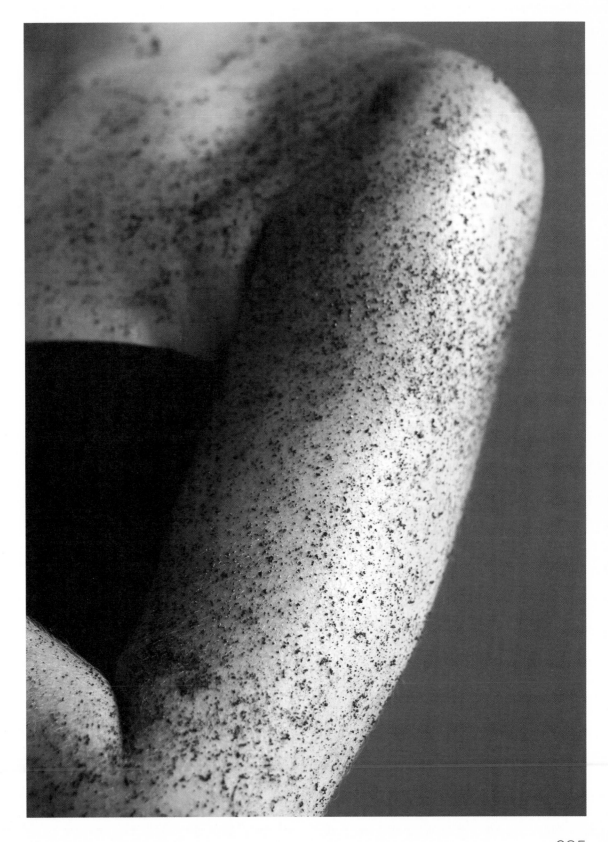

Clarifying Green Clay Powdered Face Mask

Lasts 2–3 uses

Equipment: small pot or airtight container

This mask is highly potent and deeply penetrative. Green clay binds to the toxins in pores and purges impurities from beneath the skin, allowing it to 'breathe'. It also soaks up excess oil, minimising the build up of dirt and the development of blemishes, and tightens the skin, improving the texture of the skin's surface and preventing the development of fine lines.

20g green clay powder
2g spirulina powder
2g moringa or gotu kola powder
2g matcha green tea powder
5g ground flaxseeds or chia seeds

2g charcoal powder (or cacao powder)
2g Himalayan pink salt
1g chamomile powder

Elevate it: 1 tsp acai or 1 tsp rosehip powder

Measure all the ingredients into a jar or a container with a lid and stir, or secure the lid and shake to combine.

To apply, mix 1–2 tablespoons of the powder with 1 tablespoon liquid of your choice (try raw or manuka honey or other natural syrups, tahini, coconut oil, almond oil, walnut oil, water, rose water or lemon juice). Use a little liquid to begin with and add more as required. You want to make a thin paste that will coat your face evenly. When you are happy with the consistency, apply the mask, avoiding contact with the eyes. Leave the mask on for 5–15 minutes and then rinse off with warm water. Follow with a toner or face spritz and then moisturiser, serum or night oil.

Deeply Hydrating Coconut & Clay Bath Soak

Lasts about 2 uses

Equipment: airtight container

This natural bath soak completely dissolves in hot water, enriching your bath with hydrating trace minerals and infusing it with calming and relaxing aromas. The French clay opens the skin's pores and draws out toxins, whilst the salts and dried flowers provide sodium (especially useful to overworked muscles) and a gentle exfoliation to further remove dirt and dead skin.

40g bath salts (such as Himalayan salt crystals, Epsom salts or dead sea salt)
150g powdered coconut milk
2 tbsp pink or white French clay
2 tbsp vanilla powder

Elevate it: 2 tbsp rose powder or rosehip powder, 1 tbsp dried lemongrass or fresh lemongrass, 2 tbsp fresh or dried flowers

Measure all the ingredients in a bowl and stir with a wooden spoon or spatula to combine. Transfer to a jar or an airtight container and store in the bathroom. To use, add 2 large handfuls to a full bath. Use your hand to move the powder around the water, encouraging it to dissolve.

To use this as a foot soak, fill a large bowl with hot water and add 1 large tablespoon bath soak. Soak your feet for 10–30 minutes, massaging them.

Almond, Jojoba, Walnut & Jasmine Night Oil

Makes approx. 40–50ml

Equipment: 25ml bottle or small pot

With so many skincare products on the market, it is hard to assess what our skin actually needs. In reality, it needs minimal attention and simple, natural ingredients that offer revitalising benefits, without the smart marketing or fancy packaging. I've called this night oil because I've incorporated relaxing aromatherapy oils and is best used on skin after cleansing.

5 tbsp almond oil
2 tbsp jojoba oil
2 tbsp walnut, macadamia or avocado oil
10 drops of jasmine essential oil
4 drops of rosemary essential oil

Elevate it: 1 tsp vitamin E oil, 1 tbsp rosehip oil

Measure all the ingredients in a small jar or container with a lid. Secure the lid and shake to combine. To use, apply to face and/or body and allow to soak in before getting into bed.

Rose, Ylang Ylang & Himalayan Pink Salt Bath Crystals

Lasts about 2 uses for the bath, or 6–8 uses for hand or foot soaks

Equipment: airtight container

When I was a child, bath time only appealed to me if it involved toys and so many bubbles there was hardly space for me. Nowadays I replace the bubble bath with these crystals – a combination of remineralising salts, dried flower petals and aromatherapy oils – for a calmer and more restorative experience.

300g Himalayan pink salt
10g pink clay
20 drops your chosen essential oils (page 303)
5 drops of rose water or orange blossom water
1 tsp jojoba or coconut oil
2g dried rose leaves

Elevate it: 2g lemongrass, 1 tbsp magnesium powder or magnesium flakes, 1 stick of charcoal, 2 tbsp arrowroot (for oily skin)

Mix all the ingredients in a bowl, and stir to combine with a wooden spoon or spatula. Transfer to a jar or an airtight container and store in the bathroom.

To use, add 2 small handfuls to a full bath and use your hand to move the powder around the water, encouraging it to dissolve. Once dissolved, hop in.

You could also make individual bath-soak bags. Place 2 tablespoons of the mixture into the centre of a muslin cloth or nut-milk bag and tie it together tightly using an elastic band, hairband or piece of string. Drop it into the bath and leave it to soak alongside you.

Body Butter & Body Lotion

Lasts about 20 uses

Equipment: jar or airtight container

Moisturising is another big part of my beauty regime and even if I have time for nothing else, I always make time to moisturise. My skin changes with the seasons and my personal hormonal cycle and alternates between being dry and sensitive and oily and prone to blemishes. I therefore need different products to meet different needs and the lotions below provide for both. The first is made with a base of nourishing avocado and shea butters, and coconut and jojoba oils, which contain antibacterial and antiviral properties and work to hydrate the skin and lock in moisture. The second has a light, refreshing base of aloe vera gel, which contains cleansing, detoxifying and anti-inflammatory properties and so is tailor-made for oily skin. I alternate as and when appropriate.

Avocado Body Butter
50g avocado butter, 50g shea butter
10g coconut oil, 1 tbsp jojoba or walnut oil
2 tbsp arrowroot (for more oily skin types)
10 drops of essential oils of your choice

Fill a small saucepan with water and bring to the boil. Place a heatproof bowl on top of the saucepan (creating a double boiler) and then add the avocado butter, shea butter, coconut oil, jojoba or walnut oil, arrowroot and essential oils of your choice (see below). Stir with a spatula to combine and then place in the fridge to cool.

Once set, use an electric or hand-held whisk to whip some air into the mixture, then transfer to an airtight container or jar with a lid and store at room temperature.

Use essential oils such as jasmine, tuberose, fern, birch, frankincense, hibiscus or geranium – depending on your mood. I often make one batch of body butter and then halve it, and make one energising and the other more relaxing.

Light Body Lotion
80g aloe vera gel, 20–30g softened coconut oil (or avocado butter, jojoba or almond oil), 10 drops of essential oils (page 303), 2 tbsp arrowroot

Measure all the ingredients into a medium bowl and, using a whisk, whip vigorously to combine. Once the mixture becomes light and fluffy, transfer it to a jar or airtight container and place in the fridge to set. Store at room temperature during the winter and in the fridge during the summer months.

Full Moon & New Moon Ceremonies

The full moon is a powerful time at which to reflect and to let go of things that no longer serve you, to free up space for things that can. Many people release these things by writing them down and then throwing them away or even burning them, but it can be as simple as just listing the things you want to let go of, either in your mind or on paper. It is fundamentally about making a solid decision and a symbolic change.

The new moon represents a new cycle and is an opportune time to acknowledge our desires and longings and turn our attention to attracting them, manifesting them and bringing them to life. It is the prime time to plant seeds and set intentions, and ensures you are in alignment with what you want and where you want to be.

There are hundreds of ways to celebrate the full and new moon, and whilst some are quite extreme, below is an outline of a simple ritual you can do anywhere, anytime, alone or with others, to tune in and align with the lunar cycles and what they symbolise.

1. Choose a time when the moon is visible to you and when the sun has completely gone down.

2. Create a calm and open space. Surround yourself with memorable items or things that bring you joy. If you have invited others, form a circle with the people around you if that feels natural.

3. Relax into the space and use meditation, breathing, aromatherapy, smudging, light and sound to create a soothing and clear space. This will help you transition from the fast pace of day-to-day life into a calmer mindset.

4. Set your intention – one of release for a full moon or one of attraction for a new moon. You can release it mentally by thinking it consciously or repeating a personal mantra, or you can release it physically by writing it down and burning it if you want to let go of it, or by letting it float in a bowl of water. If you don't have anything you want to let go of, or anything you want to attract, this suggests you are content and don't want to change anything. List or think about the things in your life you are grateful for and perhaps repeat a simple mantra of appreciation and acknowledgement.

5. End the ceremony with a cleansing herbal drink or a wholesome selection of natural foods.

Nature's Pantry & Daily Goods

Ingredients

Building sturdy foundations to support your daily habits is vital. Keeping stocked up on natural and functional ingredients is half the work done, and means you'll never be too far from some quick and easy nourishment. Whilst a kitchen filled with convenience foods is, well, convenient, this makes it all too easy to settle for nutritionally substandard options instead of preparing something with more sustenance. When you stock up on more natural provisions that are intended to serve many purposes in and around the body, you'll also begin to align with both nature and your own intuition. The simplest way to identify more functional provisions is to look for those that are whole, unaltered and naturally occurring – kept exactly (or as closely to) the way nature intended. Whilst most ingredients are now readily available all-year round, it is good to be mindful about sourcing local and seasonal ingredients where possible, as they not only contain the nutrition you *need* at each different stage of the year, but also, taste ten times better.

What follows is a brief breakdown of the ingredients that I use day to day, which form the basis of many of the recipes in this book. The 'daily goods' recipes guide you in making several essentials from scratch, which help you to avoid processed ingredients and are useful to keep in stock to save time and effort later on.

Fresh Produce – Fresh fruits and vegetables form the basis of most of the recipes in this book. They really bring a meal to life and each ingredient is a perfectly formed portion of vital vitamins and minerals; it couldn't be simpler.

Fermented Vegetables – Fermented vegetables are teeming with good bacteria, active enzymes and probiotics, produced by their own elements and natural juices. They can aid digestion, elimination and detoxification and help ensure the gut is in optimal health to receive and absorb vital vitamins and minerals. Kombucha (page 318), Water Kefir (page 317), Sauerkraut (page 316), miso, kimchi and various pickles are a few of my favourites.

Sea Vegetables – Produce from the ocean is rich in minerals such as iron, magnesium, calcium, protein, and vital vitamins and comes in dried, powdered or capsule form. Dried goods require various soaking and cooking methods, whilst powders (such as the superfood algae spirulina) come ready to use. Look for hijiki, wakame, nori, chlorella, arame, kombu, kelp and dulse.

Fats & Oils – Fats have been much maligned but good fats are essential for our wellbeing. Our cell membranes are made up of fats and many vitamins and minerals are fat soluble, meaning they need fats in order to be absorbed and used. Fats nourish skin, hair and nails and fuel many internal processes. Always use unrefined and nutrient-dense fats, and try to avoid trans fats and hydrogenated fats. Coconut oil, extra virgin olive oil, organic or raw butter, avocados, cacao butter and nut and seed oils (such as flaxseed, sesame, walnut and almond) are delicious for cooking or flavouring foods, and contain a host of other health benefits.

Nuts & Seeds – Nuts and seeds are great sources of healthy fats and plant-based proteins, and since proteins are the building blocks of the body, it's important that we consume enough to support cell growth, repair and renewal. I always keep almonds, cashews, Brazil nuts, pistachios, walnuts, pecans, sunflower seeds, pumpkin seeds, sesame seeds, hemp seeds, linseeds and chia seeds on hand to enjoy either as a quick snack, to make plant-based milks or yogurts (pages 304–307) or to use in other drinks, main meals and baked goods. Many people soak and activate raw nuts and seeds (page 300) because the phytates they contain are reduced during this process, making them easier to digest and their nutrients easier to absorb.

Animal Products – None of the recipes in this book contain meat, although it is often suggested as an option. I have recently begun to make far more conscious decisions when buying meat and fish. I choose organic, free-range produce where possible, and ensure it comes from a responsible source. It is important to me that an animal has been reared ethically and sustainably, without the interference of hormones, antibiotics, steroids or other methods used to produce mass-marketed meat more quickly and economically, but as a consequence, more unnaturally.

As for eggs and dairy, I use organic, free-range eggs, preferably from local suppliers, and avoid including dairy in my diet almost entirely. Personally, it has bad effects on my skin and I have found that I can live without it. In this book, I replace dairy with plant-based alternatives, but you can of course use dairy options. It is not so much a choice of being healthier as there are constantly conflicting views about what is healthy and what is unhealthy, but for me, it is more about the concept, the manufacturing processes and the morals of the intensive farming methods behind these products.

Instead of eggs (in baking), you can use chia seeds or milled linseeds, which, when soaked, swell to form a gel-like coating that acts in a similar way to bind ingredients together. Use 2–3 tbsp water to 10 tbsp chia seeds or ground linseeds, and soak for at least 20 minutes before folding into a recipe.

Instead of cheese, I use a combination of herbs, nuts and nutritional yeast, or flavoured stocks (made with garlic, onions and herbs) to add a subtle cheesiness. See page 313 for my alternative to Parmesan and grated cheese.

Grains & Pseudograins – Grains, pseudograins and psuedocereals (which are technically seeds but have similar physical characteristics to grains), have been a staple part of many traditional diets for centuries, used to provide protein and fibre, amongst other phytonutrients. Nowadays, grains are modified for economical advantages and efficiency, which means a lot of their goodness is lost or otherwise affected. Whilst oats, corn and rice surely have their place in modern diets, psuedograins such as brown, black or wild rice, millet, quinoa, buckwheat and amaranth, also have a lot to offer. They are lower in starch, have more flavour and are naturally free from gluten – an increasingly common modern-day irritation for many. If a recipe in this book calls for a specific grain or psuedograins, you can easily replace it with your own preferences without affecting the recipe.

Baking Essentials – I like to use buckwheat flour, brown rice flour, quinoa flour, cassava flour, arrowroot or ground nuts for baking, in place of white flour or wheat flours. Other gluten-free flour options include amaranth, millet, bean, teff, chickpea (gram) and coconut. Be aware that ground nuts become stale far more quickly than grain flour, so only grind them as you need them. Bicarbonate of soda and baking powder are helpful in encouraging baked goods to perform better, ensuring they rise and bind together efficiently. Vinegar (I like apple cider) reacts with these ingredients to help give cake mixture an extra lift, which is advisable if you prefer not to use eggs (simply add 1 tablespoon vinegar to any batter and stir to combine). You will also find psyllium husk powder helps things like breads bind and develop an airy, light and stable consistency.

Plant-Based Liquids – I always keep plant-based liquids: milks (pages 304–306), coconut water, fresh fruit juices and aloe vera juice in the fridge to make smoothies, juices, tonics or lattes, or when cooking or baking.

Herbs, Spices & Other Seasonings – Most herbs and spices are more nutritious when fresh, but I keep a combination of fresh, dried and ground options in my pantry, including: allspice, aniseed, basil, black pepper, cardamom, cayenne pepper, chilli, cinnamon, coriander, cumin, fennel, garlic, ginger, milk thistle, mint, oregano, parsley, rosemary, sage, sumac, thyme and turmeric. I use them for making tonics, lattes and teas and to add to dressings, soups, main meals, desserts and baked goods.

Salt (sodium) contains minerals and other essential trace elements that stimulate our digestive enzymes, helping our bodies to assimilate the vitamins and nutrients from the food we consume. Always opt for a natural form, such as rock salt or sea salt, over standard table salt, which is a manufactured form of sodium that mimics the taste of naturally occurring salts, but lacks the nutrition. Natural salts are traditionally dried by the sun and air, and therefore retain all the essential trace elements desired to help our bodies to function fully. I have included sea salt in the recipes in this book as it is generally the easiest and most affordable salt to source, but feel free to replace this with other natural salts, such as Himalayn pink salt or rock salt.

Miso is a Japanese seasoning made by fermenting soya beans with salt and koji, a type of fungus. I use both the brown and white styles of miso to add an earthy 'umami' flavour and depth to my food.

Organic Dijon mustard, wholegrain mustard or mustard seeds bring flavour and a subtle heat to anything they are added to. I use them mainly in dressings and sauces.

Natural Sweeteners – In place of heavily processed, refined sugars, I use coconut sugar, coconut nectar, raw organic honey or manuka honey, Medjool dates (or tougher dates soaked in hot water to soften), fresh fruits or homemade fruit cordials (pages 322-323). Other options include agave syrup, date syrup, rice syrup, stevia and palm jaggery (rapadura sugar). For most sweet recipes I use coconut sugar, as it is physically most similar to granulated sugar, meaning it works well in baked goods. For sauces, dressings and desserts, I prefer to use coconut sugar boiled with water to make a coconut syrup (roughly 80g sugar to 50g water). You can use whichever natural sweeteners appeal to you most, and if you're concerned by low or high GI foods, do some further research before making a decision. I personally see sweeteners as pretty equal, and only choose to avoid white or processed sugars as they lack the nutrients and fibre of more natural and less refined alternatives.

At the end of the day, sugar is sugar, and anything sweet will have some kind of effect on your blood sugar levels and insulin response. The aim is to keep sweetness, even from natural sources, to a minimum, to help wean your taste buds away from depending on or craving sugar. You'll soon realise you need less of it, and when using natural ingredients, you'll be able to taste and appreciate their true flavours more.

Vanilla, as well as adding flavour and healing benefits also brings a subtle sweetness to recipes. I use vanilla powder but you can use the same amount of extract, paste or the seeds from fresh vanilla pods, depending on what is more convenient and available to you.

Elevate It Ingredients: Medicinal Plants & Holistic Herbalism – Whilst most edible plants have the ability to nourish, some are also believed to heal, providing not only sustenance and nutrients but also positive influences on our cellular, physiological and psychological activity, altering and enhancing the ways in which our bodies and minds operate and interact. A plant's compounds can initiate a response within us, and the make-up and energy of different types of plants react differently in the body; some are energising, others are deeply relaxing. In traditional herbal medicine, many plants are used for restoring internal balance, eliminating toxins and preventing disease.

What I have discovered so far about herbs and their holistic uses comes from constant enquiry and personal experience, combined with teachings from several different herbal systems, from Ayurveda to Traditional Chinese Medicine. So far, aside from traditional kitchen herbs, I mostly use tonic herbs, nervines and adaptogens, but there are, of course, many other types of medicinal ingredients to discover*.

Tonic herbs are strengthening herbs that enhance and balance emotional, physical and spiritual energy and tone certain organs and systems in the body. Adaptogens are uplifting herbs that work to restore balance in the body and mind and help us to adapt to stress by increasing the body's resistance to physical, emotional and environmental stressors. And nervines are herbs that sooth and calm the nervous system, helping to reduce stress, anxiety, nervousness and other neurological issues.

Whilst the foundations of the recipes in this book call for more conventional ingredients, there are suggested ways to 'elevate' them by including powerful medicinal plants (roots, herbs, berries and other plant forms) in several forms, and from several herbal systems. I've listed the ingredients that I use most and just a few of their uses, but experiment with them and take time to educate yourself to find something that truly serves you. They work wonders by themselves but many are also known to work synergistically together, harmonising with one another to heighten their nutritional potential.

*   *The Healing Power of Ginseng, by Paul Bergner and Adaptogens by David Winston and Steven Maimes are great books to explore if you want to do further research.*

Ashwagandha: Relieves stress and anxiety, uplifts moods, restores balance, reduces inflammation, improves brain function and concentration, boosts our immune system and helps to combat both physical and adrenal fatigue.

Astragalus: Boosts immune system, reduces stress and anxiety, uplifts mood, reduces inflammation, anti-ageing and relieves cold and flu symptoms.

Bee pollen: Highly energising, anti-inflammatory, boosts immune system, deeply detoxifying, balances hormones, reduces stress and improves circulation.

Cacao: Supports muscle function, uplifts mood, strengthens nerves, reduces stress, balances hormones, aphrodisiac, anti-ageing, regulates appetite and enhances energy.

Chaga: Highly detoxifying, boosts immune system, relieves stress, aids digestion, reduces inflammation, enhances physical and mental endurance and boosts brain function.

Chamomile: Reduces stress and anxiety, relaxing, aids digestion, anti-inflammatory, heals wounds and infections and balances hormones.

Cordyceps: Boosts immune system, rejuvenates skin, protects against allergies and irritations, deeply detoxifying, anti-ageing and enhances energy levels.

Ginseng: Enhances fertility, relieves indigestion, uplifts mood, reduces stress, improves brain function, anti-inflammatory.

Gotu kola: Boosts brain function, reduces anxiety, detoxifies the body, calms the nervous system, promotes sound sleep and heals wounds and skin conditions.

He shou wu: Tonifying, boosts immune system, highly energising, enhances strength and stamina, supports vitality, reduces stress and supports skin renewal and rejuvenation.

Holy basil (tulsi): Reduces anxiety, balances hormones, reduces fatigue and relieves fever and headaches.

Lemon verbena:- Reduces inflammation, aids digestion, regulates appetite and relieves stress and anxiety.

Lemongrass: Aids digestion, uplifts mood, cleanses and detoxifies and boosts immune system.

Lion's mane: Boosts brain function, strengthens nerves, reduces stress and anxiety, boosts immune system, reduces fatigue and enhances gut health.

Liquorice: Reduces indigestion and heartburn, supports adrenal fatigue, boosts immunity and relieves pain (inc. menstrual tension).

Maca: Natural aphrodisiac, balances hormones, elevates endorphins, anti-ageing, enhances fertility, reduces fatigue, improves brain function and enhances energy.

Marshmallow root: Aids respiratory issues, soothes congestion, anti-inflammatory, aids digestion, supports skin health and soothes symptoms of colds and flu.

Milk thistle: Deeply cleansing and detoxifying, anti-ageing, soothes skin conditions and aids digestion.

Mucuna pruriens: Strengthens nervous system, reduces stress and anxiety, a natural source of L-dopamine, balances hormones, uplifts mood and enhances energy and endurance.

Nettle: Aids digestion, treats skin irritations, boosts immune system and reduces inflammation.

Pine pollen: Boosts immune system, antiageing, detoxifying, anti-inflammatory, boosts metabolism, natural aphrodisiac, balances hormones, uplifts mood and improves endurance.

Reishi: Detoxifying, balances hormones, reduces

fatigue, soothes skin irritations, relieves stress and anxiety and supports sound sleep.

Rhodiola: Enhances energy, uplifts mood, reduces anxiety and boosts brain function.

Rose: Uplifts mood, reduces stress and feelings of negativity and anxiety, boosts confidence, strengthens nerves and heals wounds and scars.

Rosehip: Aids digestion, relieves constipation, boosts immune system and reduces inflammation.

Shilajit: Anti-ageing, reduces stress and anxiety by increasing parasympathetic activity, reduces fatigue, enhances energy and protects against cellular damage.

Schizandra: Deeply cleansing and detoxifying, anti-ageing, boosts brain function, relieves stress and anxiety, uplifts mood, supports sound sleep and increases stamina.

Slippery elm: Aids digestion, reduces stress and anxiety and is anti-inflammatory.

St Johns wort: Treats depression, reduces mood swings, relieves anxiety, balances hormones and reduces inflammation.

Tocotrienols: Supports skin health and rejuvenation, anti-ageing, reduces fatigue, strengthens immune system, boosts brain function and supports cardiovascular health.

Triphala (a combination of amla, bibhitaki and haritaki): Deeply cleansing and detoxifying, aids digestion and is anti-inflammatory.

Turmeric: Anti-ageing, deeply cleansing and detoxifying, reduces inflammation, uplifts mood and enhances brain function and memory.

Valerian: Aids sleep and reduces anxiety.

To use herbs to treat specific and more serious conditions, or if you are pregnant or nursing, consult a doctor, alternative medicine expert, herbalist or other healthcare practitioner, as all herbs differ in potency and different people may respond differently to them. Always start by taking small doses and build it up over time.

Kitchen Practices

Apart from sourcing and stocking up on helpful and healthful ingredients, there are simple acts that you can make an integral part of your kitchen routines, channelling your energy to adopt more natural and sustainable ways of cooking and eating. Whilst making a lot of changes may seem overwhelming, these are simple methods that will end up saving you time in the long run, ensuring you get the most out of your food, whilst also enjoying your time in the kitchen and even reducing waste.

Buy Responsibly & Mindfully

I try to buy organic produce whenever possible, but I don't let it stress me out too much. Simply put, organic ingredients are those that have been grown without the interference of pesticides, but organic or not, be sure to wash all fresh produce before eating it to remove any other harmful chemicals and dirt. If you are eating the entire ingredient, this step is crucial, whilst fruits and vegetables with thick outer layers of skin are less of a concern.

When possible, buy bulk amounts of dried or ambient ingredients (such as grains, pseudograins, legumes, oils, natural sweeteners, nuts and seeds) from markets, supermarkets or health-food stores that offer bulk food dispensers for you to take just the amount you need. If you can buy in bulk, transfer your ingredients into airtight jars at home, to keep them organised and fresh. If you buy packaged ingredients, remove the packaging and store them in jars too. Doing this will make the ingredients more visible, and that way you are far more likely to actually use them.Save your jars. If you buy products in jars, once you finish the contents rinse the jars and reuse them.

Pickle, Ferment & Preserve

Before fridges and freezers were invented, people found ways to naturally prevent foods from going off. Pickling, fermenting and preserving are ancient methods that reduce waste, add flavour and preserve a food's nutrients whilst also encouraging the development of good bacteria and natural probiotics. See pages 316–321 for recipes on pickling and fermenting.

Sterilise Jars

Jams and other glassware are useful for storing or serving foodstuffs and for packaging natural, homemade skincare treatments. To sterilise jars, preheat the oven to 140°C and fill your jar with boiling water. Let the jar stand for 1–2 minutes and then drain the water. Put on a baking tray and then place in the oven for 2–5 minutes, until completely dry. Allow to cool before filling.

Freeze
Whilst freezing food is thought to destroy some of its goodness, I'm always willing to sacrifice it for convenience's sake. It's a great way to extend shelf life and find new uses for certain ingredients – most commonly, smoothies and soups. I like to chop fresh fruits and vegetables — such as bananas, mangos, avocados, berries, cucumbers and fresh herbs and place them in the freezer, spread out on a cooling rack or sheets of baking paper to ensure they don't clump together whilst they freeze. I also often freeze stock, plant-based milks and leftover juice in ice-cube trays. Once frozen, I transfer them all to ziplock freezer bags or containers. Freezing leftover cooked food is also a great way to reduce waste and always have something nutritious available on demand as alternatives to shop-bought frozen ready-meals.

Cook In Bulk & Reuse Leftovers
Whenever you have the chance to cook with unlimited resources, take the opportunity to cook more food than you may immediately need. Portion any leftovers into containers and either store in the fridge for a few days (depending on the ingredients) or store in the freezer for a later date. If you have just a few leftovers, work out ways to turn them into something new.

Soak, Activate & Sprout
Soaking, activating and sprouting raw nuts, seeds, dried legumes, grains and pseudograins is important in order to reduce anti-nutritional compounds such as phytates, which bind to certain vitamins and minerals and prevents them from being fully absorbed and used by the body. Soaking these ingredients heightens the potency and potential of each one and also makes them easier to digest, reducing the risk of inflammation in the gut and ensuring your body can access their full nutritional offering. Activating is a method of drying ingredients that have been soaked, which is usually done in a dehydrator but can also be done in an oven on the lowest temperature, or at room temperature.

Sprouting involves soaking and rinsing ingredients until they develop a 'tail'. It's not the end of the world if you don't do this (I am rarely organised enough to do so) but it can be incredibly beneficial, especially if you find nuts, grains and seeds difficult to digest. For most nuts, seeds, legumes, grains and pseudograins, it is best to soak them for a minimum of 6–8 hours, preferably overnight (which is possibly the easiest option provided you plan ahead). You can cut the soaking time for cashews to as little as 2 hours, and Brazil nuts, toasted grains, pseudograin flakes and oats don't require any soaking at all.

Nature's Pantry & Daily Goods

Waste Less

There are many parts of fresh fruits and vegetables that get discarded but which actually have many purposes. The ends of a cucumber, strawberry tops and fruit peels can be used to infuse water. Carrot tops, beetroot ends, sweet potato ends, cauliflower leaves, broccoli stalks, fennel fronds and many other parts of a vegetable can be used to make broths (page 315) or teas (pages 119–121). Wilting greens and cauliflower or broccoli leaves that aren't fresh enough to use in a salad can be used to make things like pesto (pages 310–311), dressings (pages 133–135), dips and spreads (pages 180–183) or can be juiced or added to smoothies.

Organise Your Kitchen Space

Your kitchen space is just as important as any other space in your home, if not more so. Creating a calm and clutter-free space in which to cook will make the experience more enjoyable, and keeping worktops clear, tidy and organised, rather than chaotic and crowded, will ensure you can easily navigate your way around the kitchen. Another tip – especially useful when introducing new ingredients – is to arrange them where you can see them, as you will be more likely to use them, if they are visible.

Kitchen Equipment

Apart from standard kitchen equipment (bowls, chopping boards, knives and baking trays), the following items have become essentials in my kitchen and have helped take my daily dietary rituals and routines to the next level.

A good-quality high-speed blender
A good-quality food processor, with several attachments
Reliable scales
Sticks of charcoal or a water filter jug
Lidded jars
A mandolin
A juicer
A reusable take-away cup for hot drinks
A glass water bottle
A small funnel (for making beauty and home products)
A selection of small cosmetic bottles with either spray-top or roll-top lids

Beauty & Home Ingredients

Making beauty and home remedies call for ingredients you are likely to have in your kitchen. Many plant-based fats and oils act as natural moisturisers to make things like body butters (page 289), and add scent and structure to things like fragrance oils (page 148) and candles. The main components for the beauty and home recipes in this book include base and carrier oils, botanical liquids and essential oils, examples of which are outlined below. Our bodies are all different, and this includes our hair, skin and nails so, just like food, what works for me might not work for you, but some of my favourite ingredients are outlined here.

Base & Carrier oils
Almond oil
Avocado butter
Beeswax
Cacao or cocoa butter
Coconut oil
Evening primrose oil
Jojoba oil
Macadamia oil
Mango butter
Olive oil
Shea butter
Soy wax
Walnut oil

Liquids & Extracts
Aloe vera
Apple cider vinegar
Fruit, vegetable and herb extracts or infusions
    (such as cucumber, chamomile, jasmine)
Orange blossom water
Rose water

Clays, Powders & Exfoliants
Arrowroot
Bentonite clay
Bicarbonate of soda
Dried plants
Green clay
Pink clay
Plant powders (such as rose, vanilla)
Salt crystals
Sugar
White clay

Essential Oils
Essential oils are highly concentrated extracts taken from flowers, fruits, leaves, roots, trees, nuts and seeds. They are extremely potent so must be diluted by safer, milder oils, known as carrier oils. Inhalation is a common way to use essential oils, but they are also powerfully cleansing and healing components to add to natural beauty and cleaning products. Opposite is a selection of my favourites with some of their main properties and uses:

Use 100 per cent natural oils and preferably organic. Use with care. Consult a herbalist if in doubt. For consumption, ingest sparingly and ensure the oils are definitely food grade.

Basil: Supports menstruation problems, soothes sore muscles, increases concentration and alertness.

Bergamot: Uplifting, cleanses skin and soothes irritations and inflammation and is calming and relaxing, reducing anxiety.

Black pepper: Detoxifying, encourages circulation, eases anxiety, aids digestion and improves mineral absorption.

Cardamom: Aids digestion, soothes unsettled stomach, reduces nausea and is uplifting.

Cedarwood: Detoxifying, improves focus, stimulates metabolism, improves digestion and heals wounds and infections.

Chamomile: Calming, relaxing, antiviral, antifungal, encourages sound sleep and boosts immune system.

Cinnamon: Reduces inflammation, boosts immune system and uplifts mood.

Clary sage: Balances hormones, anti-bacterial (heals wounds and infections), relieves stress and aids digestion.

Coriander: Clears skin and strengthens hair, soothes sore joints and muscles, aids digestion and encourages confidence and control.

Eucalyptus: Deeply cleansing, used to treat sinus irritations and allergies.

Fennel: Heals wounds and infections, boosts circulation, stimulates metabolism and relieves digestive issues.

Frankincense: Relieves indigestion, relieves inflammation, balances hormones, uplifting, boosts immune system and heals wounds and infections.

Geranium: Balances hormones, reduces stress, reduces inflammation, improves circulation and is calming.

Grapefruit: Boosts concentration and alertness, cleansing, regulates appetite, curbs sugar cravings and reduces fluid retention.

Jasmine: Increases concentration, reduces stress, balances mood and reduces fatigue.

Lavender: Calming, relieves stress, relieves headaches, encourages sound sleep and is good for skin.

Lemongrass: Calming, aids digestion, boosts complexion, relieves muscle tension, kills bacteria and boosts energy.

Palo santo: Boosts immune system, anti-inflammatory, fights infection, stimulates the nervous system and reduces stress.

Patchouli: Grounding, boosts immune system, reduces inflammation, uplifts mood, heals wounds and infections and reduces tension.

Rose: Balances hormones, uplifts mood, soothes skin conditions, cleanses and clears skin and soothes nerves.

Rose geranium: Stimulates metabolism, soothes skin conditions, moisturising, anti-bacterial and calming.

Rosemary: Detoxifying, improves memory, aids digestion, relieves muscular tension and lowers cortisol – reducing stress.

Sandalwood: Boosts immune system, calming, grounding, enhances concentration, heals scars and improves concentration.

Spearmint: Cooling, energising, good for oral health, aids digestion and soothes respiratory issues.

Valerian: Calming, relaxing, reduces anxiety, soothes unsettled stomach and encourages sound sleep.

Ylang ylang: Uplifts mood, balances hormones, relieves inflammation and boosts energy.

Daily Goods Recipes

Milks & Yogurts

Plant-based milks form the basis of many recipes in this book, and since so manufactured products are sweetened and heavily processed, there's nothing better than making these milks and yogurts yourself. They're simple to make and if you're put off by the soaking process or the need for a nut milk bag, you'll be pleased to know you can 'milk' without either. Whilst soaking makes for better digestibility and easier absorption, plant-based milks can still thrive without this step, and as for the nut-milk bag, you can in fact use a jelly strainer or a standard sieve to get just as good results.

Whether you need an ice-cold drink, a creamer for your coffee, a base for your smoothies or a liquid to loosen soups and sauces, plant-based milks are incredibly versatile and provide flavour, texture and goodness. They are concentrated sources of healthy fats, protein, vitamins and minerals and come in an easy-to-use form that should definitely become a part of your daily routines in some way or another.

Plant-based yogurts are made using pretty much the same methods and ingredients as milks, and offer much the same benefits for the body and mind. Kept a little thicker, these yogurts provide the prospect of more of a meal, serving as a suitable bed for fruits, granolas, compotes, jams and other toppings, or as a topping or side offering for both savoury meals and desserts.

Making Milks

Main Ingredients
Nuts or seeds

Sweeteners
Medjool dates, natural syrups, dried apricots, dried figs, raisins, goji berries, fresh fruits

Flavourings
Plant powders (such as tonic herbs
    and adaptogens)
Fresh or dried fruits, vegetables, herbs, spices,
    flowers, roots and other botanicals
Food-grade essential oils

Liquids
Filtered water
Coconut water
Liquid probiotics

Ratios
Nut milks require more liquid than seed milks, but other than that, there is no official protocol to follow. If you fancy a richer, creamier milk, add your liquid gradually until you are pleased with the result. If you like your milks lighter, add more liquid until you are content. And for a runny cream option to serve in or on desserts, reduce the quantity of liquid by one-quarter and use your intuition to reach the perfect consistency for your specific needs.

Nut Milk *(Makes approx. 1 litre)*
Put 200g mixed or single type of nuts (ideally soaked for a minimum of 6 hours) and 1 litre filtered water (reserving some to control the thickness of your milk gradually) into your blender and blend on a high speed for 3–4 minutes, until the mixture becomes smooth and a light shade of white. Strain (either through a nut-milk/jelly bag or a sieve), rinse the blender before returning the milk to the blender and blending again for 1–2 minutes. Taste and add more water if needed. Add any flavourings and sweeteners of choice and blend for a further minute, until you are happy with the consistency and flavour. Strain again, transfer the mixture to a sterilised bottle or jar with a lid and store in the fridge for 3–4 days.

Lazy Boy Nut Milk
For a quicker option, blend 2 tbsp of nut butter (preferably raw, but roasted will also work) with 150ml filtered water on a high speed for 2–3 minutes. Strain and transfer to a bottle or jar with a lid and store in the fridge for 3–4 days.

Seed Milk *(Makes approx. 1 litre)*
Put 50g mixed or single type of seeds (I like golden linseeds or flaxseeds, sesame seeds, sunflower seeds, hemp seeds, pumpkin seeds) and 1 litre filtered water in a blender and blend on a high speed for 1 minute. Leave to sit for a few moments and then blend for a further minute. Strain the mixture (either through a nut-milk/jelly bag or a sieve), rinse the blender and then blend again, for 1 minute. Strain, rinse the blender again and blend for a third time, this time adding any flavourings and natural sweeteners of your choice. Strain and transfer straight to a sterilised bottle or jar with a lid. Store in the fridge for 3–4 days.

Lazy Boy Seed Milk
For a quicker option, blend 2 tbsp tahini or sunflower or pumpkin seed butter (preferably raw, but roasted will also work) with 150ml filtered water on a high speed for 2–3 minutes. Strain and transfer straight to a bottle or jar with a lid and store in the fridge for 3–4 days.

Coconut Milk
Blend 50g young Thai coconut flesh/meat, 80g desiccated coconut or 100g toasted coconut flakes (preheat the oven to 170°C to toast the coconut flakes on a baking tray for 10 minutes, until they begin to brown) and 1 litre filtered water (or coconut water) on a high speed for 1–2 minutes, until smooth. (Use boiling water if using desiccated or toasted coconut). Add extra water or coconut water if it's too thick, alongside any flavourings and sweeteners of your choice. Blend for 1 minute to combine. If using coconut flesh, transfer the mixture directly into a bottle or jar with a lid. If using desiccated or toasted coconut, strain the mixture into a jug (through your nut-milk/jelly bag or a sieve), rinse the blender before you blend again for 1–2 minutes. Strain into a bottle or jar with a lid. Store in the fridge for 3–4 days.

Oat Milk

Blend 200g gluten-free jumbo oats with 1 litre filtered water on a high speed for 2–3 minutes, until the mixture becomes smooth and a light shade of white. Strain (either through a nut-milk/jelly bag or a sieve), rinse the blender and then blend for 1–2 minutes. Pause the machine and taste the mixture, then add more water as needed. At this stage, add any flavourings and natural sweeteners of your choice and blend for a further 1 minute, until you are happy with the consistency and flavour. Strain again, transfer the mixture to a sterilised bottle or jar with a lid and store in the fridge for 3–4 days.

Flavoured Milks (Serves 1)

To make a flavoured milk, choose one of the following flavour combinations and put all of the ingredients in a blender and blend on a high speed for 1–2 minutes. You can add ice to the blender for a chilled drink. Transfer to a sterilised bottle or jar with a lid and store in the fridge for 3–4 days.

Avocado, Wheatgrass & Matcha milk

250ml plant-based milk, ½ tsp wheatgrass powder, ½ tsp matcha powder, 2 tbsp avocado.

Cucumber Coconut Milk

250ml coconut milk and 20g grated cucumber.

Fig & Brazil Nut Milk

250ml brazil nut milk, 1 tsp vanilla powder and 1 fresh or dried fig.

Ginger Nut Milk

250ml nut milk, 1 tbsp ground ginger or fresh ginger juice and ½ Medjool date or raw honey.

Hazelnut, Chia & Mocha Milk

150ml hazelnut milk, 1 tbsp chia seeds, 1 tsp raw cacao powder, 1 tsp vanilla powder, ½ tsp maca powder, 1 Medjool date, 1 tsp nut butter (optional) and 1 shot of coffee (or 1 tbsp instant coffee or chicory powder).

Minted Charcoal Milk

250ml plant-based milk, a handful of fresh mint leaves, ½ tsp activated charcoal powder and 1 tsp vanilla powder.

Pecan & Cashew Milk

250ml pecan and cashew milk (use 120g pecans and 60g cashews), 1 tsp vanilla powder, 1 Medjool date or other natural sweetener and a pinch of salt.

Rose, Cherry & Brazil Nut Milk

250ml plant-based milk, 1 tsp rose water, 6 stoned and chopped cherries, 1 tsp acai powder (or pulp), 1 tsp maca powder and 1 tsp acerola cherry powder.

Salted Coconut Almond Milk

250ml almond milk with 150ml coconut water, ½ tsp vanilla powder, 1 date and a pinch of salt.

Strawberry Hemp Milk

30g grated raw beetroot, 150g strawberries, 250ml hemp milk, 120ml filtered water or coconut water, 1 date or 20g fresh pineapple or apple (to sweeten), 1 tsp bee pollen and 1 tsp lime juice.

Toasted Coconut & Bee Pollen Milk

250ml toasted coconut milk, 1 tsp vanilla powder, ½ tsp bee pollen and a pinch of salt.

Elevate it: Elevate any of these milks even further by adding other plant powders, such as adaptogens, tonic herbs or powders or pastes (pages 297–298).

Simple Coconut Yogurt (Serves 2)

Put 10g chia seed gel or whole chia seeds, 180g coconut milk (the solid part of a can), 80ml coconut drinking milk, ½ Medjool date or 1 tsp natural syrup, 1 tbsp melted coconut oil, 1 probiotic capsule or 1 tsp liquid probiotics, (optional) in a blender for 3–4 minutes, until smooth. Set in the fridge for a minimum of 2 hours. Once set, blend again for a further 30 seconds, gradually adding the remaining drinking coconut milk to loosen the mixture until it reaches your desired consistency.

Cashew or Almond Yogurt (Serves 2)

Put 250g cashews or blanched almonds, ideally soaked 150ml boiling water (or plant-based milk), 8g chia seed gel or whole chia seeds, 1 Medjool date (or natural syrup), ½ tsp lemon juice, 1 tsp vanilla powder and a pinch of salt in a blender and blend all the ingredients on the highest speed for 3–4 minutes. (You can elevate it by adding ½ tsp psyllium husk or 2 tsp ground flaxseeds or ½ tsp ashwagandha powder.) If using psyllium husk/ground flaxseeds, add to the blender after the initial stage and blend for a further 30 seconds. Refrigerate for 20 minutes until the mixture has set or keep in the fridge until needed.

Smooth Chia Seed Yogurt *(Serves 1)*
Put 250ml unsweetened plant-based milk, 4 tbsp whole chia seeds, 2 Medjool dates, 1 tsp vanilla powder, 1 tsp ground cinnamon (and for a chocolate version, add 2 tbsp cacao powder) in a blender, blending on a high speed for 3–4 minutes, until smooth. The chia seeds should be completely broken down.

Elevate it: You can elevate it by adding 1 tsp maca powder, 1 tsp mucuna pruriens, 1 tsp tocos powder, 1 tsp ashwagandha powder, 1 tbsp ground flaxseeds or golden linseeds.

Enjoy instantly or transfer to a bowl, jar or airtight container and place in the fridge to set and chill. Store in the fridge for 3–4 days.

Butters & Pastes

These recipes provide concentrated levels of natural and lively ingredients and offer alternatives to standard butter, shop-bought nut butters (which are commonly either highly processed or highly priced) and other powerful pastes that make cooking and creating with plants effortlessly easy.

Nut & Seed Butters

Roast a combination of the following nuts and/or seeds on a baking tray in a preheated oven at 140°C/gas mark 1, for 10–15 minutes, until they begin to brown. Next, transfer to a blender and pulse the ingredients for 5–10 minutes (this will depend on the nature of the nuts and seeds you use), until they come together in a smooth and runny paste. Season with a little salt and add any extra oils, a little natural sweetener or herbs or spices (in fresh, ground or extract form) of choice. Transfer to a jar or an airtight container and allow to cool before storing in the fridge. Enjoy straight from the jar, added to lattes, smoothies, soups or dressings, or used in or on top of breakfasts, savoury meals or desserts.

Brazil, Almond & Macadamia Nut Butter
(*Serves 2–4*)
Follow the method above, using 100g Brazil nuts, 150g macadamia nuts, 100g almonds, and salt, to taste. (You can elevate it by adding 1 tsp vanilla powder, dried flowers, dried fruit, 1 tsp natural sweetener, 1 tbsp cacao powder or paste, ½ tsp ground turmeric, ½ tsp ground paprika, a pinch of chilli to taste, 1 tbsp nutritional yeast, a handful of fresh basil leaves, 1 tbsp beetroot powder or grated raw beetroot).

Cinnamon Pecan Butter (*Serves 2–4*)
Follow the method for Nut & Seed Butter using 400g pecans, a pinch of salt, 1 tsp vanilla powder, 1 tsp ground cinnamon and 1 tsp maca powder. (You can elevate it by adding dried flowers, dried fruit, 1 tsp natural sweetener, 1 tbsp cacao powder or paste).

Avocado 'Butter' (*serves 10–20*)
Very different to nut and seed butters, this spread is much lighter and creamier and tastes just like salted butter. It is delicious on bagels, bread, toast, crackers, bread rolls, pancakes or added to main meals in the place of traditional butter is brimming with healthy fats. Put the flesh of ½ ripe avocado, 180g coconut oil and a pinch of salt in a high-speed blender for 2–3 minutes, until smooth and fully combined. (You can elevate it by adding 5g dried nori, pinch of spirulina, pinch of he shou wu, pinch of Ashwagandha powder or 1 tsp natural sweetener). Ensure there are no lumps of avocado remaining, as this will make it more difficult to spread as a butter alternative. Transfer to a jar or airtight container and store in the fridge for up to 1 month.

Herbal Plant Pastes (*Makes 20–25 servings*)
This recipe was inspired by the Ayurvedic remedy chyawanprash (a traditional herbal 'jam' made from honey, fat, sesame oil and various herbs and spices). It was first developed as a quick prepared formula to support many ailments, and creating similar pastes from scratch makes navigating tonic herbs and adaptogens easier than ever.

Making a paste from your favourite powders is an easy way to use them. Use ½–1 spoonful in smoothies, tucked into porridge, spread onto toast, stirred through tea, hot water or hot milk or eat straight from the pot when you're in search of something sweet or need a little mental or physical boost. This paste satisfies cravings whilst also flooding the system with powerful plant extracts.

Put 50g honey or other natural sweetener, 20g melted coconut oil, 1 tsp sesame or walnut oil, 4 tsp he shou wu powder, 2 tsp chaga powder, 2 tsp maca powder, pinch of black pepper, 2 tsp ginseng powder, 2 tsp ashwagandha powder, 2 tsp ground cardamom, 2 tsp vanilla powder, 2 tsp ground cinnamon, 2 tsp ground ginger, 4 tsp pine pollen, 2 tsp mucuna pruriens powder, 1 tsp triphala powder, pinch of salt and a pinch of ground turmeric in a small bowl and mix together using a spatula or wooden spoon. (You could elevate it by adding 2 drops food-grade essential oils). Mix and spread vigorously for 1–2 minutes until all of the ingredients are combined, and the mixture develops into a gummy consistency.

Pour into a jar or a small pot with a lid and store in the fridge or at room temperature.

Condiments

I know how addictive condiments can be. Before I discovered the power and possibilities of cooking and creating with plants, I used to fill my plate with so much mayonnaise you couldn't see my actual food. Thankfully, there are ways to create your favourite condiments using highly nutritious ingredients, which will elevate your meals rather than spoiling them.

Avocado Mayonnaise *(Serves 10–15)*
Put the flesh of 2 ripe avocados, 1 tsp lemon juice, a splash of apple cider vinegar and a pinch of salt in to a blender and blend on a medium speed, gradually adding 125ml olive oil, a few drops at a time. As you add the oil, increase the speed of the blender and blend for 1–2 minutes, until the mixture is combined and smooth. Transfer to a small bowl or an airtight container and store in the fridge until ready to serve. Over time the mixture will begin to brown. Drizzle with lemon juice to prevent this and eat within 2–3 days.

Beetroot Tomato Ketchup *(Serves 4)*
Heat 2 tbsp olive oil in a saucepan over a medium heat and, once hot, add ½ onion, diced. Fry for a few minutes and then add ¼ tsp ground coriander, pinch of ground cinnamon, 1 tsp paprika, pinch of chilli powder or chilli flakes, pinch of ground ginger, 1 tsp celery salt or salt, black pepper to taste, 1 tbsp fresh coriander leaves, ½ garlic clove, crushed (optional), 3 tsp apple cider vinegar, 80g chopped tomatoes, 80g grated raw beetroots and 6–8 tbsp water.

Simmer for 15–20 minutes until the tomatoes soften and the beetroot is cooked through. Transfer to a blender and blend on the highest speed for 30–40 seconds, until smooth. Place in the fridge to chill before serving.

Cashew Almond Mayonnaise (Serves 20)
Preheat the oven to 140°C/gas mark 1. Arrange 50g skinned almonds on a baking tray and toast in the oven for 10–15 minutes then allow to cool for 10–12 minutes. Transfer to a blender. Add 80g cashews (soaked), a pinch of salt, 2 tbsp fresh lemon juice, 2–3 tsp apple cider vinegar, 130ml extra virgin olive oil and 80ml boiling water (added gradually as required) to a blender and blend on the highest speed for 2–3 minutes until smooth and fully combined. (You can elevate it by adding ½ dried chipotle pepper, 1 crushed garlic clove, ½ –1 tsp Dijon mustard.) Transfer to a dish or airtight container and chill in the fridge.

Tomato & Goji Chilli Jam *(Serves 10)*
Heat 2 tbsp olive oil in a saucepan over a medium heat and,once hot, add 200g chopped cherry tomatoes, 1 chopped fresh chilli or 1–2 tsp chilli flakes, 2 chopped red peppers, 100g goji berries and a splash of water. Simmer for 10 minutes, stirring continuously, then add 1 tsp grated fresh ginger or ground ginger, 1 crushed garlic clove, 1 tbsp chia seeds, salt, 1 tsp apple cider vinegar and 4–6 tbsp natural sweetener. Simmer for 25–30 minutes, until the mixture thickens, stirring continuously. Once thickened, for a smoother result you can run the mixture through a blender. Transfer to a jar or airtight container and chill in the fridge.

Herbal Sunflower Chutney *(Serves 6–8)*

Put 15g fresh mint leaves, 10g fresh coriander leaves, 10g spinach, juice of 2 limes, ½ green chilli, 10 tbsp olive or coconut oil, 120g sunflower seeds, 1 large garlic clove, 1 tsp natural syrup, 1 tbsp ground ginger (or 2.5cm piece of fresh ginger) and 3 tbsp avocado in a blender with 4 tbsp boiling water and blend until smooth. You may need to stop and scrape down the sides a few times, and if the mixture isn't blending smoothly, gradually add a little more boiling water. Once smooth, transfer to a serving pot and chill in the fridge until ready to serve.

Mango Chutney *(Serves 6–8)*

Put 5tbsp apple cider vinegar, pinch of salt, ½ tsp lemon juice and 1 tbsp onion seeds in a small saucepan and simmer over a low heat. Add 1 tsp ground cardamom, ¼ tsp ground cumin, ¼ tsp ground coriander, 200g chopped mango, 20g grated raw beetroot (optional), 5cm piece of fresh ginger, grated, and 40–50g coconut sugar. Bring to the boil, then reduce the heat and simmer for 40–45 minutes. Once cooked, run through a blender for a smoother result or transfer to a jar or airtight container and chill in the fridge until ready to serve.

Pesto

I don't think I have ever made two pestos the same, as every time I make it I use whatever I have in my kitchen and never really follow a recipe. Traditionally, pesto is made from oil, basil, pine nuts, garlic and cheese, but you can add so much more to it to further enhance the nourishment without affecting the taste. Play around with whichever ingredients you desire or need using up, following this very rough guide. To make a simple pesto sauce for pasta dishes or to stir through warm vegetables or other sides, add the flesh of half an avocado and a large splash of water, or use plant-based milk to thin the pesto.

Seasoning:
Nutritional yeast (or Parmesan cheese), salt, pepper, tamari or garlic.

Herbs & spices:
I like to use basil, mint, coriander, parsley, lemon thyme, wild garlic, ginger or chilli.

Vegetables & leaves:
Spinach, kale, dandelion, nettle, chard, broccoli, unused leaves of vegetables (such as cauliflower, beetroot and carrot).

Oils:
I tend to use about 60–80ml extra virgin olive oil and occasionally add a dash of avocado, chia seed or walnut oil.

Nuts & seeds:
I use 1–2 handfuls of almonds, cashews, Brazil nuts, walnuts, macadamia nuts, pine nuts, sunflower seeds, hemp seeds or pumpkin seeds.

Acidic ingredients:
Try using apple cider vinegar, lemon juice, lime juice or orange juice.

Elevate it: Spirulina powder, wheatgrass powder, chlorella powder, he shou wu powder and Shilajit powder.

Sundried Tomato Pesto

Blend 80g sundried tomatoes, 60g fresh tomatoes (any size, roughly chopped), 1 handful fresh basil leaves, 80ml extra virgin olive oil, 50g almonds or cashews, 1 tsp lemon juice or ¼ tsp apple cider vinegar, 1 crushed garlic clove, 2 tbsp nutritional yeast and a generous

Nature's Pantry & Daily Goods

pinch of salt together in a blender, until blended but still chunky .

Basil, Spinach & Almond Pesto
Blend 2 large handfuls of basil, 1 handful of spinach, 1 handful or almonds, 60ml extra virgin olive oil, 1 tsp lemon juice, 2 tbsp nutritional yeast, 1 crushed garlic clove, and a generous pinch of salt together in your blender, until thick and smooth.

Herbal Hemp & Lemon
Blend 100g nuts or seeds, 80ml extra virgin olive oil, 2 tbsp hemp seeds, 1 large handful of fresh basil leaves, 5g fresh mint, 4g fresh lemon balm leaves (or lemongrass), 1 handful of spinach, 2 tsp lemon juice, 1 crushed garlic clove, 2 tbsp nutritional yeast, ½ tsp apple cider vinegar and a generous pinch of salt together in a blender, until thick and smooth.

Kale, Pumpkin Seed & Walnut Pesto
Blend 1 handful of kale, 10–20g broccoli stalk, 2 handfuls of pumpkin seeds, 1 handful of walnuts, 2 handfuls of fresh basil leaves, 80ml olive oil, 1 tsp lemon juice, 2 tbsp nutritional yeast, 1 crushed garlic clove and a generous pinch of salt together in a blender, until thick and smooth.

Watercress & Nettle Pesto
Blend 2 large handfuls of fresh basil leaves, 1 handful of watercress, about 10 nettles (making sure to handle them with care), 60ml extra virgin olive oil, 1 handful of almonds or pine nuts, 1 tsp lemon juice, 2 tbsp nutritional yeast, 1 crushed garlic clove and a generous pinch of salt together in a blender, until thick and smooth. If you can't find nettles or they are out of season, use other greens.

Below
Sun-dried tomato pesto (page 310)

Powders & Toppings

Powders are for you if you're highly stressed and/or pressed for time. They are low maintenance and life-giving, and come as concentrated forms of our favourite plants, meaning you get more benefits by using less. Although often costly to pay for upfront, a little goes a long, long way. Nowadays, you can buy all kinds of powder combinations, meaning you don't have to fork out on a full bag of several ingredients, but when you buy products like these, you're paying for a lot of labour, transportation, branding, marketing and packaging. Making your own powder mixes is far more affordable and also means you can personalise them to your tastes and everchanging needs.

Powder Blends For Instant Drinks

Use one, several or all of these ingredients to create diverse plant powders. Mix equal amounts or experiment with different amounts, and take no more than 1–2 tsp per day.

Beauty: Ground flaxseeds, ground chia seeds, shizandra berry powder, pine pollen, acai powder, goji berry powder and pearl powder.

Brain: Cacao powder, astragalus powder, maca powder, rhodiola powder, he shou wu powder, shilajit powder, pine pollen, chaga powder and beetroot powder.

Body: Pea protein, ground almonds, wheatgrass powder, triphala powder, coconut milk powder, matcha powder and cordyceps powder.

Deep sleep: Ground fennel seeds, lavender, ground chamomile, triphala powder, mucuna pruriens and magnesium powder.

Digestive aid: Probiotic powder, triphala powder, activated charcoal powder, ground flaxseeds, spirulina powder, moringa powder, chlorella powder and wheatgrass powder.

Immunity & detoxification: Ginseng powder, maca powder, ground ginger, pine pollen, chaga powder, ashwagandha powder, baobab powder, ashitaba powder, spirulina powder and activated charcoal powder.

Mood: Tocos powder, maca powder, mucuna pruriens powder, Ashwagandha powder, pine pollen, lion's mane (mushroom) powder, gotu kola powder and ashitaba powder.

Caution: Tonic herbs and adaptogen powders are highly powerful and since you don't find them in everyday products, it may take a while for your body to get used to them (although, personally, it didn't for me). Be intuitive and do speak to a healthcare specialist or your doctor before consuming if you are on medication or pregnant, as drastic dietary changes are not always advised.

Powdered Instant 'Coffee' (Makes enough for 12–15 servings)

Put 1 tsp vanilla powder, 6 tbsp chicory powder (or instant coffee), 1 tsp coconut sugar (optional), 1 tsp maca powder and 2 tbsp coconut milk powder (optional) in a small bowl and combine. (You can elevate it by adding 4 tbsp reishi mushroom powder, 4 tbsp he shou wu powder). Transfer to a jar or airtight container. Use 1–1½ tbsp per mug, and just add hot water or hot plant-based milk. Stir or use a small hand whisk until dissolved, or blend in a high-speed blender for a frothier result.

Plant-Powered Protein Powders (Makes enough for 25 servings)

Put 150g pea protein isolate or brown rice protein isolate, 40g coconut milk powder, 20g ground flaxseeds or golden linseeds, 50g hemp protein powder (or ground hemp seeds), 20g chia seed protein powder (or ground chia seeds), 1 tsp ground cinnamon and 2 tbsp cacao powder in a small bowl and stir to combine. (You can elevate it by adding 2 tsp reishi mushroom powder, 2 tsp lion's mane mushroom powder, 2 tsp maca powder, 2 tsp wheatgrass powder.) Transfer to a pot, bowl or container and store at room temperature. Add to smoothies or you can shake up with water, coconut water or almond milk for an even more powerful protein hit.

Herb-Infused Oil
These oils can be used to season cooking, or drizzle over finished salads, toasts, vegetables, side dishes, pasta dishes and risottos. I like to use basil, oregano and rosemary. Wash 8 sprigs fresh herbs (or about 30 leaves) and then dry them with kitchen paper to ensure they are 100% dry. Place into a bottle and use a funnel or a small jug to add 400ml extra virgin olive oil (or avocado, walnut or hemp oil), making sure the oil covers the herbs. Leave to infuse at room temperature or in the fridge for 2–3 days, then enjoy. Elevate the flavour by adding dried plants or plant powders such as fresh lemongrass, fresh turmeric, spirulina powder, shilajit powder, reishi powder, he shou wu powder, chilli flakes, dried flower petals, chaga root or astragalus root. Use within a month.

Herbal Salt Mix
Mixing dried herbal ingredients to your choice of natural salt is a simple way to add extra flavour and nutrients to your meals. You could do the same with coconut sugar, adding whole vanilla pods, cinnamon sticks or dried flowers.

In a small bowl, mix together 50g salt (I like Himalayan pink salt or local, organic sea salt), 25g dried herbs and/or dried flowers. Transfer to a pot, bowl or container and store at room temperature.

Suggestions for other herbal mixes
Basil, marjoram and oregano
Mint, parsley and marigold
Rose petal and thyme
Coriander and cumin
Rosemary, sage and garlic powder
Spirulina and nori

Nut Parmesan Sprinkle (*Makes enough for 10–12*)
Put 200g raw or toasted nuts, a generous pinch of salt, 2 tbsp nutritional yeast, 1 tsp lemon juice and 2 tsp hemp seeds (optional) in a food processor, blender or a small, electric herb grinder and pulse for 30–40 seconds, until the nuts are completely broken down into crumbs. Transfer to a jar or an airtight container and store in the fridge for up to 2 weeks. Use to garnish savoury snacks, sides and main meals.

Coconut 'Bacon' (*Serves 2*)
Preheat the oven to 160°C/gas mark 3. Put 3 tbsp tamari, 1 tsp natural syrup, ½–1 tsp smoked paprika, ½ tsp reishi or shilajit powder, 1–2 tsp nutritional yeast and freshly ground black pepper, to taste, in a bowl and stir to combine. Toss in 50g raw coconut flakes and use your hands to coat them fully in the marinade. Spread out evenly on a baking tray and bake for 10 minutes, stirring after 5 minutes. Remove from the oven and allow to cool and crisp up before using. Enjoy as a snack alternative to crisps, or use as a topping for salads, soups, pasta dishes and other main meals.

Baked Goods

Some shop-bought baked goods have lost their purity and true purpose, due to businesses being more concerned about making a profit than a healthier human race. It may sound blunt but it's true. Some baked goods are plagued with fillers, artificial raising agents, gums and sugars, leaving no room for the nutritious ingredients our bodies actually need.

Magic Seed 'Bread' Rolls (*Makes 4*)
Preheat the oven to 200°C/gas mark 6 and line a baking tray with baking paper.

Put 100g cassava flour (tapioca flour – other gluten-free flours work), 2 tbsp psyllium husk powder (optional), 3 eggs, 4 tbsp ground flaxseeds or golden linseeds, 1 tbsp extra virgin olive oil and 1 tsp baking powder in a bowl.

(*Elevate it:* You can elevate it by adding 1 tsp activated charcoal, 1 grated raw beetroot, a handful of spinach or kale (finely chopped), a handful of chopped olives and a handful of chopped dried fruit.)

Stir to combine all the ingredients, using a spatula or wooden spoon. Stir vigorously for about 4 minutes until the mixture thickens and becomes more dough-like.

Next, beat 1 egg in a small bowl or jug, using a fork. Set aside.

Spoon the dough mixture onto the prepared baking tray to make 4–5 individual rolls. The mixture will seem a little sloppy, but it will totally transform in the oven. Working quickly so the rolls don't loose their shape, brush each one gently with the beaten egg and sprinkle each one with some sesame seeds, a little extra salt and some dried herbs, if desired. Bake for 20–25 minutes until golden brown. Leave to cool for 10–20 minutes before slicing.

Instead of making rolls, you could spread it flat across your baking tray and, once baked, cut it into squares to make sandwich bread. You could also spread into circles to form a pizza base, or form into small balls to make dough balls.

Miracle Bread (*Makes 1 loaf*)
Preheat the oven to 180°C/gas mark 4 and grease a loaf tin with a little coconut oil.

Put 150g raw almonds, 100g quinoa flakes (or oats or buckwheat flakes) and 130g pumpkin seeds in a food processor. Blend for 1–2 minutes to a flour-like consistency, then transfer to a large mixing bowl.

Add 140g sunflower seeds, 150g flax or golden linseeds, 3 tbsp psyllium husk powder, 3 tbsp nutritional yeast, a small handful of fresh basil leaves, 2 tbsp dried basil or a mixture of dried herbs, ½ tsp salt, freshly ground black or cayenne pepper, to taste, 2 tbsp chia seeds, 2 tbsp black onion seeds and 2 tbsp sesame seeds and stir thoroughly until everything is fully combined. Gradually pour in 350ml water, stirring constantly with a wooden spoon or spatula until the mixture becomes doughy (you may not need to use all the water). Let it stand for 5–10 minutes. When the mixture begins to come together, use your hands to knead it for a couple of minutes, in the bowl.

Transfer the mixture to the prepared loaf tin and gently push the mixture down firmly with the back of a spoon, spatula, or your hands. Bake for 45 minutes, until the top begins to brown. Insert a knife in the middle and if it comes out clean, remove the bread from the oven and leave to cool.

Once cool enough to handle, transfer to a cooling rack. Slice immediately for some warm fresh bread, or leave to cool before slicing and storing, either in the fridge or the freezer.

Broths

Homemade broths are generally more nutritionally charged and flavoursome than shop-bought stocks and powdered stock cubes. In our lazy, modern ways, we have dropped the habit of making them from scratch, which was formerly an intuitive kitchen ritual for most people. Vegetable broths are rich in vitamins, and seaweed broth (see page 122) is incredibly high in iron and trace minerals. Animal broths contain all of the above and are also high in essential fats and collagen, which support gut health and vibrant skin, whilst also providing the body with vital fats that make it possible for our cells to assimilate certain micronutrients. Broths are a great way to use up all kinds of leftovers, and a glass a day, either straight or added to smoothies, soups and other meals, can do wonders all round.

Meat & Fish Broths

Heat 1 tbsp coconut oil in a large saucepan or stockpot and, once hot, throw in 1 chopped carrot, ½ onion (chopped), 1 celery stick (chopped), a large handful of kale stalks, 1 tbsp apple cider vinegar, a handful of bay leaves and 4–5 sprigs of fresh herbs. Sauté for 5–10 minutes and then add 1–2kg animal or fish bones (leftover from meals or from a butcher or fishmonger). Fill the pan with just enough cold water to cover the bones and vegetables and bring to the boil. (If any useable meat escapes from the bones, retrieve it and save it for salads and other meat-based meals). Once boiling, reduce the heat and then simmer with the lid on for a minimum of 4 hours for fish stock and 8 hours for meat stock, ideally. If you can, leave it over a low heat for 12 –24 hours, depending on the size of the bones.

Vegetable Broth

Chop 500g vegetables into pieces about 3–4cm wide. Heat 20g coconut oil in a large saucepan or stockpot and once hot, add the vegetables, fresh herbs of your choice, 2 garlic cloves and 1tsp salt or tamari. (You can elevate it by adding 20–30g seaweed, 10g chaga root or powder). Sauté for about 5–10 minutes and then add enough water to cover the vegetables. Bring to the boil for 15–20 minutes, then strain through a sieve and transfer to a jar or airtight container. Let it cool before securing with a lid and storing in the fridge.

Pickles, Quickles & Fermented Foods

Pickling and fermenting are ingenious ancient rituals, which involve preserving ingredients for a long period of time to retain and even enhance their goodness and to prevent them from expiring. Many modern commercial preservation products often contain a lot of refined sugars, acidity regulators, flavourings and other artificial ingredients, which is why it's advisable to make your own from scratch.

Basic Pickled Vegetables

Experiment with infusing your pickles with herbs and spices, such as fennel seeds, mustard seeds, coriander seeds, onion seeds, dill, basil, rosemary, mint, sliced fresh ginger, sliced fresh turmeric or chilli flakes.

Makes enough brine to pickle 400g fresh produce in 1x1.5-litre sterilised jar (see page 299 for sterilising instructions).

Combine 250ml apple cider vinegar, 250ml water, 20–40g coconut sugar (to taste) and 1 tbsp salt in a jug, stirring until all of the sugar and salt is dissolved.

Prepare 400g of your vegetables of choice. (I like to use raw carrots, beetroot, chicory, fennel and red onions.) Wash them thoroughly, peel, remove any tough parts of ends and slice either into chunks, discs or thin wedges, depending on the shape of your produce. Pack the vegetables into a sterilised jar or divide between several jars.

To prepare the brine, transfer the vinegar mixture to a saucepan and bring to the boil. Once boiling, gently pour the vinegar mixture into the jar (or jars), ensuring the produce is fully submerged and covered by the brine. Secure the lid(s) and leave to cool at room temperature. Once cool, transfer to the fridge and ideally enjoy within 1–2 months.

Pickled Ginger *(Serves 30–40)*

Peel 400g fresh ginger and, using a vegetable peeler or mandolin, slice the ginger thinly. Transfer to a bowl, sprinkle with the 1 tsp salt and stir to coat. Set aside for 10–30 minutes to allow the salt to extract the ginger's liquid.

Using your hands, squeeze the ginger to release any further liquid. Transfer the ginger to a sterilised jar (or several jars), discarding its liquid.

In a saucepan, stir 250ml rice wine or apple cider vinegar, 200ml water and 30–40g coconut sugar and bring to the boil until the sugar has dissolved. Pour the vinegar mixture into the jar with the ginger and set aside to cool for 5–10 minutes. Seal with a lid and place in the fridge for 24 hours. Store in the fridge for up to 2 months.

Quickled Cucumber *(Serves 20)*

Wash and halve 400g cucumber lengthways and then widthways. Scrape out the seeds (save these for a smoothie) and then slice thinly, lengthways, into half moons. Transfer to a bowl and add 250ml apple cider vinegar, 250ml water, 30–40g coconut sugar, ½ tsp chilli flakes, 1 tbsp grated fresh ginger, 1 tsp salt. Transfer to a sterilised jar (page 299) with a lid, or an airtight container, and store in the fridge for up to a month.

Sauerkraut

Optional Flavourings – turmeric, ginger, garlic, mustard seeds, fennel seeds, coriander seeds, caraway seeds, edible flowers, dried seaweed or fresh or dried herbs.

Equipment: 1 × 2 litre jar or 2 × 1 litre jars

Finely slice the 1 red or white cabbage and 200–400g other vegetables, using a sharp knife or a mandolin. Remove the hard centre of the cabbage and save it for later as it comes in useful when packing your jars. Place all of the vegetables into a large bowl with 2 tsp salt and any herbs or spices of your choice (I like to use turmeric, ginger, garlic, mustard seeds, fennel seeds, coriander seeds, caraway seeds, edible flowers, dried seaweed or fresh or dried herbs). Then begin to mash and massage with your hands or a flat-ended rolling pin for a minimum of 10 minutes, to release all of the vegetables' natural juices.

Once the vegetables have softened and there is a considerable amount of liquid, pack the vegetables into 1 × 2-litre (or 2 × 1-litre) sterilised jars, making them as compact as possible. Once full, pour the liquid into the jar(s) to just about cover the vegetables. Here, take the hard bit of your cabbage (and perhaps any other discarded vegetable ends), and place it on top of the sauerkraut – it will act as a plug to hold the vegetables in place when the lid is secured, ensuring they stay submerged in the brine.

Secure the lid and place your jars in a baking tray or other dish, as you will often notice frothing and leakage during the fermentation process. Leave for 3–10 days to ferment at room temperature, preferably somewhere warm but not hot, and away from direct sunlight. 'Burp' your sauerkraut every day by gently releasing the lid to let a little air out, but don't open the lid fully or for more than a second. After 3 days, taste your sauerkraut, and if you want to allow the flavours to develop further, leave for longer. Once satisfied with the taste, transfer to the fridge and store for up to 6 months.

My favourite alternatives are Beetroot Nori Sauerkraut (using cabbage, beetroot, carrots and dried nori) and Golden Sauerkraut (using cabbage, grated turmeric and mustard seeds).

Water Kefir *(Makes approx. 1 litre)*
Water kefir is a probiotic beverage made from water kefir grains or powdered starter cultures (both of which are a symbiotic group of beneficial bacteria that create probiotics and enzymes as a side product of breaking down natural sugar). Fermenting these grains using water and natural sugars creates a naturally

fizzy drink that is high in the probiotics and enzymes essential for optimal gut health. Easier to make than Kombucha (page 318), water kefir is a simple process that provides refreshing and revitalisng alternatives to commercial soft drinks and fizzy drinks. You can drink it straight or you can add it to other drinks, such as iced teas, juices, smoothies or even cocktails. Start with just half a glass per day until your system is used to it.

Dissolve 50g coconut sugar in 100ml boiling water, either boil in a saucepan over a medium heat or boil the kettle and dissolve the sugar in a large heatproof bowl or jug.

Once the sugar has completely dissolved, add 650ml of filtered water to the sugar solution, to make the liquid up to 750ml. (Alternatively, add 900ml water if you want to make a weaker drink, but if using the grains for the first time, less water is advised for a strong fermentation.) Transfer the solution to a 1-litre sterilised jar, then add 45–50g hydrated water kefir grains, ½ citrus fruit of your choice, 5–10g ginger and 3 tbsp raisins, goji berries, chopped apricots or chopped dates. Cover with a muslin cloth or cheesecloth and secure with a rubber band. Leave in a mildly warm place for up to 72 hours. (I generally brew mine for 48 hours.)

After 48 hours, see how it tastes and if you are satisfied, strain through a plastic sieve. Otherwise, leave it for another 24 hours before straining. Discard the fruits but keep your kefir grains as you can reuse them eternally (see Storing Your Grains). Pour the kefir into 2 x 500ml sterilised swing-top glass bottles and store in the fridge.

For a Second Fermentation
Whilst the water kefir can be enjoyed as it is, after its initial fermentation, you can ferment it a second time, which allows you to add flavour to your water kefir and more carbonation to develop, producing a fizzier result.

For the secondary fermentation, pour either 4 tablespoons pure, natural fruit juice of your choice or about 50g fresh fruit into 2 × 500ml sterilised swing-top glass bottles. Divide the water kefir between bottles, filling them to 1–2.5cm below the top. Seal the bottles and leave them to ferment for a further 48–72 hours at room temperature. Once a day, release any pressure that builds up inside the bottle by quickly and slightly opening the lid to let out some air.

After this second fermentation, transfer the bottles to the fridge to chill and to slow down the fermentation process.

Once ready to enjoy, open over a sink in case there is a build-up of pressure!

Flavouring the Second Fermentation
For fresh fruit (per 750ml –1-litre batch water kefir): 50g smashed blueberries, 50g smashed raspberries, 50g smashed strawberries, 1–2 passion fruits, ½ fresh mango, chopped.

For fruit juice (use roughly 80-100ml fruit juice per 750ml–1-litre batch water kefir): ginger juice (around 20ml may be strong enough if only using ginger), apple juice, orange juice, cucumber juice.

For purées (use 4 tbsp fruit purée per 750ml–1-litre batch water kefir). For example, 3 passion fruit blended with 100ml water.

Tips & flavour variations
Add fresh lemon juice and a little natural sweetener to a glass and fill with unflavoured water kefir (after first or second fermentation).

Add raisins, dates, cinnamon sticks and orange peel after the first fermentation, and ferment a second time. After the second fermentation, add a few drops of food-grade cinnamon or orange essential oil and a little natural sweetener, to create a subtle cola flavour.

Infuse water kefir with rose petals, rose water, smashed blueberries, smashed raspberries and a little beetroot juice, or sliced beetroot to colour.

Consult your doctor if on medication, pregnant or just generally new to water kefir and unsure about using it.

Storing Your Grains
Water kefir grains are live and natural, and there is no 'off' switch to their activeness. It is common to brew continuously, but there are a few options for storing your grains, and taking a break from brewing.

Option 1: Make a solution of sugar water, transfer to a sterilised jar, add the grains and store in the fridge. It's safe to store like this for up to 3 weeks. Repeat this every 3 weeks to refresh the water and keep the grains active.

Option 2: After the fermentation process, rinse the grains thoroughly through a plastic sieve using filtered water. Lay them on a piece of unbleached parchment paper, somewhere where they won't be disturbed, to dry out. Dry at room temperature for 3–5 days, depending on the room temperature. Once fully dry, transfer to a freezer bag or in clingfilm, and store in the fridge for up to 6 months, or in the freezer for an unlimited time. When ready to make water kefir again, rehydrate the grains in sugar solution to reactivate. Note: the grains may not produce a strong fermentation, and it may take a few batches to 'strengthen' them again as they feed off the natural sugar solution.

Kombucha *(Makes approx. 2 litres)*
Kombucha has been produced and enjoyed for thousands of years. It is a probiotic drink, and is honoured for improving digestion and nutrient assimilation. The living bacteria produced during fermentation are essential for a healthy gut, and ultimately, for healthy cellular and organ function all round, keeping the brain and body thriving. Modern diets do not tend to offer enough of these crucial enzymes, and today's popular processed convenience foods contain ingredients that actually destroy whatever enzymes we do have inside us still fighting to thrive. The more probiotic help and bacterial support our gut can get, the better we will function. Period.

Just a sip of kombucha instantly enlivens my cells and I feel buzzy, uplifted and more active than ever. Kombucha is also known to have

Nature's Pantry & Daily Goods

antiviral and antibacterial properties, and can support liver function, improving the body's detoxification process by preventing bad bacteria from thriving and flushing out toxins. The acids produced can also strengthen the gut lining and help regrowth and repair if it is under stress or if good bacteria have been harmed and destroyed (by toxins from modern diets or things like antibiotics or medication).

Made from sugar, tea and a SCOBY (a Symbiotic Culture Of Bacteria and Yeast), kombucha is so simple to make, and you can use green tea and coconut sugar for added benefits, if, like me, you aren't comfortable with the concept of using white refined sugar. Be assured, though, that the SCOBY feeds off the sugar, so you don't actually consume the sugar and it doesn't have the same effect on blood sugar levels. The longer the tea ferments, the less sugar it will contain, and after about 10–12 days, there will be hardly a trace of sugar left.

Serve kombucha cold over ice, add to cocktails or add to sparkling water for a fizzier option. Store in the fridge until finished – there is no expiry.

To make, bring 2 litres water to the boil, either boiling the water in kettle loads or using a large saucepan over a high heat.

Place 6 teabags or 2–3 tbsp loose tea and 150–180g coconut sugar into a 2.5–litre sterilised glass container. Pour the boiling water into your container. Leave the tea to brew for 30 minutes, stirring occasionally. Remove/strain the teabags/leaves and then let the tea cool completely until it is only slightly warm to touch.

Add 1 large SCOBY (you can buy these online or from many health-food stores, see page 327 for suppliers), placing it at the top of your container with the lightest side upwards (if you can distinguish between the two – it's not always obvious and isn't crucial). The SCOBY should float at the top or in the middle of the tea. Cover the top of the container with a muslin cloth and secure with a rubber band. Leave in a cool, dark place for 10–20 days –

I usually brew mine for 12–18 days, but the flavour will depend on the temperature and exact size of the scoby. After 10 days, taste your kombucha to see if it is ready. It should look cloudier in colour and taste slightly sweet, slightly tangy and a little like apple cider vinegar (though it shouldn't taste like sweet tea). You can decide whether you want to leave it to brew for longer (the longer you leave it, the less sweet it will taste and the more vinegary it will become). The fermentation time depends on a few factors, such as the temperature of the environment (warmer temperatures speed fermentation), but most importantly, your taste preferences.

You may see a lot of activity in the brewing container, which is the new SCOBY forming (known as the baby SCOBY, which develops as a by-product of the original SCOBY). You will end up with two scobys after fermentation.

For a single fermentation, remove the SCOBYs when you are happy with the taste and pour the kombucha into 2–3 × 1-litre sterilised swing-top bottles. Seal the lids and store in the fridge – the kombucha will get fizzier over time.

For a Second Fermentation
A second fermentation involves flavouring your kombucha and leaving it to ferment for a further 3–5 days at room temperature. Divide the chosen fruit (see Flavouring the Second Fermentation below) between 2–3 × 1-litre sterilised swing-top bottles and then fill with your single-fermentation kombucha. Seal with a lid and leave to ferment at room temperature for a further 3–5 days.

To avoid the bottles exploding, each day, 'burp' the bottles to release some air (which builds up and creates intense pressure).

After 3–5 days, store the kombucha in the fridge.

Flavouring the Second Fermentation
You can infuse your kombucha with whole fruits, fruit purées or fruit juices, to add flavour and enhance its nutritional capabilities. Whole fruits should be washed and either sliced or gently mashed in order to release the flavours. Fruit purées can be made by blending fruit with just

Nature's Pantry & Daily Goods

enough water to create a thin paste and fresh fruit juices should ideally be freshly made or be cold-pressed, organic and unpasteurised. Try to avoid using just citrusy fruits as they will alter the flavour and power of the good bacteria in the kombucha.

For fresh fruit (per 2.5-litre kombucha): 100g smashed blueberries, 100g smashed raspberries, 100g smashed strawberries, 3 passion fruits, 1 mango, chopped.

For fruit juice (use roughly 120–150ml fruit juice per 2.5-litre batch kombucha): ginger juice (use less if only using ginger – around 20ml per bottle), apple juice, orange juice, cucumber juice.

For purées (per 2.5-litre batch kombucha): for example, use 2 tbsp fruit purée per bottle, 3 passion fruits blended with 100ml water.

Favourite Flavour Combinations
These are a few of my favourite options. Play around with quantities of each to suit your own personal taste.

Passion fruit purée, passion fruit seeds
    and ginger juice
Mango and passion fruit seeds
Passion fruit, blueberry and raspberry
Mixed berry
Blood orange and dried hibiscus
Mango and lime
Apple and ginger

Tips
After 3 days, move the bottles to the fridge, to stunt the fermentation process. Leave the fruit to infuse and strain before serving, or strain before storing in the fridge.

Be careful when opening as the pressure may have built up. Open it over the sink and facing away from you.

Consult your doctor if on medication, pregnant or just generally new to kombucha and unsure about using it. Start with just half a glass per day until your system is used to it.

How to Reuse, Store or Share Your SCOBYs
For each future batch of kombucha, you should use the mother and baby SCOBYs together until the baby has grown to more or less the same size. Once this has happened, you can throw the mother out or give it away to someone who wants to start brewing. Ensure that you start off with small brews the first time you use the 'baby' alone, and gradually increase the volume that you brew as the 'baby' grows. SCOBYs are live and natural so there is no 'off' switch. They don't do well in the fridge so the best thing to do is carry on brewing. Whilst the normal brewing time for a batch of kombucha is 7–30 days, you can brew for up to 6 weeks if you are going away, but it will then need to be 'fed' again with fresh tea after the 6 weeks. The longer you leave your kombucha to brew, the stronger and more potent it will become and the less sweet it will be. If it's too vinegary, you can dilute it with water or sparkling water before enjoying. If you want to store the SCOBY, remove the SCOBY from the jar, separate the mother and the baby and put them into the same jar, with enough brewed kombucha to cover it. Seal with a lid and keep in the fridge for up to 6 months. When you want to brew a new batch of kombucha, remove the SCOBY from the fridge and bring to room temperature before adding it to the sweetened and cooled tea.

Continuous Brewing & Batch Brewing
There's a lot of information online about batch brewing and continuous brewing. For me, I like to do batch brewing as it's slightly easier to handle and keep track of. Continuous means you add sweet tea to the batch of kombucha, however much you took out. This starts the fermentation again but some people say the caffeine and sugar is higher as the fresh tea doesn't ferment as much – I'm not sure about this. Batch brewing on the other hand involves bottling *all* of the tea and then starting again from scratch.

Once you've starting brewing kombucha, decide whether you want to do a continuous brew or a batch brew. To continue brewing, only bottle 1 litre of the kombucha, and replace it with 1 litre new sugar and tea (halve the original quantities to make the tea (page 319), allow it to cool entirely and then add it to the brewing vessel). Ferment for 1–5 days (or more if you can handle a stronger taste), draw more from the batch and put into bottles and repeat if you want to continue.

If you want to do a batch method (which I prefer and which is better for 1–2 people), draw all of the kombucha out and put into bottles, then start over from scratch from the beginning. There is no mixing of fermented tea with new tea and this way it is easier to keep track of the fermenting time.

Natural Botanical Cordials

Cordials are traditionally concentrates made from sugars and flavourings (for soft drinks) or wines and spirits (for alcoholic drinks). They have been produced and consumed for generations to make delicious drinks, but made with the right ingredients they also have the power to soothe, nourish and heal. I use coconut sugar or natural syrups rather than refined sugars, and I use considerably less of them than is suggested in traditional recipes. You can use cordials to make instant hot or cold drinks (adding them to hot water, cold water, coconut water or sparkling water), mix them with alcohol to make cocktails or even use them as flavoured syrups for breakfasts or desserts.

Each recipe makes around 10–20 servings

Fundamental Ingredients
500ml water, 50g coconut sugar, fresh fruit juice or fresh fruits of choice, additional flavours (such as fresh herbs, tonic herbs, fresh spices, teas, roots, fresh or dried flowers, floral waters).

Apple, Marshmallow Root & Mint Cordial
Put 50g coconut sugar, 500ml water, 100g grated apple, 5g marshmallow root and 2–4 sprigs of fresh mint into a small saucepan. Place it over a medium–high heat and bring to the boil. When it starts to bubble, reduce the heat and let the syrup simmer for 5–10 minutes, to infuse. Strain through a fine sieve into a jar or an airtight container and allow to cool before storing in the fridge. (You can elevate it by adding 1 tbsp lemon balm or 10g lemongrass root.)

Chai Concentrate
Put 50g coconut sugar (or natural syrup), 200ml black tea (made with 200ml water and 1 teabag), Cacao Nib Tea (page 120) or Chaga Astragalus Tea (page 120), 1–2 tsp ground cinnamon, 1–2 tsp ground cardamom, 1 tbsp vanilla powder, ½ tsp ground ginger, ½ tsp ground nutmeg, ½ tsp ground cloves and ½ tsp ground allspice into a small saucepan.

Place it over a medium–high heat and bring to the boil. When it starts to bubble, reduce the heat and let the syrup simmer for 5–10 minutes, to infuse. Strain through a fine sieve into a jar or an airtight container and allow to cool before storing in the fridge. To enjoy, mix 1–2 tsp chai concentrate with hot or cold water or plant-based milk.

Cold-Brewed Coffee Concentrate
Fill a 500ml jar with 450ml water. Add 50g ground coffee beans and stir to combine. Place the lid on your jar and leave to sit at room temperature for 6–24 hours. Strain the coffee through a fine sieve, nut-milk bag or a cheesecloth into a bowl or jug. Rinse the jar and transfer the coffee back into it, then stir in 2–4 tbsp natural sweetener. Store in the fridge for 1–2 weeks. To enjoy, simply fill a glass to halfway with the cold-brew coffee and top it up with cold water or plant-based milk.

Ginger, Hibiscus & Aloe Cordial

Put 50g coconut sugar, 500ml water, 2 tsp lemon or lime juice, 20g dried hibiscus, 40g fresh ginger and 10–15g aloe gel or aloe vera juice into a small saucepan. Place the pan over a medium–high heat and bring to the boil. When it starts to bubble, reduce the heat down and let the syrup simmer away for 5–10 minutes (to infuse). Strain through a fine sieve into a jar or an airtight container and allow to cool before storing in the fridge.

Elevate it: Elevate it with a dash of liquid probiotics, rose water, orange blossom water, food-grade essential oils or schizandra tincture.

Grape, Ginger & Turmeric Cordial

Put 50g coconut sugar, 500ml water, 50g white or red grapes, 10g grated fresh ginger and 5g grated fresh turmeric into a small saucepan. Place it over a medium–high heat and bring to the boil. When it starts to bubble, reduce the heat and let the mixture simmer for 5–10 minutes, to infuse. Strain through a fine sieve into a jar or an airtight container and allow to cool before storing in the fridge.

Mint & Lemon Cordial

Put 50g coconut sugar, 500ml water, the juice of 1 lemon and a handful of fresh mint leaves into a small saucepan. Place it over a medium–high heat and bring to the boil. When it starts to bubble, reduce the heat and let the syrup simmer for 5–10 minutes, to infuse. Strain through a fine sieve into a jar or an airtight container and allow to cool before storing in the fridge.

Elevate it: Elevate it by adding 10g lemongrass root, 1 tbsp lemon balm or 5g astragalus root.

Rose, Beetroot & Berry Cordial

Put 50g coconut sugar, 500ml water, 5g dried rose petals, 30g grated raw beetroot and a handful of blueberries or raspberries into a small saucepan. Place it over a medium–high heat and bring to the boil. When it starts to bubble, reduce the heat and let the syrup simmer for 5–10 minutes, to infuse. Strain

through a fine sieve into a jar or an airtight container and allow to cool before storing in the fridge.

Elevate it: You can elevate it by adding 1 tbsp acai powder or pulp or 1 tsp rose water.

Rosemary & Mint Syrup

Put 50g coconut sugar, 500ml water, 2 sprigs of fresh rosemary and 6 sprigs of fresh mint into a small saucepan. Place it over a medium–high heat and bring to the boil. When it starts to bubble, reduce the heat and let the syrup simmer for 5–10 minutes – to infuse. Strain through a fine sieve into a jar or an airtight container and allow to cool before storing in the fridge.

Alcoholic Cordials

For alcoholic cordials, put 500ml pure vodka into a glass bottle and add fruit and herbs of your choice. Seal and store for 4–6 weeks and then strain. Add a little natural sweetener (about 2–6 tbsp) and then reseal and store for a further 2–4 weeks, until infused. To serve, simply dilute with tonic water, pure fruit juices or other mixers of choice.

Glossary

Ayurveda

Ayurveda, a Sanskrit word that can be translated as 'the science or wisdom of life', is an ancient health system originating in India over 5,000 years ago. It considers health as the dynamic integration between our environments, our bodies, our minds and our spirits. Recognising that human beings are part of nature, Ayurveda takes into account the unique nature of each person and situation, considering the individual's physiology and lifestyle habits as well as the season, the geography, the climate, and other factors that are often overlooked in modern healthcare. Ayurveda believes the Universe is governed by three constitutional energies: Vata (Wind), Pitta (Fire) and Kapha (Earth) – known as doshas or 'types'. These primary forces are responsible for the characteristics of our mind and body, and whilst it is understood that each person possesses all three of these energies, often one or two will be more predominant, and that is known as a person's Ayurvedic constitution, or *prakriti*. Understanding your *prakriti* (which is apt to change and adapt) helps to determine the most sensible lifestyle choices for you. There are seven doshas – Single: Vata, Pitta, Kapha; Duo: Vata/Pitta, Pitta/Kapha, Kapha/Vata; and Tri-doshic: Vata/Pitta/Kapha. Once you understand your *prakriti*, you can use Ayurvedic rituals and ingredients intended to pacify each dosha by boosting digestive health and building strength so that your body can carry out the natural healing it was designed to do. Many rituals and recipes in this book have been inspired by Ayurvedic teachings.

Bodywork

In alternative medicine, bodywork refers to a variety of therapies that involve working on the human body, usually to assess, ease and improve a person's physical and/or mental state. The therapies often improve posture, reduce both physical and mental stress and tension, ease pain or injuries, improve circulation, enhance energy levels and bring awareness to the mind–body connection to promote natural healing. These therapies are not used to cure illnesses directly, but are used to relax and restore balance within the body and mind, which, as a result, can prevent illness or promote healing. Acupressure, acupuncture, shiatsu, craniosacral therapy, massage (most techniques) and reflexology are amongst the most common.

Chakras

Chakras are known in Indian traditions as centres of the body in which energy flows through. Similarly to meridians, chakras can become blocked, which can prevent the flow of energy, leading to both physical and mental illness or unrest. There are seven chakras in the body and each one represents certain characteristics and a persons characteristics can relate to a blockage or imbalance in certain chakras. For example, the root chakra (located at the base of the spine) represents a sense of feeling grounded and secure and a blockage or imbalance in this chakra will be recognisable in someone experiencing worry, fear or anxiety. There are exercises and ingredients that can help you to return to a state of balance, and whilst chakral energy is not a main focus in this book, many of the recipes and rituals can help to restore balance.

Do-In

Do-In (also known as dao yin or tao yin in Chinese and Taoist teachings) is a combination of energising exercises, meridian stretches, breath work, meditative techniques, self-massage and acupressure. It is designed to increase the flow of energy around the body and to refresh, revitalise and invigorate. Some exercises can be energising (ideal for the morning), some can enhance concentration (ideal during the day) and others are more relaxing (ideal for evenings), but all are aimed to be calming, soothing and strengthening. Do-In exercises take very little time and effort and are effective ways to increase the flow of energy around the body.

Energy Work

Energy work refers to healing therapies that consider the human energy field, energy channels and the flow of energy (known as qi, chi or prana in ancient Eastern teachings), and it works to detect and move energy around the body to correct imbalances and unblock stagnant energy. Some treatments involve the touch of an energy worker, whilst others involve just the energy of their hands hovering close to the client. There are also methods of self-treatment (such as tapping and shaking). Acupuncture, crystal healing, reiki, qi gong, vibrational energy, EFT, chakra healing and vibrational medicine are common examples of energy work.

Fuctional foods

I use the word functional to describe ingredients that I believe possess and bring a particularly special purpose to a recipe. Not only do they provide nutrients, vitamins and minerals, they can have deeper impacts within the body, such as aiding digestion, balancing hormones, cleansing the system, fighting toxins and improving moods, to name a few. Most fresh, natural ingredients rich in life-giving nutrients count as functional, to me, but adaptogens and tonic herbs take things a step further.

Herbalism & Herbal Medicine

Herbal medicine is a form of alternative medicine that studies the medicinal and therapeutic abilities of plants and the relationship between plants and humans. Herbalism uses natural herbs to support, prevent and/or heal certain imbalances within the body.

Holistic & Holism

Holism encapsulates the theory that parts of a whole are interconnected and cannot exist or be understood fully when they are observed independently. In holistic medicine, nutrition and other therapies, the treatment of a person as a whole is observed, taking into account many factors of their lives, from their physical health, mental health, past experiences and their genes to their diet and lifestyle habits, relationships and other social factors, rather than just physiological symptoms. It is thought that, to truly heal, we need to look at the dynamic play of all aspects of a person's life, as each person's system is unique and thus requires more individualised treatment. The basis of this book is to bring awareness to how things are connected, and to encourage you to understand your individual self more thoroughly in order to take care of yourself and feel your best.

Inversions

An inversion is a pose in yoga where the heart is above the head and the head and chest are over the pelvis. Such poses are honoured for improving stamina, circulation, lymphatic drainage and confidence, as well as stimulating the nervous system, boosting the flow of oxygen around the body and bringing a sense of clarity and balance to the mind. The more challenging inversions tend to be energising and invigorating, whilst the more gentle inversions tend to be relaxing and calming.

Makko Ho Stretches

Makko ho is a shiatsu stretching technique. I first discovered these yoga-like stretches whilst training to become a shiatsu practitioner at the beginning of 2017. Meridian stretches are intended to improve the flow of energy (qi/chi/prana) around the body, to restore energetic balance and remove any energy blockages (which can be caused by stress, trauma and detrimental lifestyle habits). Makko ho stretches can help to relieve stress and calm the mind and by addressing each of the body's meridians, they approach particular parts of the body that correlate with each meridian. You will find a few of my favourite meridian stretches in this book.

Mantras & Mantra Meditation

A mantra is a sacred word or phrase that is typically repeated over and over again during meditation. It can be as simple as a single sound formed from a single letter or syllable, or it can be a word or a more complicated phrase that resonates with the speaker, either in meaning or vibrational frequency.

Some mantras are Sanskrit whilst others are not. Some are personal and very unique whilst others can be more generic, like Om or Shanti, for example. Mantras are traditionally used to encourage a sense of focus, clarity and intention. Mantra meditation (where you repeat a mantra for a certain amount of time) is intended to focus the brain on a single task, reducing stress by slowing thoughts and silencing overactive minds. Some mantras are also thought to be more powerful at attracting specific things, depending on their nature.

There are many different types of mantras. I practice Vedic meditation, which involves a mantra I was given based on the year I was born and the year in which my teacher began training in Vedic meditation. You can ask a teacher or you can find mantras online that are connected to your year of birth, or which just seem meaningful to you at certain times.

Some Sanskrit mantras may not make any sense to you at first but if you spend some time researching, you will find translations and symbolic explanations. Certain mantras will also resonate with your nervous system, through frequency and vibration of the sound created when each one is uttered, either aloud or in your head. Some people like to keep their mantra the same, whilst others may constantly change theirs or incorporate new ones and practise with several. You don't necessarily have to meditate with your mantra, instead you could have a mantra written down and placed somewhere you can see it, or you might repeat your mantra every morning (either aloud or in your head), or at the beginning of, or during, a yoga class.

Meridians

A meridian is an energy channel or pathway in the body through which life-energy flows. There are 12 main meridians and each runs through all the major parts of the body. Each meridian is a yin-yang pair, meaning each yin organ is paired with a yang organ. Energy flows through the 12 meridians. In traditional Chinese and Japanese alternative medicine practices, certain problems in certain organs can be treated by working the corresponding meridian channels, often through meridian stretches, acupuncture or acupressure.

Qnola

Qnola is a range of quinoa-based breakfast goods, free from gluten, dairy and refined sugar. I began developing unique recipes for quinoa-based granola as a simple breakfast option for myself, and went on to launch Qnola officially as a brand in 2014. The award-winning products offer a healthier alternative to processed cereals and are stocked in some of the worlds largest supermarkets and department stores.

Suppliers & Resources

Whilst I frequently shop in supermarkets, I like to support smaller companies as much as I can, buying from local suppliers who source from local growers or manufacturers. Whilst most ingredients in this book are easy to come by and available from local shops, supermarkets, farmers' markets and health-food stores, I source the more specialised ingredients from the following suppliers, most of whom are online.

www.sunpotion.com: For adaptogens, superfood powders, tonic herbs and general inspiration.

www.buywholefoodsonline.com: For bulk wholefood ingredients and medicinal plant powders, such as nuts, flours,herbs, spices, natural sweeteners, roots and adaptogens.

www.dragonherbs.com: For medicinal plants, tonic herbs, adaptogens and other plant powders.

www.indigo-herbs.co.uk : For medicinal plants, herbs, tonic herbs, adaptogens, superfoods, tinctures and teas.

www.gracefruit.com: For natural cosmetic ingredients such as carrier oils, butters, essential oils and containers.

www.nhrorganicoils.com: For organic essential oils and food-grade essential oils.

www.suppliesforcandles.co.uk: For candle making equipment, including wooden and cotton wicks, glass containers, soy wax, beeswax, oils and dried botanicals.

www.happykombucha.co.uk: For brewing and fermenting equipment and kefir grains.

www.muji.com: For spray-top bottles and containers for self-made home and beauty products.

My journey has developed and been inspired largely by the journeys of others. Here is a brief list of some of the most transformational and helpful books I have read. I recommend these resources if you are truly interested in gaining a deeper understanding in some of the topics I have covered in this book. And the apps which I find are particularly useful for guided meditation are Headspace, Buddhify and Inscape.

Cleanse, Nurture and Restore, by Pukka Herbs founder Sebastian Pole,

The Slow Down Diet, by Marc David

Wellth, by Jason Wachob

The Sleep Revolution and *Thrive*, by Arianne Huffington

The New Health Rules, by Frank Lipman M.D & Danielle Claro

Moon Time, by Johanna Paungger & Thomas Poppe

Mind Your Body, by Andrew Scott & Sarah Wale

Intuitive Eating, by Evelyn Trebole & Elyse Resch

The Monk Who Sold His Ferrari, by Robin Sharma

Skin Cleanse, by Adina Grigore

Neals Yards Remedies: Healing Foods, by Susannah Steel

Clean, by Alejandro Junger

Aromatherapy – a guide for home use, by Christine Westwood

Adaptogens, by David Winston

Herbs for Stress and Anxiety, by Rosemary Gladstar

The Healing Power of Ginseng & the Tonic Herbs, by Paul Bergner

Acknowledgements

This is not an acknowledgements page solely for the book, but since the book is practically an extension of my entire life so far, it is an opportunity for me to thank all the people who have impacted my journey in some way. Particular gratitude goes to:

Mama Sue and Dada Bob – my realest guides, and gurus in their own ways. Nothing is as pure or constructive as your love and support and somehow you have mastered the perfect balance of giving me and the girls the space and freedom to do anything we want to do, whilst nurturing us no end. You keep me so grounded; I love you 60/10.

Ju Ju and Jo Jo – for keeping me company for the last 24 years and for getting me like no one else does. For all the moments we've experienced in ways that only sisters can, and for your unwavering love, support and encouragement. Everything would be a third of what it is without you.

Sharb – living proof that the unplanned things are the best things, and that there is so much out there beyond what we can dream of, desire or hope for. I can't list all the reasons I love you here, but I hope I tell you enough day to day. Thank you for being who you are and for helping me to be who I am. Puss och kram skumbanan.

Lydia – the little lady boss who has made all of this possible and is a true driving force behind Qnola. Your support and passion mean more than anything, and I'm so proud of you and grateful that you chose to join me on this journey. We're a small team, but we're a dream team.

Lucie – Qnola's first employee. From hernias and broken arms, to quinoa parties and the most supportive hugs I've ever received, you were and always will be a big part of Qnola.

Coleman – for being more me than anyone else on this planet, and for being my best friend at the time a girl needs a best friend the most. For all the Qnola events you kept me company at, for the packaging drafts when Qnola was just an idea, and for all the times in between.

Elly – a true part of me; my third sister. For the last 24 years, for the travels that changed my life, and for being the first person to go to Waitrose to buy a pack of Qnola (and you, Joey!).

Eva – soul sister 1. I've never been so sure about a person as quickly as I was about you. You are such a shining light and you've guided my path more than you probably realise.

Bonnie - soul sister II. For the company in New York, for your bright and hearty energy, for your constant support and for bringing 'Burgs' by Mt. Wolf into my life.

Kate – soul sister III. The way we were brought together so naturally was further proof for me that the Universe gives you exactly what you need, exactly when you need it. Our spontaneous journey has been so interesting and authentic and I wish I could bottle your bountiful energy into a calming remedy I could share with the masses.

Pip – If only everyone were as real as you. You have mastered the ability to possess significant knowledge, good vibes and an expert ability to laugh at yourself all at once, and that inspires me more than anything. Thank you for being so grounding and so giving. I love what we're building together.

Bex – for being my first Qnola customer via Instagram and for being such a positive driving force in my life. If you hadn't asked me to make Qnola for you, it probably never would have left my kitchen.

Leah – for the moon walks, the woo-woo talks and for sharing the business struggles with me. Qnola has been more manageable and more fun thanks to you.

Jada – for always lifting me up. For your positive vibes, your empowering pep talks and your infectious passion for making changes and achieving dreams.

Georgia D – for your design expertise, for your constant enthusiasm and for taking the entire family to take a selfie with Qnola when it launched in Waitrose.

Esme, Laura, Liv and Ryan – for making me, me.

All the lady bosses in my life — with open hearts and genuine intention, you gave me inspiration and confidence and helped me take the initial steps to create what I can now call a business. In particular: Rimi, Lily, Bethany, Natali, Chi, The Hardihood Girls, Holly, Marina, Alexandra, Melissa and Fleur.

All of my lovely bookers at IMG – for all the amazing opportunities you've given me and for your constant support in everything I do.

All of my regular teachers at Yogahome, in particular Isabell, Eryck, Nova, Shira, Scarlett and Aleksei. Tara Stiles, Mike Taylor and Sam Berlind at Strala Yoga. Tracey Kriller and the British School of Shiatsu. Manu and Paolo at DeRose. And the entire Lululemon community, including Danielle Mika, and Ryan Leier – a one-of-a-kind yogi.

Rita, Clare, Louie, Rosie, Clara and Lizzie – for bringing this book to life beyond my imagination, and for making the entire process smooth, easy and fun. Vicky – for asking me to write this book almost three years ago and for waiting patiently for me to start doing it. It has become something far more interesting than it would have been back then! Thank you for giving me this opportunity. And Sophie – for being such a calming and open editor, and for not running a mile when I handed over an extra 100,000 words with the first draft of my manuscript.

Felicity and Jess – for not only understanding but also sharing my vision for this book, for helping me to articulate my initial ideas and for supporting me every single step of the way.

And to all of you; my returning Qnola customers, my regular blog visitors and, now, readers or givers of this book. I hope my products and projects have and will continue to serve you well.

Further thanks to blok London, tempo pilates, bodyism, lagree and ethos gym, for helping me stay active during the recipe testing stages of writing this book; to Bug clothing for providing some beautiful threads for our shoots; and to Poppy France on hair and make-up.

First published in Great Britain in 2018 by
Kyle Books, an imprint of Kyle Cathie Ltd
192-198 Vauxhall Bridge Road
London SW1V 1DX
general.enquiries@kylebooks.com
www.kylebooks.co.uk

10 9 8 7 6 5 4 3 2 1

ISBN 978 0 85783 442 3

Inside Design & Art Direction: Clare Newsam
Photographer: Rita Platts
Food Stylists: Rosie Ramsden and Lizzie Kamentzky
Props Stylist: Louie Waller
Project Editors: Vicky Orchard and Sophie Allen
Editorial Assistants: Isabel Gonzalez-Prendergast and Sarah Kyle
Production: Nic Jones, Gemma John and Lisa Pinnell

A Cataloguing in Publication record for this title is available from the British Library.

Colour reproduction by ALTA Image, London
Printed and bound in China by 1010 Printing International Ltd